FUTURE
English for Results
3

Irene E. Schoenberg
with Meg Brooks
and Margot Gramer

Series Consultants
Beatriz B. Díaz
Ronna Magy
Federico Salas-Isnardi

Future 3
English for Results

Pearson Education, 221 River Street, Hoboken, NJ 07030 USA

Staff credits: The people who made up the *Future* team, representing editorial, production, design, manufacturing, and marketing, are Pietro Alongi, Rhea Banker, Peter Benson, Nancy Blodget, Elizabeth Carlson, Jennifer Castro, Tracey Munz Cataldo, Natalia Cebulska, Aerin Csigay, Mindy DePalma, Dave Dickey, Gina DiLillo, Warren Fischbach, Pam Fishman, Nancy Flaggman, Irene Frankel, Shelley Gazes, Gosia Jaros-White, Mike Kemper, Niki Lee, Melissa Leyva, Stefan Machura, Amy McCormick, Linda Moser, Liza Pleva, Joan Poole, Sherry Preiss, Stella Reilly, Mary Rich, Lindsay Richman, Barbara Sabella, Katarzyna Starzynska-Kosciuszko, Loretta Steeves, Kim Steiner, Alexandra Suarez, Katherine Sullivan, Paula Van Ells, and Marian Wassner.

Cover design: Rhea Banker
Cover photo: Kathy Lamm/Getty Images
Text design: Elizabeth Carlson
Text composition: Word & Image Design Studio Inc.
Text font: Minion Pro

Library of Congress Cataloging-in-Publication Data
A catalog record for the print edition is available from the Library of Congress.

Printed in the United States of America
ISBN 13: 9780134696164 (Student Book with MyEnglishLab)
ISBN 10: 0134696166 (Student Book with MyEnglishLab)

ISBN 13: 9780134659534 (Student Book with Essential Online Resources)
ISBN 10: 0134659538 (Student Book with Essential Online Resources)

An adult course book for today has many layers and only a very talented editor can make it succeed. Kim Steiner is such an editor, and it is a pleasure to express my gratitude for her hard work in putting this book together. I am grateful for her research, creativity, humor, and thoughtfulness.

In addition, I would like to thank the following people: Irene Frankel for her inspiration, insight, and guidance throughout this series; Rhea Banker, Michael Kemper, Mindy DePalma, and Barbara Sabella for their work on the book design, layout, and art; and Penny Steiner-Grossman, Ed. D, Assistant Dean for Educational Resources, Albert Einstein College of Medicine, for her advice on the medical and health units. In addition, the publisher and I would like to thank the White Plains Public Library and the Chalmer Davee Library for granting us permission to reproduce photos of their beautiful murals and decor.

Irene E. Schoenberg, author of *Future* Student Book 3

Contents

To the Teacher

Welcome to *Future*
English for Results

Future is a six-level, four-skills course for adults and young adults correlated to state and national standards. *Future* supports Workforce Innovation and Opportunity Act (WIOA) goals and prepares adults for College and Career Readiness (CCRS), English Language Proficiencies (ELP), job skills, standardized tests, and EL-Civics. It incorporates research-based teaching strategies, corpus-informed language, and the best of modern technology.

KEY FEATURES

Future provides everything your students need in one integrated program.

In developing the course, we listened to what teachers asked for and we responded, providing six levels, more meaningful content, a thorough treatment of grammar, explicit skills development, abundant practice, multiple options for state-of-the-art assessment, and innovative components.

Future serves students' real-life needs.

We began constructing the instructional syllabus for *Future* by identifying what is most critical to students' success in their personal and family lives, in the workplace, as members of a community, and in their academic pursuits. *Future* provides outstanding coverage of life-skills competencies, basing language teaching on actual situations that students are likely to encounter and equipping them with the skills they need to achieve their goals. The grammar and other language elements taught in each lesson grow out of these situations and thus are practiced in realistic contexts, enabling students to use language meaningfully, from the beginning.

Future grows with your students.

Future takes students from absolute beginner level through low-advanced proficiency in English, addressing students' abilities and learning priorities at each level. As the levels progress, the curricular content and unit structure change accordingly, with the upper levels incorporating more academic skills, more advanced content standards, and more content-rich texts.

Future is fun!

Humor is built into each unit of *Future*. Many of the conversations, and especially the listenings, are designed to have an amusing twist at the end, giving students an extra reason to listen—something to anticipate with pleasure and to then take great satisfaction in once it is understood. In addition, many activities have students interacting in pairs and groups. Not only does this make classroom time more enjoyable, it also creates an atmosphere conducive to learning in which learners are relaxed, highly motivated, and at their most receptive.

Future puts the best of 21st-century technology in the hands of students and teachers.

In addition to its expertly developed print materials and audio components, *Future* goes a step further.

- Every **Student Book** comes with **Essential Online Resources** and optional **MyEnglishLab** for use at home, in the lab, or wherever students have access to a computer. The online resources can be assigned by teachers and used both by students who wish to extend their practice beyond the classroom and by those who need to "make up" what they missed in class.
- The **Tests and Test Prep** book comes with the *Future* Exam*View*® *Assessment Suite*, enabling teachers to print ready-made tests, customize these tests, or create their own tests for life skills, grammar, vocabulary, listening, and reading.
- The **Companion Website** provides a variety of teaching support, including a PDF of the Teacher's Edition and Lesson Planner notes for each unit in the Student Book.

Future provides all the assessment tools you need.

- The **Placement Test** evaluates students' proficiency in all skill areas, allowing teachers and program administrators to easily assign students to the right classes.
- The **Tests and Test Prep** book for each level provides:
  - **Printed unit tests** with accompanying audio CD. These unit tests use standardized testing formats, giving students practice "bubbling-in" responses as required for CASAS and other standardized tests. In addition, reproducible test prep worksheets and practice tests (in the online resources) provide invaluable help to students unfamiliar with such test formats.
  - The *Future* Exam*View*® *Assessment Suite* is a powerful program that allows teachers to create their own unique tests or to print or customize already prepared tests at three levels: pre-level, at-level, and above-level.
- **Performance-based assessment:** Lessons in the Student Book end with a "practical assessment" activity such as Role Play, Make It Personal, or Show What You Know. Each unit culminates with both a role-play activity and a problem-solving activity, which require students to demonstrate their oral competence in a holistic way. The **Teacher's Edition and Lesson Planner** provides speaking rubrics to make it easy for teachers to evaluate students' oral proficiency.
- **Self-assessment:** For optimal learning to take place, students need to be involved in setting goals and in

monitoring their own progress. *Future* has addressed this in numerous ways. In the Student Book, checkboxes at the end of lessons invite students to evaluate their mastery of the material. End-of-unit reviews allow students to see their progress in grammar and writing. After completing each unit, students go back to the goals for the unit and reflect on their achievement. In addition, the Essential Online Resources and MyEnglishLab provide students with continuous feedback (and opportunities for self-correction) as they work through each lesson. The Workbook contains the answer keys, so that students can check their own work outside of class.

Future addresses multilevel classes and diverse learning styles.

Using research-based teaching strategies, *Future* provides teachers with creative solutions for all stages of lesson planning and implementation, allowing them to meet the needs of all their students.

- The **Multilevel Communicative Activities Book** provides an array of reproducible activities and games that engage students through different modalities. Teachers' notes provide multilevel options for pre-level and above-level students, as well as extension activities for additional speaking and writing practice.
- The **Teacher's Edition and Lesson Planner** offers pre-level and above-level variations for every lesson plan, as well as numerous optional and extension activities designed to reach students at all levels.
- The **Transparencies and Reproducible Vocabulary Cards** include picture and word cards that will help kinesthetic and visual learners acquire and learn new vocabulary. Teachers' notes include ideas for multilevel classes.
- The **Essential Online Resources** included with the Student Book have extraordinary tools for individualizing instruction, as well as providing immediate feedback. All new reading and writing printable activities support College and Career Readiness goals (for levels 1–5). Multiple life-skills and listening activities with listen, record, and compare functions allow students to practice these skills outside of class. In addition, the audio files for the book are available in the Essential Online Resources, enabling students to listen to any of the material that accompanies the text.
- The **MyEnglishLab** option includes everything in the Essential Online Resources and much more. Readings with interactive activities and feedback (for all units in levels 1–5) support College and Career Readiness skills. Grammar Coach video presentations and additional online interactive activities for all of the grammar lessons give students extra grammar practice.

- The **Workbook with Audio**, similarly, allows students to devote their time to the lessons and specific skill areas that they need to work on most. In addition, students can replay the audio portions they want to listen to as many times as necessary, choosing to focus on the connections between the written and spoken word, listening for grammar, pronunciation, and/or listening for general comprehension.

Future's persistence curriculum motivates students to continue their education.

Recent research about persistence has given us insights into how to keep students coming to class and how to keep them learning when they can't attend. Recognizing that there are many forces operating in students' lives—family, jobs, childcare, health—that may make it difficult for them to come to class, programs need to help students:
- Identify their educational goals.
- Believe that they can successfully achieve them.
- Develop a commitment to their own education.
- Identify forces that can interfere with school attendance.
- Develop strategies that will help them try to stay in school in spite of obstacles.

Future addresses all of these areas with its persistence curriculum. Activities found throughout the book and specific persistence activities in the back of the book help students build community, set goals, develop better study skills, and feel a sense of achievement. In addition, the Essential Online Resources and MyEnglishLab are unique in their ability to ensure that even those students unable to attend class are able to make up what they missed and thus persist in their studies.

Future supports busy teachers by providing all the materials teachers need, plus teacher support.

The **Student Book**, **Workbook with Audio**, **online resources**, **Multilevel Communicative Activities Book**, and **Transparencies and Reproducible Vocabulary Cards** were designed to provide teachers with everything they need in the way of ready-to-use classroom and homework materials so they can concentrate on responding to their students' needs.

Future provides ample practice with flexible options to best fit the needs of each class.

The Student Book provides 60–100 hours of instruction. It can be supplemented in class by using:
- Teacher's Edition and Lesson Planner expansion ideas
- Transparencies and Reproducible Vocabulary Cards
- Workbook exercises
- Multilevel Communicative Activities

- Tests
- Essential Online Resources activities, as well as Student Book audio
- MyEnglishLab activities
- Activities on the Companion Website (futureenglishforresults.com)

TEACHING MULTILEVEL CLASSES

Teaching tips for pair and group work

Using pair and group work in an ESL classroom has many proven benefits. It creates an atmosphere of liveliness, builds community, and allows students to practice speaking in a low-risk environment. Many of the activities in *Future* are pair and small-group activities. Here are some tips for managing these activities:

- Limit small groups to three or four students per group (unless an activity specifically calls for larger groups). This maximizes student participation.
- Change partners for different activities. This gives students a chance to work with many others in the class and keeps them from feeling "stuck."
- If possible, give students a place to put their coats when they enter the classroom. This allows them to move around freely without worrying about returning to their own seats.
- Move around the classroom as students are working to make sure they are on task and to monitor their work.
- As you walk around, try to remain unobtrusive, so students continue to participate actively, without feeling they are being evaluated.
- Keep track of language points students are having difficulty with. After the activity, teach a mini-lesson to the entire class addressing those issues. This helps students who are having trouble without singling them out.

Pairs and groups in the multilevel classroom

Adult education ESL classrooms are by nature multilevel. This is true even if students have been given a placement test. Many factors—including a student's age, educational background, and literacy level—contribute to his or her ability level. Also, the same student may be at level in one skill, but pre-level or above-level in another.

When grouping students for a task, keep the following points in mind:

- *Like-ability* groups (in which students have the same ability level) help ensure that all students participate equally, without one student dominating the activity.
- *Cross-ability* groups (in which students have different ability levels) are beneficial to pre-level students who need the support of their at- or above-level classmates. The higher-level students benefit from "teaching" their lower-level classmates.

For example, when students are practicing a straightforward conversation substitution exercise, like-ability pairings are helpful. The activity can be tailored to different ability levels, and both students can participate equally. When students are completing the more complex task of creating their own conversations, cross-ability pairings are helpful. The higher-level student can support and give ideas to the lower-level student.

The *Future* Teacher's Edition and Lesson Planner, the Teacher's Notes in the Multilevel Communicative Activities Book, and the Teacher's Notes in the Transparencies and Reproducible Vocabulary Cards all provide specific suggestions for when to put students in like-ability versus cross-ability groups, and how to tailor activities to different ability levels.

Level	Description	CASAS Scale Scores
Intro	True Beginning	Below 180
1	Low Beginning	181–190
2	High Beginning	191–200
3	Low Intermediate	201–210
4	High Intermediate	211–220
5	Low Advanced	221–235

Unit Tour

Unit Opener

Each unit starts with a full-page photo that introduces the theme and vocabulary of the unit.

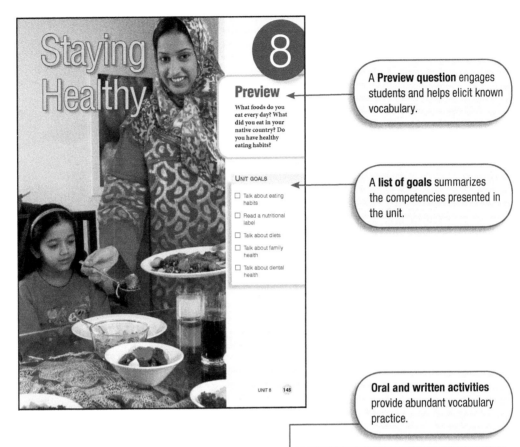

A **Preview question** engages students and helps elicit known vocabulary.

A **list of goals** summarizes the competencies presented in the unit.

Oral and written activities provide abundant vocabulary practice.

Vocabulary

Theme-setting vocabulary is presented in picture dictionary format.

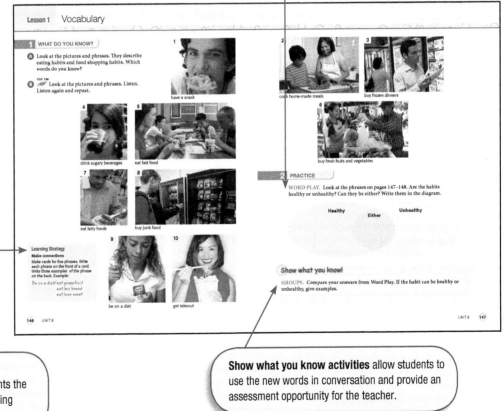

Vocabulary learning strategies give students the tools to continue learning outside of class.

Show what you know activities allow students to use the new words in conversation and provide an assessment opportunity for the teacher.

Listening and Speaking

Three listening lessons present the core competencies and language of the unit.

Before You Listen activities encourage critical thinking and introduce new language and concepts.

The **Pronunciation Watch** and exercises focus on the sound patterns, stress, and intonation of English.

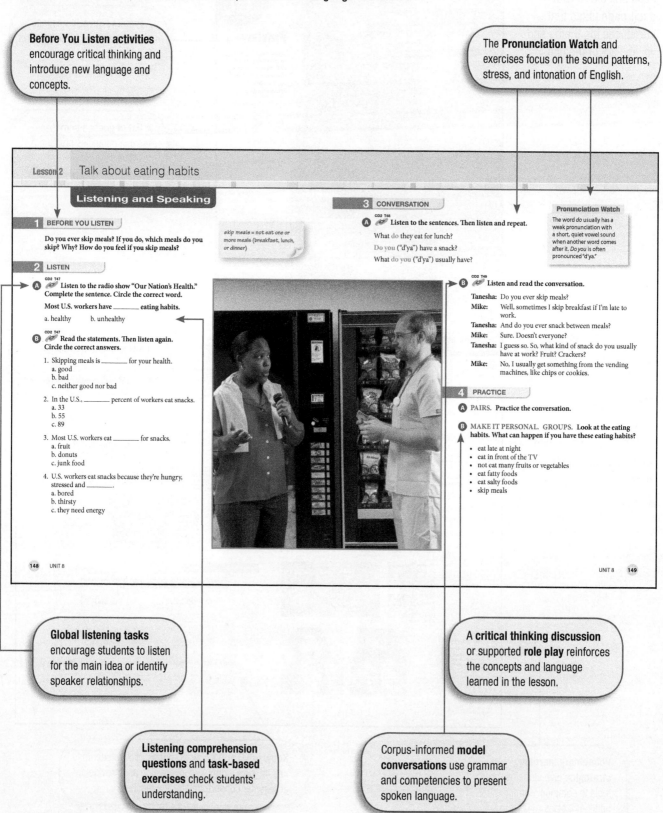

Lesson 2   Talk about eating habits

Listening and Speaking

1 BEFORE YOU LISTEN

Do you ever skip meals? If you do, which meals do you skip? Why? How do you feel if you skip meals?

skip meals = not eat one or more meals (breakfast, lunch, or dinner)

2 LISTEN

CD2 T47

A Listen to the radio show "Our Nation's Health." Complete the sentence. Circle the correct word.

Most U.S. workers have _____ eating habits.

a. healthy   b. unhealthy

CD2 T47

B Read the statements. Then listen again. Circle the correct answers.

1. Skipping meals is _____ for your health.
   a. good
   b. bad
   c. neither good nor bad

2. In the U.S., _____ percent of workers eat snacks.
   a. 33
   b. 55
   c. 89

3. Most U.S. workers eat _____ for snacks.
   a. fruit
   b. donuts
   c. junk food

4. U.S. workers eat snacks because they're hungry, stressed and _____.
   a. bored
   b. thirsty
   c. they need energy

3 CONVERSATION

CD2 T48

A Listen to the sentences. Then listen and repeat.

What do they eat for lunch?

Do you ("d'ya") have a snack?

What do you ("d'ya") usually have?

Pronunciation Watch

The word *do* usually has a weak pronunciation with a short, quiet vowel sound when another word comes after it. *Do you* is often pronounced "d'ya."

CD2 T49

B Listen and read the conversation.

Tanesha: Do you ever skip meals?
Mike: Well, sometimes I skip breakfast if I'm late to work.
Tanesha: And do you ever snack between meals?
Mike: Sure. Doesn't everyone?
Tanesha: I guess so. So, what kind of snack do you usually have at work? Fruit? Crackers?
Mike: No, I usually get something from the vending machines, like chips or cookies.

4 PRACTICE

A PAIRS. Practice the conversation.

B MAKE IT PERSONAL. GROUPS. Look at the eating habits. What can happen if you have these eating habits?

- eat late at night
- eat in front of the TV
- not eat many fruits or vegetables
- eat fatty foods
- eat salty foods
- skip meals

148   UNIT 8

UNIT 8   149

Global listening tasks encourage students to listen for the main idea or identify speaker relationships.

A **critical thinking discussion** or supported **role play** reinforces the concepts and language learned in the lesson.

Listening comprehension questions and **task-based exercises** check students' understanding.

Corpus-informed **model conversations** use grammar and competencies to present spoken language.

Grammar

Each unit presents three grammar points in a logical, systematic grammar syllabus.

Grammar charts present the target grammar point.

Grammar Watch notes call attention to specific aspects of the grammar point.

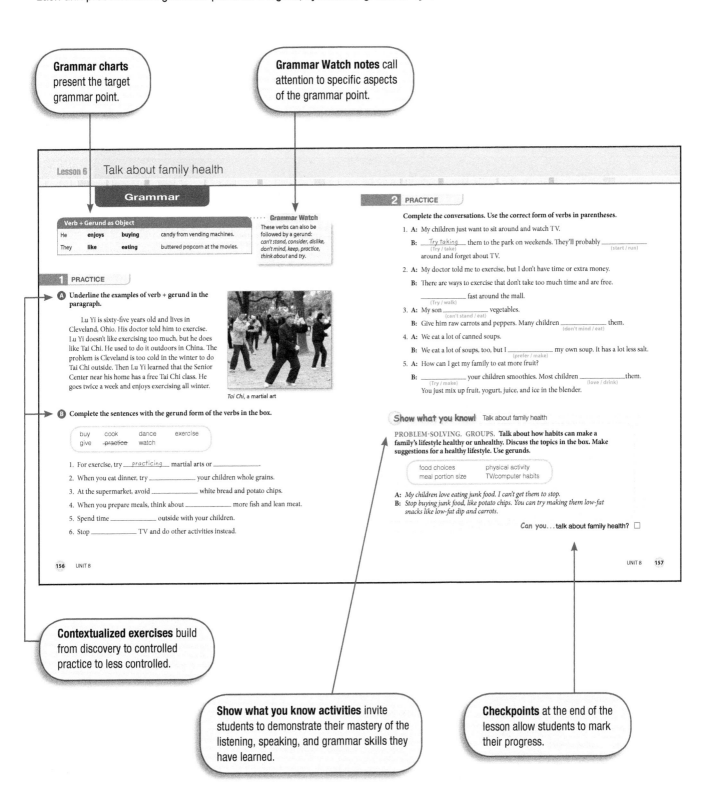

Lesson 6 Talk about family health

Grammar

Verb + Gerund as Object

| He | enjoys | buying | candy from vending machines. |
| They | like | eating | buttered popcorn at the movies. |

Grammar Watch

These verbs can also be followed by a gerund: *can't stand, consider, dislike, don't mind, keep, practice, think about* and *try*.

1 PRACTICE

A Underline the examples of verb + gerund in the paragraph.

Lu Yi is sixty-five years old and lives in Cleveland, Ohio. His doctor told him to exercise. Lu Yi doesn't like exercising too much, but he does like Tai Chi. He used to do it outdoors in China. The problem is Cleveland is too cold in the winter to do Tai Chi outside. Then Lu Yi learned that the Senior Center near his home has a free Tai Chi class. He goes twice a week and enjoys exercising all winter.

Tai Chi, a martial art

B Complete the sentences with the gerund form of the verbs in the box.

| buy | cook | dance | exercise |
| give | ~~practice~~ | watch | |

1. For exercise, try _practicing_ martial arts or _____.
2. When you eat dinner, try _____ your children whole grains.
3. At the supermarket, avoid _____ white bread and potato chips.
4. When you prepare meals, think about _____ more fish and lean meat.
5. Spend time _____ outside with your children.
6. Stop _____ TV and do other activities instead.

2 PRACTICE

Complete the conversations. Use the correct form of verbs in parentheses.

1. **A:** My children just want to sit around and watch TV.
   B: _Try taking_ (Try / take) them to the park on weekends. They'll probably _____ (start / run) around and forget about TV.

2. **A:** My doctor told me to exercise, but I don't have time or extra money.
   B: There are ways to exercise that don't take too much time and are free.
   _____ (Try / walk) fast around the mall.

3. **A:** My son _____ (can't stand / eat) vegetables.
   B: Give him raw carrots and peppers. Many children _____ (don't mind / eat) them.

4. **A:** We eat a lot of canned soups.
   B: We eat a lot of soups, too, but I _____ (prefer / make) my own soup. It has a lot less salt.

5. **A:** How can I get my family to eat more fruit?
   B: _____ (Try / make) your children smoothies. Most children _____ (love / drink) them. You just mix up fruit, yogurt, juice, and ice in the blender.

Show what you know! Talk about family health

PROBLEM-SOLVING. GROUPS. **Talk about how habits can make a family's lifestyle healthy or unhealthy. Discuss the topics in the box. Make suggestions for a healthy lifestyle. Use gerunds.**

| food choices | physical activity |
| meal portion size | TV/computer habits |

A: *My children love eating junk food. I can't get them to stop.*
B: *Stop buying junk food, like potato chips. You can try making them low-fat snacks like low-fat dip and carrots.*

Can you... talk about family health? ☐

156 UNIT 8

UNIT 8 157

Contextualized exercises build from discovery to controlled practice to less controlled.

Show what you know activities invite students to demonstrate their mastery of the listening, speaking, and grammar skills they have learned.

Checkpoints at the end of the lesson allow students to mark their progress.

Life Skills

The Life Skills lesson in each unit focuses on functional language, practical skills, and authentic printed materials such as instructions, labels, and diagrams.

Short speaking activities encourage students to think critically about the Life Skills topic.

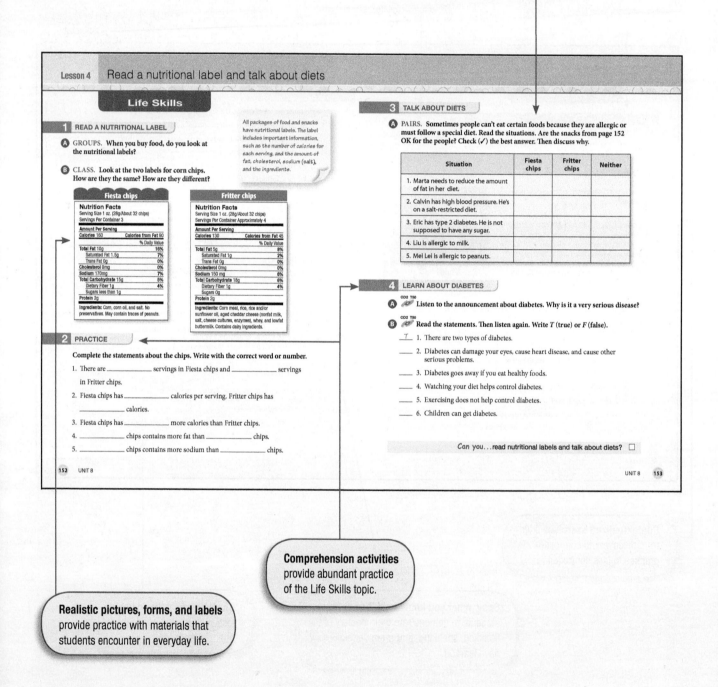

Lesson 4 Read a nutritional label and talk about diets

Life Skills

1 READ A NUTRITIONAL LABEL

A GROUPS. When you buy food, do you look at the nutritional labels?

B CLASS. Look at the two labels for corn chips. How are they the same? How are they different?

All packages of food and snacks have nutritional labels. The label includes important information, such as the number of calories for each serving, and the amount of fat, cholesterol, sodium (salt), and the ingredients.

Fiesta chips

Nutrition Facts
Serving Size 1 oz. (28g/About 32 chips)
Servings Per Container 3

Amount Per Serving
Calories 160   Calories from Fat 90
                          % Daily Value
Total Fat 10g   16%
  Saturated Fat 1.5g   7%
  Trans Fat 0g   0%
Cholesterol 0mg   0%
Sodium 170mg   7%
Total Carbohydrate 15g   5%
  Dietary Fiber 1g   4%
  Sugars less than 1g
Protein 2g

Ingredients: Corn, corn oil, and salt. No preservatives. May contain traces of peanuts.

Fritter chips

Nutrition Facts
Serving Size 1 oz. (28g/About 32 chips)
Servings Per Container Approximately 4

Amount Per Serving
Calories 130   Calories from Fat 45
                          % Daily Value
Total Fat 5g   8%
  Saturated Fat 1g   2%
  Trans Fat 0g   0%
Cholesterol 0mg   0%
Sodium 150 mg   6%
Total Carbohydrate 18g   6%
  Dietary Fiber 1g   4%
  Sugars 0g
Protein 2g

Ingredients: Corn meal, rice, rice and/or sunflower oil, aged cheddar cheese (nonfat milk, salt, cheese cultures, enzymes), whey, and lowfat buttermilk. Contains dairy ingredients.

2 PRACTICE

Complete the statements about the chips. Write with the correct word or number.

1. There are _____ servings in Fiesta chips and _____ servings in Fritter chips.

2. Fiesta chips has _____ calories per serving. Fritter chips has _____ calories.

3. Fiesta chips has _____ more calories than Fritter chips.

4. _____ chips contains more fat than _____ chips.

5. _____ chips contains more sodium than _____ chips.

3 TALK ABOUT DIETS

A PAIRS. Sometimes people can't eat certain foods because they are allergic or must follow a special diet. Read the situations. Are the snacks from page 152 OK for the people? Check (✓) the best answer. Then discuss why.

Situation	Fiesta chips	Fritter chips	Neither
1. Marta needs to reduce the amount of fat in her diet.			
2. Calvin has high blood pressure. He's on a salt-restricted diet.			
3. Eric has type 2 diabetes. He is not supposed to have any sugar.			
4. Liu is allergic to milk.			
5. Mei Lei is allergic to peanuts.			

4 LEARN ABOUT DIABETES

A CD2 T50 Listen to the announcement about diabetes. Why is it a very serious disease?

B CD2 T50 Read the statements. Then listen again. Write *T* (true) or *F* (false).

_T_ 1. There are two types of diabetes.

____ 2. Diabetes can damage your eyes, cause heart disease, and cause other serious problems.

____ 3. Diabetes goes away if you eat healthy foods.

____ 4. Watching your diet helps control diabetes.

____ 5. Exercising does not help control diabetes.

____ 6. Children can get diabetes.

Can you... read nutritional labels and talk about diets? ☐

Comprehension activities provide abundant practice of the Life Skills topic.

Realistic pictures, forms, and labels provide practice with materials that students encounter in everyday life.

Reading

High-interest articles introduce students to cultural concepts and useful, topical information. Students read to learn while learning to read in English.

Comprehension questions check understanding of the article and build reading skills.

Essential **reading skills** such as finding the main idea, scanning for information, and getting meaning from context are introduced and practiced.

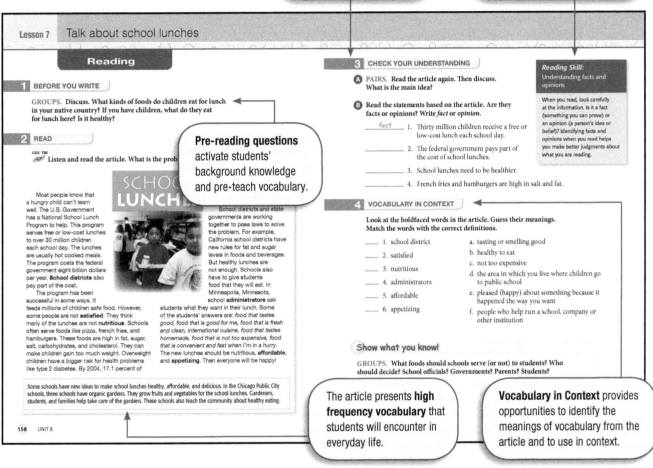

Pre-reading questions activate students' background knowledge and pre-teach vocabulary.

The article presents **high frequency vocabulary** that students will encounter in everyday life.

Vocabulary in Context provides opportunities to identify the meanings of vocabulary from the article and to use in context.

Writing

The concepts that students have learned in the unit are applied in the writing lesson.

In **Before You Write**, students generate ideas and read a model.

After they write, students **check their writing** for clarity and errors in spelling, punctuation, and grammar.

Review & Expand

The final page of the unit allows students to review and expand on the language, themes, and competencies they have worked with throughout the unit.

> Lively **role-play activities** motivate students, allowing them to feel successful. Teachers can use these activities to assess students' mastery of the material.

> Cross-references direct students to the **Grammar Review**, the **Persistence Activity** and the **Team Project** for that unit.

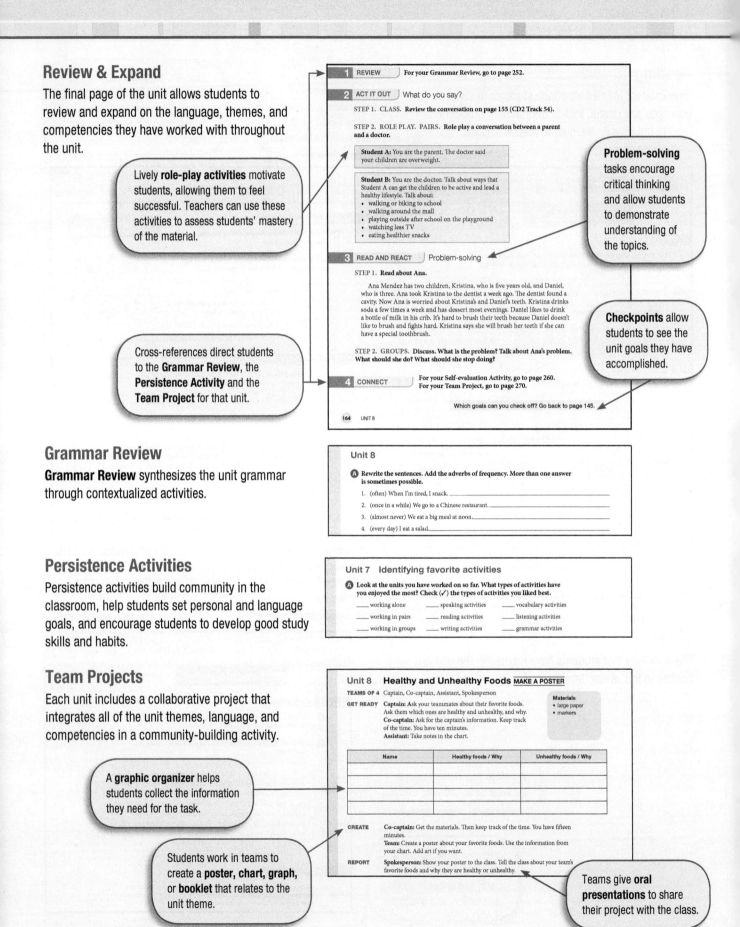

1 REVIEW For your Grammar Review, go to page 252.

2 ACT IT OUT What do you say?

STEP 1. CLASS. Review the conversation on page 155 (CD2 Track 54).

STEP 2. ROLE PLAY. PAIRS. Role play a conversation between a parent and a doctor.

Student A: You are the parent. The doctor said your children are overweight.

Student B: You are the doctor. Talk about ways that Student A can get the children to be active and lead a healthy lifestyle. Talk about:
- walking or biking to school
- walking around the mall
- playing outside after school on the playground
- watching less TV
- eating healthier snacks

3 READ AND REACT Problem-solving

STEP 1. Read about Ana.

Ana Mendez has two children, Kristina, who is five years old, and Daniel, who is three. Ana took Kristina to the dentist a week ago. The dentist found a cavity. Now Ana is worried about Kristina's and Daniel's teeth. Kristina drinks soda a few times a week and has dessert most evenings. Daniel likes to drink a bottle of milk in his crib. It's hard to brush their teeth because Daniel doesn't like to brush and fights hard. Kristina says she will brush her teeth if she can have a special toothbrush.

STEP 2. GROUPS. Discuss. What is the problem? Talk about Ana's problem. What should she do? What should she stop doing?

4 CONNECT For your Self-evaluation Activity, go to page 260. For your Team Project, go to page 270.

Which goals can you check off? Go back to page 145.

164 UNIT 8

> **Problem-solving** tasks encourage critical thinking and allow students to demonstrate understanding of the topics.

> **Checkpoints** allow students to see the unit goals they have accomplished.

Grammar Review

Grammar Review synthesizes the unit grammar through contextualized activities.

Unit 8

A Rewrite the sentences. Add the adverbs of frequency. More than one answer is sometimes possible.

1. (often) When I'm tired, I snack._____
2. (once in a while) We go to a Chinese restaurant._____
3. (almost never) We eat a big meal at noon._____
4. (every day) I eat a salad._____

Persistence Activities

Persistence activities build community in the classroom, help students set personal and language goals, and encourage students to develop good study skills and habits.

Unit 7   Identifying favorite activities

A Look at the units you have worked on so far. What types of activities have you enjoyed the most? Check (✓) the types of activities you liked best.

____ working alone   ____ speaking activities   ____ vocabulary activities

____ working in pairs   ____ reading activities   ____ listening activities

____ working in groups   ____ writing activities   ____ grammar activities

Team Projects

Each unit includes a collaborative project that integrates all of the unit themes, language, and competencies in a community-building activity.

> A **graphic organizer** helps students collect the information they need for the task.

> Students work in teams to create a **poster, chart, graph,** or **booklet** that relates to the unit theme.

Unit 8   Healthy and Unhealthy Foods MAKE A POSTER

TEAMS OF 4 Captain, Co-captain, Assistant, Spokesperson

GET READY **Captain:** Ask your teammates about their favorite foods. Ask them which ones are healthy and unhealthy, and why.
Co-captain: Ask for the captain's information. Keep track of the time. You have ten minutes.
Assistant: Take notes in the chart.

Materials
- large paper
- markers

Name	Healthy foods / Why	Unhealthy foods / Why

CREATE **Co-captain:** Get the materials. Then keep track of the time. You have fifteen minutes.
Team: Create a poster about your favorite foods. Use the information from your chart. Add art if you want.

REPORT **Spokesperson:** Show your poster to the class. Tell the class about your team's favorite foods and why they are healthy or unhealthy.

> Teams give **oral presentations** to share their project with the class.

MyEnglishLab

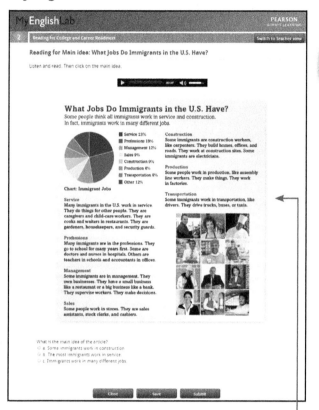

MyEnglishLab delivers rich online content to engage and motivate **students**.

Grammar Coach videos give additional grammar presentations and practice.

MyEnglishLab also provides students with:
- rich interactive practice in listening, speaking, vocabulary building, and life skills
- immediate and meaningful feedback on wrong answers
- grade reports that display performance and time on task

Reading and writing lessons, based on College and Career Readiness Standards (CCRS), develop essential skills for academic and career readiness.

MyEnglishLab delivers innovative teaching tools and useful resources to **teachers**.

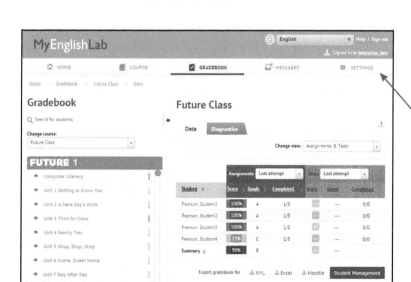

With **MyEnglishLab**, teachers can:
- view student scores by unit and activity
- monitor student progress on any activity or test
- analyze class data to determine steps for remediation and support

Scope and Sequence

UNIT	VOCABULARY	LISTENING	SPEAKING AND PRONUNCIATION	GRAMMAR
Pre-Unit **Getting Started** *page 2*	Clarification questions	• Listen to clarification questions in classroom contexts	• Ask for clarification	• *Wh-* questions • *Yes/No* questions • Introduction to noun clauses • Introduction to reported speech
1 **In the Neighborhood** *page 5*	Countries	• Listen to a conversation about people making new acquaintances • Listen to a radio announcement about the West-Indian Day parade • Listen to a conversation about people's past habits	• Make small talk • Talk about life in the U.S. • Talk about holidays and celebrations • Compare your life now with your life in the past • Word stress • Pronunciation of *used to*	• Simple present • Quantifiers • *Used to*
2 **Dreams and Goals** *page 25*	• Educational goals • Goals at work • Community goals	• Listen to a conversation about people going back to school • Listen to a conversation about looking for a job • Listen to a radio announcement for a community center	• Talk about your hopes and dreams • Talk about going back to school • Talk about future plans • Talk about looking for a better job • Talk about community services • Pronunciation of *will* • Pronunciation of *going to*	• *Will/will probably/might/won't* • The future with *be going to* • Present continuous for the future
3 **School Days** *page 45*	School activities	• Listen to a radio talk show about parental involvement in school • Listen to a conversation about bullies at school • Listen to a conversation between a parent and a school counselor	• Talk about why children fall behind in school • Talk about ways to help children in school • Talk about library services • Talk about dealing with bullies • Talk about things teachers and counselors should do to help children • Talk about ways that children can continue their education • Word stress in two-syllable nouns • Word stress in phrasal verbs	• Inseparable and separable phrasal verbs • Simple past review: Regular and irregular verbs • *Should* and *Have to*
4 **Getting a Job** *page 65*	Qualities of employees	• Listen to a radio commercial for a technical school • Listen to a conversation at a job interview • Listen to a radio talk show about illegal interview questions	• Talk about your work experience • Describe your work history • Talk about positive work behavior • Pronunciation of the final *-s* • Penultimate stress in words ending with *-sion* or *-tion*	• Present perfect: *Yes/No* questions with *ever* and *never* • Present perfect: Statements with *for* and *since* • *Be* + adjective + infinitive

LIFE SKILLS	READING	WRITING	PROBLEM SOLVING/ NUMERACY	PERSISTENCE
	• Scanning for specific information			• Community building
• Identify countries on a world map • Follow a recipe • Handle food safely	• Read about new communities in the U.S. • *Reading Skill:* Understanding the main idea	• Write about your life now and in the past • Describe your life in your native country • Describe your life in the U.S.	• Give advice to someone who recently moved to the U.S.	• Ask and answer questions with a partner about yourselves • Write a poem about yourself
• Set goals • Talk about obstacles and supports	• Read about entrepreneurs • *Reading Skill:* Predicting	• Write about your goals • Describe the steps you will take to reach your goals	• Give advice to someone who wants to change careers	• Categorize goals • Set goals • Set time limits for goals • Talk about obstacles and supports
• Understand the letter grading system • Read a report card • Listen to a school telephone recording • Role-play a parent-teacher meeting	• Read a letter from a parent to a teacher • Read a tutor sign up sheet • Read an article about library services • *Reading Skill:* Using what you know	• Write a letter to a librarian asking for improvements to services	• Talk about local school problems and what parents can do • Talk about problems children sometimes have at school and suggest solutions • Give advice to a parent	• Identify your resources for learning English
• Read and complete a job application	• Read a letter of recommendation • Read an online job advertisement • Read an article about job interviews • *Reading Skill:* Making inferences	• Write a list of questions and answers for a job interview • Write a thank-you letter for a job interview • Describe your qualifications • Use correct letter format	• Talk about how to respond to job interview questions • Give advice to someone filling out a job application	• Check the progress of your goals

Text in red = Civics and American culture

UNIT	VOCABULARY	LISTENING	SPEAKING AND PRONUNCIATION	GRAMMAR	
5 **Traveling** *page 85*	People, things, and places in an airport	• Listen to an airport announcement • Listen to a telephone conversation about friends' travel arrangements • Listen to a telephone conversation about travel delays	• Give and follow instructions at an airport • Talk about airline travel • Identify personal belongings • Talk about delays and cancellations • Make polite requests and ask for permission • Pronunciation of *can* • Sentence stress	• *Can/could:* Affirmative and negative statements • *Be able to:* Affirmative and negative statements • Possessive adjectives and possessive pronouns • Polite requests with *would/could/will/can* • Requests for permission with *could/can/may*	
6 **Getting a Good Deal** *page 105*	Problems with purchases	• Listen to a conversation about a broken appliance • Listen to a conversation about problems with cell phone service • Listen to a customer making an exchange	• Talk about product defects • Talk about getting a good deal • Talk about problems with cell phone service • Compare prices and quality • Compare shopping experiences • Make an exchange • Pronunciation of *th-* • Linking consonants to vowels	• Noun clauses • Comparative adjectives • *As . . . as* with adjectives	
7 **Getting There Safely** *page 125*	Things and places on the road	• Listen to a traffic report • Listen to a police officer interview drivers after an accident • Listen to a radio report about steps to take after a car accident	• Talk about car maintenance • Describe a traffic accident • Identify steps to take after an accident • Talk about driving costs • Pronunciation of *a/an/the* • Vowel sounds of unstressed syllables	• *A, An, The* • Past continuous • Present time clauses	
8 **Staying Healthy** *page 145*	Health habits	• Listen to a radio report about eating habits • Listen to a radio announcement about diabetes • Listen to a radio announcement about family health • Listen to a conversation about dental health	• Talk about eating habits • Talk about nutrition and special diets • Talk about family health • Talk about healthy food substitutes • Talk about dental health • Pronunciation of *do* • Intonation with *Yes/No* and *Wh-* questions	• Adverbs of frequency • Verb + gerund as object • Gerunds	

LIFE SKILLS	READING	WRITING	PROBLEM SOLVING/ NUMERACY	PERSISTENCE
• Read screen instructions • Read a bus terminal map	• Read an article about traveling safely • *Reading Skill:* Getting meaning from context	• Write about a problem you had when you traveled • Describe the problem	• Solve a travel problem	• Identify what is important to you
• Read a newspaper sales ad • Read a rebate	• Read a warranty • Read an article about comparison shopping • *Reading Skill:* Using formatting clues	• Write about shopping experiences • Compare two stores	• Talk about problems with cell phone service • Give advice to people with phone service problems • Compare price and quality • Give advice to people buying a refrigerator	• Identify what you have learned so far
• Identify parts of a car	• Identify causes of car accidents • *Reading Skill:* Interpreting charts	• Write a letter to the mayor of your city about a traffic problem • Explain the problem • Suggest a solution	• Identify common car problems • Talk about ways to drive defensively • Talk about ways to save money on gas and cars • Give advice to someone who hit a parked car	• Identify your favorite activities
• Read a nutritional label	• Read about school lunches • *Reading Skill:* Understanding facts and opinions	• Describe your eating habits • Write about your diet in your native country and in the U.S.	• Give advice to a parent about dental care	• Identify ways to reduce stress

Text in red = Civics and American culture

UNIT	VOCABULARY	LISTENING	SPEAKING AND PRONUNCIATION	GRAMMAR	
9 **On the Job** *page 165*	Job skills	• Listen to an employer train an employee • Listen to an employee ask for time off • Listen to an employee respond to correction	• Identify your strengths in the workplace • Ask for clarification • **Talk about expectations on the job** • Respond appropriately to correction by an employer • Give and follow instructions • **Sentence stress to clarify**	• *One/Ones* • Verb + object + infinitive • Reported speech: commands and requests with *tell/ask*	
10 **Going to the Doctor** *page 185*	Places in a hospital	Listen to conversations about • rescheduling a doctor appointment • describing symptoms • medical procedures and concerns	• **Talk about problems with making or going to doctor's appointments** • Reschedule a doctor's appointment • **Talk about feelings about doctors** • Talk about symptoms • Talk about medical procedures and concerns • **Pronunciation of /d/ /t/ /ɪd/ sound in verbs ending with *-ed*** • **Time length of stressed and unstressed syllables**	• Participial adjectives • Present perfect continuous • Gerunds after prepositions	
11 **Money Matters** *page 205*	Money and banking	• Listen to a radio commercial for banking services • Listen to a customer open a bank account • **Listen to a radio talk show about budgeting** • Listen to a conversation about rental housing	• Open a checking account • Use checking accounts safely • Talk about uses and risks of credit cards • **Budget your expenses** • Ask about appliances and utilities • Talk about housing • **Intonation with *if-* clauses**	• Present real conditional • Future real conditional • Gerunds and infinitives as objects of verbs	
12 **Washington, D.C.** *page 225*	Places in or near Washington, D.C.	• Listen to a conversation about friends comparing trips to Washington, D.C. • Listen to a tour guide talk about a travel itinerary • Listen to a tour guide talk about President Lincoln	• **Talk about favorite places** • **Talk about famous places you have visited** • **Talk about the government** • **Talk about fereral holidays** • **Talk about rights and freedoms** • Talk about famous U.S. presidents • **Pronunciation of *did you*** • **Word stress in compound words**	• Superlatives: *-est, least, most, one of the most* • Simple present passive • Past passive	

LIFE SKILLS	READING	WRITING	PROBLEM SOLVING/ NUMERACY	PERSISTENCE
• Identify safety hazards at work • Interpret a safety poster • Interpret safety signs	• Read about health in the workplace • *Reading Skill:* Skimming	• Write about good and bad things about a job • Write about your feelings about the job	• Talk about your biggest problems at work and give suggestions • Identify situations in workplaces that cause stress or can harm your health and suggest solutions	• Identify times you succeeded at something
• Recognize places in a hospital • Identify parts of the body • Read and complete a medical history form	• Read about immunizations • *Reading Skill:* Using graphics	• Write about an experience with a doctor	• Problem-solve how to calm children getting an immunization • Problem-solve a situation with diabetes	• Identify things you are an expert at
• Read a checking statement • Read utility bills	• Read an advertisement for free checking • Read an article about using credit cards wisely • *Reading Skill:* Understanding Author purpose	• Write about your financial goals	• Read a checking statement • Write ways to avoid problems with identity theft • Read a budget worksheet • Budget your expenses • Read utility bills • Problem-solve ways to save money on utilities • Problem-solve ways for someone to get out of debt	• Reflect on your dreams, hopes, and goals • Review what you have learned in class • Identify how the things you learned in class have helped you reach your goals
• Read a subway map • Ask for and listen to directions • Identify the three branches of U.S. government • Identify federal holidays • Identify Presidents George Washington and Abraham Lincoln	• Read an article about the freedom of religion in the United States • *Reading Skill:* Summarizing	• Write about rights and freedoms • Explain why one right or freedom is important to you	• Give advice to travelers who are late for their flight	• Make a poster of your accomplishments and memories from class

Text in red = Civics and American culture

Correlations

UNIT	CASAS Reading Basic Skill Content Standards	CASAS Listening Basic Skill Content Stadards
1	**U1:** R1.2, 1.3, 2.2, 2.4, 3.1, 3.2, 3.6, 3.8, **L1:** 1.4, 3.3, 3.10, 3.12, 3.13, **L2:** 1.4, 3.10, 3.12, 6.5, **L3:** 3.3, 3.10, 3.12, **L4:** 1.4, 3.3, 3.10, 3.12, 3.13, 6.1, 7.2, 7.9, **L5:** 1.4, 3.10, **L7:** 2.7, 3.10, **L8:** 1.4, 6.6, **L9:** 3.3, 3.12, **SWYK Review & Expand:** 3.3, 3.10, 3.13, 6.6	**U1:** L2.1, 4.1, 4.2, 4.3, L1:1.1, **L2:** 1.1, 1.4, 1.6, 2.4, 2.7, 2.8, 3.1, 3.2, 3.3, 3.5, 3.6, 4.7, 6.1, 6.2, 6.3, **L4:** 1.1, 1.4, 2.4, 2.7, 2.8, 2.9, 3.1, 3.2, 3.5, 3.6, 4.5, 4.7, 6.1, 6.2, 6.8, **L5:** 1.1, 1.4, 2.4, 2.7, 2.8, 2.9, 3.1, 3.2, 3.3, 3.6, 4.11, 6.1, 6.2, **L6:** 4.7, **L8:** 1.1, 1.4, 1.5, 2.4, 2.7, 2.8, 2.9, 3.1, 3.2, 3.6, 4.5, 4.7, 6.1, 6.2, 6.3, 6.6, **L9:** 4.7, **SWYK Review & Expand:** 4.7, 6.6
2	**U2:** R1.2, 1.3, 2.2, 3.1, 3.2, 3.6, 3.8, **L1:** **1.4**, 2.12, 3.3, 3.10, 3.12, 3.13, 3.14, **L2:** 1.4, 2.5, 3.10, **L3:** 3.3, 3.10, 3.14, **L4:** 1.4, 2.12, 3.10, 3.12, 3.13, 4.4, 6.1, 7.1, 7.2, 7.9, **L5:** 1.4, 3.10, **L6:** 3.14, 7.4, **L7:** 3.3, **L8:** 3.3, **L9:** 1.4, **L10:** 3.10, 4.8, **SWYK Review & Expand:** 3.3, 3.10	**U2:** L2.1, 4.1, 4.2, 4.3, **L1:** 1.4, 4.7, **L2:** 1.4, 2.4, 2.7, 2.8, 2.9, 3.1, 3.2, 3.3, 4.5, 4.11, 6.2, 6.3, 6.5, 6.6, **L3:** 3.9, **L4:** 1.4, 2.4, 2.7, 2.8, 2.9, 3.1, 3.2, 3.9, 4.7, 6.1, 6.2, 6.3, 6.5, 6.8, 6.10, **L5:** 1.4, 1.5, 2.4, 2.7, 2.8, 2.9, 3.1, 3.2, 3.9, 4.5, 4.11, 6.2, 6.3, 6.6, **L6:** 3.9, **L7:** 3.3, 3.5, **L9:** 1.4, 2.4, 2.7, 2.8, 2.9, 3.1, 3.2, 3.9, 4.5, 4.11, 6.2, 6.3, **SWYK Review & Expand:** 3.9, 4.7, 6.6
3	**U3:** R1.2, 1.3, 2.2, 3.1, 3.2, 3.6, 3.8, 3.10, **L1:** 3.3, 3.12, 4.1, 6.1, 7.8, **L2:** 1.4, 3.12, **L3:** 3.15, 4.1, **L4:** 1.4, 2.12, 3.12, 3.13, 6.1, 7.2, 7.9, **L5:** 3.3, 4.1, 6.1, 7.8, **L6:** 1.4, 3.12, **L7:** 3.3, **L8:** 4.1, **L9:** 1.4, 3.12	**U3:** L2.1, 4.1, 4.2, 4.3, **L2:** 1.4, 1.6, 2.3, 2.4, 2.7, 2.8, 2.9, 3.1, 3.2, 3.3, 3.5, 4.11, 6.2, 6.3, **L4:** 1.4, 1.6, 2.3, 2.4, 2.7, 2.8, 2.9, 3.1, 3.2, 3.3, 3.5, 4.7, 4.11, 6.1, 6.8, 6.10, **L6:** 1.4, 2.3, 2.4, 2.7, 2.8, 2.9, 3.1, 3.2, 3.3, 3.5, 4.11, 6.2, 6.3, 6.6, **L8:** 6.6, **L9:** 1.4, 1.6, 2.3, 2.4, 2.7, 2.9, 3.1, 3.2, 3.3, 4.11, 6.2, 6.3, **SWYK Review & Expand:** 4.7, 6.6
4	**U4:** R1.2, 1.3, 2.2, 3.1, 3.2, 3.3, 3.6, 3.10, **L1:** 1.4, 3.12, 3.13, 7.1, **L2:** 1.4, **L3:** 2.5, 3.9, **L4:** 4.1, 4.4, 4.7, 6.2, **L5:** 1.4, 3.9, 3.12, **L6:** 3.9, 4.3, 7.1, **L7:** 1.4, 3.12, 3.13, 6.1, 7.2, 7.9, **L8:** 4.1, 4.3, 6.1, **L9:** 1.4, **L10:** 3.9	**U4:** L1.4, 2.1, 4.1, 4.2, 4.3, **L1:** 2.3, L2:1.2, 2.3, 2.4, 2.7, 2.8, 2.9, 3.1, 3.2, 4.11, 6.1, 6.2, 6.3, 6.6, **L3:** 3.5, 3.9, **L5:** 2.3, 2.4, 2.7, 2.8, 2.9, 3.1, 3.2, 3.9, 4.11, 6.1, 6.2, 6.3, 6.5, 6.6, **L6:** 3.9, 6.6, **L7:** 2.3, 2.4, 2.7, 2.8, 2.9, 3.1, 3.2, 3.4, 6.8, 6.10, **L9:** 2.3, 2.4, 2.7, 2.8, 2.9, 3.1, 3.2, 4.11, 6.1, 6.2, 6.3, 6.5, **SWYK Review & Expand:** 6.6
5	**U5:** R1.2, 1.3, 2.2, 2.12, 3.1, 3.2, 3.6, 3.8, **L1:** 1.4, 3.3, 3.12, 3.13, 6.1, **L2:** 1.4, 2.5, 3.3, **L3:** 2.5, 3.3, **L4:** 3.12, 4.8, 4.9, **L5:** 1.4, 3.3, **L6:**3.10, **L7:** 1.4, 3.10, 3.13, 6.1, 7.2, 7.9, **L8:** 3.3, 3.10, **L9:** 1.4, **L10:** 3.12	**U5:** L2.1, 4.1, 4.2, 4.3, **L2:** 1.4, 2.3, 2.4, 2.7, 2.8, 2.9, 3.1, 3.2, 3.3, 3.5, 3.9, 4.11, 6.1, 6.2, 6.3, 6.5, 6.6, **L3:** 3.5, **L4:** 6.6, **L5:** 1.4, 2.3, 2.4, 2.7, 2.8, 2.9, 3.1, 3.2, 3.3, 3.9, 4.11, 6.1, 6.2, 6.3, 6.5, **L6:** 6.6, **L7:** 1.4, 2.3, 2.4, 2.7, 2.8, 2.9, 3.1, 3.2, 3.3, 3.4, 3.9, 4.11, 6.6, 6.8, 6.10, **L9:** 1.4, 2.3, 2.4, 2.7, 2.8, 2.9, 3.1, 3.2, 3.3, 3.9, 4.11, 6.1, 6.2, 6.3, 6.5, **L10:** 6.6, **SWYK Review & Expand:** 6.6
6	**U6:** R1.2, 1.3, 2.2, 2.12, 3.1, 3.2, 3.6, 3.8, 3.9, **L1:** 1.4, 3.12, **L2:** 1.4, 3.10, **L3:** 3.3, 3.10, 3.12, 4.1, **L4:** 1.4, 3.10, 3.13, 6.1, 7.2, 7.9, **L5:** 1.4, 3.12, 4.4, **L6:** 3.3, 3.12, 4.4, 6.2, 7.13, **L7:** 3.3, 4.4, 6.2, **L8:** 1.4, 3.3, 3.10, 4.4, **L9:** 3.10, **L10:** 3.3	**U6:** L2.1, 4.1, 4.2, 4.3, **L2:** 1.4, 2.3, 2.4, 2.7, 2.8, 2.9, 3.1, 3.2, 3.9, 4.11, 6.1, 6.2, 6.3, **L4:** 1.4, 2.3, 2.4, 2.7, 2.8, 2.9, 3.1, 3.2, 3.9, 4.7, 4.11, 6.5, 6.8, 6.10, **L5:** 1.4, 2.3, 2.4, 2.7, 2.8, 2.9, 3.1, 3.2, 3.9, 4.11, 6.1, 6.2, 6.3, 6.6, **L6:** 3.10, 6.6, **L8:** 1.4, 2.3, 2.4, 2.7, 2.8, 2.9, 3.1, 3.2, 3.9, 4.11, 6.1, 6.2, 6.3, 6.5, 6.6, **L9:** 4.5, **SWYK Review & Expand:** 4.7, 6.6
7	**U7:** R1.2, 1.3, 2.2, 2.12, 3.1, 3.2, 3.6, 3.8, 3.9, 3.10, **L1:** 1.4, 3.12, **L2:** 1.4, 3.12, 4.4, **L3:** 3.3, 3.12, **L4:** 3.3, 3.12, 3.13, **L5:** 1.4, 3.3, 3.12, **L6:** 3.3, **L7:** 1.4, 3.13, 6.1, 7.2, 7.9, **L8:** 3.3, **L9:** 1.4, **L10:** 3.3	**U7:** L2.1, 4.1, 4.2, 4.3, **L1:** 1.4, **L2:** 1.4, 2.3, 2.4, 2.7, 2.8, 2.9, 3.1, 3.2, 3.3, 3.9, 4.11, 6.1, 6.2, 6.6, **L5:** 1.4, 2.3, 2.4, 2.7, 2.8, 2.9, 3.1, 3.2, 3.3, 3.9, 4.11, 6.1, 6.2, 6.6, **L7:** 1.4, 2.3, 2.4, 2.7, 2.8, 2.9, 3.1, 3.2, 3.3, 3.5, 3.9, 4.11, 6.10, **L9:** 1.4, 2.3, 2.4, 2.7, 2.8, 2.9, 3.1, 3.2, 3.3, 3.9, 4.11, 6.1, 6.2, **SWYK Review & Expand:** 6.8
8	**U8:** R1.2, 1.3, 2.2, 2.12, 3.1, 3.2, 3.6, 3.8, 3.9, 3.10, **L1:** 1.4, 3.12, **L2:** 1.4, 3.3, 3.12, **L3:** 3.3, **L4:** 2.7, 3.12, 4.1, **L5:** 1.4, 3.12, **L6:** 3.3, 3.12, **L7:** 1.4, 3.12, 3.13, 6.1, 7.2, 7.9, 7.10, **L8:** 1.4, 3.3, 3.12, **L9:** 3.3, **L10:** 3.3, **SWYK Review & Expand:** 3.3	**U8:** L2.1, 4.1, 4.2, 4.3, **L1:** 1.4, **L2:** 1.4, 2.3, 2.4, 2.7, 2.8, 2.9, 3.1, 3.2, 3.9, 4.6, 4.7, 4.11, 6.1, 6.2, 6.5, **L5:** 1.4, 2.3, 2.4, 2.7, 2.8, 2.9, 3.1, 3.2, 3.9, 4.6, 4.7, 4.11, 6.1, 6.2, 6.5, 6.6, **L7:** 1.4, 2.3, 2.4, 2.7, 2.8, 2.9, 3.1, 3.2, 3.9, 6.1, 6.5, 6.8, 6.9, 6.10, **L8:** 1.4, 2.3, 2.4, 2.7, 2.8, 2.9, 3.1, 3.2, 3.9, 4.6, 4.7, 4.11, 6.1, 6.2, **SWYK Review & Expand:** 6.6
9	**U9:** R1.2, 1.3, 2.2, 2.12, 3.1, 3.2, 3.6, 3.8, 3.9, **L1:** 1.4, 3.12, **L2:** 1.4, 3.12, **L3:** 3.3, 3.10, **L4:** 1.4, 3.10, 3.12, 3.13, 6.1, 7.2, 7.9, **L5:** 3.3, **L6:** 1.4, 3.12, **L7:** 3.3, 3.12, **L8:** 3.3, 7.1, **L9:** 1.4, 3.3, 3.12,	**U9:** L2.1, 4.1, 4.2, 4.3, L1:1.4, **L2:** 1.4, 2.3, 2.4, 2.7, 2.8, 2.9, 3.1, 3.2, 3.9, 3.13, 4.6, 4.11, 5.4, 5.5, 5.6, 6.2, 6.6, 6.7, **L3:** 4.11, 6.6, 6.7, **L4:** 1.4, 2.3, 2.4, 2.7, 2.8, 2.9, 3.1, 3.2, 3.9, 3.13, 4.6, 6.8, 6.9, **L6:** 1.4, 2.3, 2.4, 2.7, 2.8, 2.9, 3.1, 3.2, 3.9, 3.13, 4.6, 6.2, 6.5, **L9:** 1.4, 2.3, 2.4, 2.7, 2.8, 2.9, 3.1, 3.2, 3.9, 3.13, 4.6, 4.11, 6.2, 6.6, **L10:** 4.11, 6.6, **SWYK Review & Expand:** 4.11, 6.6
10	**U10:** R1.2, 1.3, 2.2, 2.12, 3.1, 3.2, 3.6, 3.8, **L1:** 1.4, 3.12, L2: 1.4, 3.10, 3.12, L3: 1.4, **L4:** 4.7, **L5:** 1.4, 3.10, 3.12, **L6:** 3.10, 3.12, **L7:** 1.4, 3.13, 6.1, 7.2, 7.9, **L8:** 3.10, **L9:** 1.4, 3.12, **L10:** 3.10	**U10:** L2.1, 4.1, 4.2, 4.3, **L1:** 1.4, 2.7, 2.8, 2.9, 3.1, 3.2, 3.9, 4.6, 4.11, 6.2, 6.6, **L3:** 1.4, **L5:** 1.4, 2.7, 2.8, 2.9, 3.1, 3.2, 3.9, 4.6, 4.11, 6.2, **L6:** 6.6, **L7:** 1.4, 2.7, 2.8, 2.9, 3.1, 3.2, 3.9, 6.1, 6.5, 6.8, 6.9, **L9:** 1.4, 2.7, 2.8, 2.9, 3.1, 3.2, 3.9, 4.6, 4.11, 6.2, **SWYK Review & Expand:** 6.6
11	**U11:** R1.2, 1.3, 2.2, 2.12, 3.1, 3.2, 3.3, 3.6, 3.8, 3.9, **L1:** 1.4, 3.12, 4.4, 4.7, **L2:** 1.4, 3.12, 4.4, **L3:** 3.12, **L4:** 1.4, 3.13, 4.4, 7.2, 7.11, **L6:** 1.4, 3.12, 4.4, 4.7, **L8:** 3.12, 4.4, 4.7, **L9:** 1.4, 2.7, 3.12, 4.4, 7.13, **SWYK Review & Expand:** 3.12, 4.4, 4.7	**U11:** L2.1, 4.1, 4.2, 4.3, L1:1.4, **L2:** 1.4, 2.3, 2.4, 2.7, 2.8, 2.9, 3.1, 3.2, 3.9, 3.13, 4.6, 6.1, 6.2, **L3:** 6.6, **L4:** 1.4, 2.3, 2.4, 2.7, 2.8, 2.9, 3.1, 3.2, 3.9, 3.13, 6.1, 6.2, 6.6, **L6:** 1.4, 2.3, 2.4, 2.7, 2.8, 2.9, 3.1, 3.2, 3.9, 3.13, 4.6, 6.1, 6.2, **L9:** 1.4, 2.3, 2.4, 2.7, 2.8, 2.9, 3.1, 3.2, 3.9, 3.13, 4.6, 6.1, 6.2, 6.6, **SWYK Review & Expand:** 6.6
12	**U12:** R1.2, 1.3, 1.4, 2.2, 2.12, 3.1, 3.2, 3.6, 3.8, 3.9, **L1:** 1.4, 3.12, **L2:** 1 .4, 3.3, 3.12, **L3:** 3.3, 3.12, **L4:** 1.4, 3.3, 3.12, 4.9, **L5:** 1.4, 3.3, 3.12, **L6:** 3.3, **L7:** 1.4, 3.13, 6.1, 7.2, 7.7, **L8:** 1.4, 3.3, 3.12, **L9:** 3.3, 3.12, 8.4	**U12:** L2.1, 4.1, 4.2, 4.3, **L1:** 1.4, **L2:** 1.4, 2.3, 2.4, 2.7, 2.8, 2.9, 3.1, 3.2, 3.9, 3.13, 4.6, 4.11, 6.1, 6.2, **L4:** 1.4, 2.3, 2.4, 2.7, 2.8, 2.9, 3.1, 3.2, 3.9, 3.13, 4.6, 4.11, 6.1, 6.2, **L5:** 1.4, 2.3, 2.4, 2.7, 2.8, 2.9, 3.1, 3.2, 3.9, 3.13, 4.6, 4.11, 6.1, 6.2, **L7:** 1.4, 3.9, 3.13, 6.8, **L8:** 1.4, 2.3, 2.4, 2.7, 2.8, 2.9, 3.1, 3.2, 3.9, 3.13, 4.6, 4.11, 6.1, 6.2, 6.6, **SWYK Review & Expand:** 6.6

CASAS Competencies	Unit CCR Standards
U1: 0.1.2, 0.1.5, 0.2.1, 0.2.4, 7.2.6, **L1:** 7.4.3, **L5:** 2.7.1, **L6:** 2.7.1, **L7:** 1.1.1, 3.5.3, **SWYK Review & Expand:** 0.1.3, 7.3.2	RI/RL.2.1, RI.3.2, RI.3.4, W.2.3, W.3.4, W.3.5, W.3.8, SL.3.1.a, SL.3.1.b, SL.3.1.c, SL.3.1.d, SL.3.2, SL.3.2.3, SL.3.4, SL.3.6, L.2.1.a, L.3.1.a, L.2.1.c, L.3.1.c, L.2.1.e, L.3.1.e, L.2.1.f, L.3.1.f, L.2.1.h, L.3.1.h, L.2.1.l, L.3.1.l, L.2.1.m, L.3.1.m, L.3.3.a, L.2.4.a, L.3.5.a, L.3.5.b, L.2.6, L.3.6
U2: 0.1.2, 0.1.3, 0.1.5, 0.2.4, **L1:** 0.2.1, 7.1.1, 7.4.3, L2: 0.2.1, 7.1.1, **L4:** 0.2.1, **L5:** 0.2.1, 4.1.3, **L6:** 4.1.3, 7.1.1, **L7:** 7.1.1, 7.1.2, 7.2.7, **L8:** 7.1.1, 7.1.2, 7.2.7, **L9:** 2.5.8, **L10:** 0.2.1, 2.5.8, 5.6.5, **SWYK Review & Expand:** 0.2.1, 7.1.1, 7.1.2, 7.3.2	RI/RL.2.1, RI.3.2, RI.3.4, RI.3.7, RL.3.7, W.2.3, W.3.4, W.3.5, W.3.8, SL.3.1.a, SL.3.1.b, SL.3.1.c, SL.3.1.d, SL.3.2, SL.3.2.3, SL.3.4, SL.3.6, L.2.1.a, L.3.1.a, L.2.1.g, L.3.1.g, L.2.1.l, L.3.1.l, L.2.1.m, L.3.1.m, L.3.3.a, L.2.4.a, L.3.5.a, L.3.5.b, L.2.6, L.3.6
U3: 0.1.2, 0.1.3, 0.1.5, 0.2.4, **L2:** 2.8.2, 2.8.8, 7.2.2, **L3:** 2.8.8, 7.2.2, **L5:** 2.5.6, **L6:** 7.2.2, **L8:** 2.8.8, 7.2.2, **L9:** 2.8.4, 2.8.6, 7.2.2, **L10:** 7.2.2, **SWYK Review & Expand:** 2.8.8, 7.2.2	RI/RL.2.1, RI.3.2, RI.3.4, W.3.1.a, W.3.1.b, W.3.1.c, W.3.1.d, W.3.4, W.3.5, W.3.8, SL.3.1.a, SL.3.1.b, SL.3.1.c, SL.3.1.d, SL.3.2, SL.3.2.3, SL.3.4, SL.3.6, L.2.1.a, L.3.1.a, L.2.1.c, L.3.1.c, L.2.1.e, L.3.1.e, L.2.1.g, L.3.1.g, L.2.1.i, L.3.1.i, L.2.1.l, L.3.1.l, L.2.1.m, L.3.1.m, L.2.2.c, L.3.2.c, L.2.2.d, L.3.2.d, L.2.2.h, L.3.2.h, L.2.2.i, L.3.2.i, L.2.2.j, L.3.2.j, L.3.3.a, L.2.4.a, L.3.5.a, L.3.5.b, L.2.6, L.3.6
U4: R0.1.2, 0.1.3, 0.1.5, 0.2.1, 4.1.6, **L1:** 7.4.3, **L2:** 4.1.5, **L4:** 4.1.2, **L6:** 4.1.5, **L7:** 4.1.5, **L9:** 4.1.5, 4.2.6, 7.3.2, **SWYK Review & Expand:** 4.1.5, 7.3.2	RI/RL.2.1, RI.3.2, RI.3.4, W.3.4, W.3.5, W.3.8, SL.3.1.a, SL.3.1.b, SL.3.1.c, SL.3.1.d, SL.3.2, SL.3.2.3, SL.3.4, SL.3.6, L.2.1.a, L.3.1.a, L.2.1.e, L.3.1.e, L.2.1.i, L.3.1.i, L.2.1.l, L.3.1.l, L.2.1.m, L.3.1.m, L.2.2.h, L.3.2.h, L.2.2.i, L.3.2.i, L.2.2.j, L.3.2.j, L.3.3.a, L.2.4.a, L.3.5.a, L.3.5.b, L.2.6, L.3.6
U5: 0.1.2, 0.1.3, 0.1.5, **L1:** 2.2.4, 2.2.7, 7.4.3, **L2:** 0.1.7, 2.2.7, **L4:** 1.3.6, 2.2.1, 2.2.2, 2.2.4, 2.2.5, **SWYK Review & Expand:** 7.3.2	RI/RL.2.1, RI.3.2, RI.3.3, RI.3.4, W.3.2.a, W.3.2.b, W.3.2.c, W.3.2.d, W.3.4, W.3.5, W.3.8, SL.3.1.a, SL.3.1.b, SL.3.1.c, SL.3.1.d, SL.3.2, SL.3.2.3, SL.3.4, SL.3.6, L.2.1.a, L.3.1.a, L.2.1.l, L.3.1.l, L.2.1.m, L.3.1.m, L.2.2.g, L.3.2.g, L.2.2.h, L.3.2.h, L.2.2.i, L.3.2.i, L.2.2.j, L.3.2.j, L.3.3.a, L.2.4.a, L.3.5.a, L.3.5.b, L.2.6, L.3.6
U6: 0.1.3, 0.1.5, **L1:** 7.4.3, **L3:** 1.7.5, **L5:** 1.3.3, 1.6.3, **L6:** 1.2.1, 1.2.2, **L7:** 1.2.1, **L8:** 1.3.3, 1.6.3, **SWYK Review & Expand:** 1.3.3, 1.6.3, 7.3.2	RI/RL.2.1, RI.3.2, RI.3.4, RI.2.5, RI.3.5, RI.2.6, W.3.2.a, W.3.2.b, W.3.2.c, W.3.2.d, W.3.4, W.3.5, W.3.7, W.3.8, SL.3.1.a, SL.3.1.b, SL.3.1.c, SL.3.1.d, SL.3.2, SL.3.2.3, SL.3.4, SL.3.6, L.2.1.a, L.3.1.a, L.2.1.j, L.3.1.j, L.2.1.l, L.3.1.l, L.2.1.m, L.3.1.m, L.2.2.h, L.3.2.h, L.2.2.i, L.3.2.i, L.2.2.j, L.3.2.j, L.3.3.a, L.2.4.a, L.3.5.a, L.3.5.b, L.2.6, L.3.6
U7: 0.1.2, 0.1.3, 0.1.5, **L1:** 7.4.3, **L2:** 1.9.6, **L3:** 1.9.6, **L4:** 1.9.9, 3.4.2, **L5:** 1.9.7, 5.3.7, **L6:** 1.9.7, 3.4.2, 5.3.7, **L7:** 1.9.7, 3.4.2, **L8:** 3.4.2, 5.1.7, **SWYK Review & Expand:** 7.3.2	RI/RL.2.1, RI.3.2, RI.3.3, RI.3.4, RI.3.7, RL.3.7, W.3.1.a, W.3.1.b, W.3.1.c, W.3.4, W.3.5, W.3.1.d, W.3.8, SL.3.1.a, SL.3.1.b, SL.3.1.c, SL.3.1.d, SL.3.2, SL.3.2.3, SL.3.4, SL.3.6, L.2.1.a, L.3.1.a, L.2.1.e, L.3.1.e, L.2.1.l, L.3.1.l, L.2.1.m, L.3.1.m, L.2.2.c, L.3.2.c, L.2.2.d, L.3.2.d, L.2.2.h, L.3.2.h, L.2.2.i, L.3.2.i, L.2.2.j, L.3.2.j, L.3.3.a, L.2.4.a, L.3.5.a, L.3.5.b, L.2.6, L.3.6
U8: 0.1.2, 0.1.3, 0.1.5, **L1:** 3.5.2, 7.4.3, **L2:** 0.2.1, 3.5.2, **L3:** 0.2.1, 3.5.2, **L4:** 3.5.1, 3.5.2, **L5:** 3.5.1, 3.5.2, 7.2.3, **L6:** 3.5.1, 3.5.2, **L8:** 3.5.4, **L9:** 3.5.4, **L10:** 0.2.1, 3.5.2, **SWYK Review & Expand:** 3.5.2, 3.5.4, 7.2.2, 7.3.2	RI/RL.2.1, RI.3.2, RI.3.4, RI.3.6, RI.2.8, W.3.2.a, W.3.2.b, W.3.2.c, W.3.2.d, W.3.4, W.3.5, W.3.8, SL.3.1.a, SL.3.1.b, SL.3.1.c, SL.3.1.d, SL.3.2, SL.3.2.3, SL.3.4, SL.3.6, L.2.1.a, L.3.1.a, L.2.1.j, L.3.1.j, L.2.1.l, L.3.1.l, L.2.1.m, L.3.1.m, L.2.2.h, L.3.2.h, L.2.2.i, L.3.2.i, L.2.2.j, L.3.2.j, L.3.3.a, L.2.4.a, L.3.5.a, L.3.5.b, L.2.6, L.3.6
U9: 0.1.3, 0.1.5, 4.4.1, 4.8.1, **L1:** 7.4.3, **L2:** 0.1.6, **L3:** 0.1.6, 0.1.7, **L4:** 7.5.4, 7.5.5, **L8:** 4.3.1, **L9:** 4.6.1, 4.8.2, 7.5.3, **L10:** 0.1.7, 4.6.1, 4.8.2, **SWYK Review & Expand:** 4.6.1, 7.3.2, 7.5.3	RI/RL.2.1, RI.3.2, RI.3.4, W.2.3, W.3.4, W.3.5, W.3.8, SL.3.1.a, SL.3.1.b, SL.3.1.c, SL.3.1.d, SL.3.2, SL.3.2.3, SL.3.4, SL.3.6, L.2.1.a, L.3.1.a, L.2.1.c, L.3.1.c, L.2.1.g, L.3.1.g, L.2.1.l, L.3.1.l, L.2.1.m, L.3.1.m, L.2.2.h, L.3.2.h, L.2.2.i, L.3.2.i, L.2.2.j, L.3.2.j, L.3.3.a, L.2.4.a, L.3.5.a, L.3.5.b, L.2.6, L.3.6
U10: 0.1.2, 0.1.3, 0.1.5, **L1:** 7.4.3, **L2:** 3.1.2, **L4:** 3.6.1, **L5:** 3.6.3, 3.6.4, L6: 3.6.3, 3.6.4, **L7:** 3.4.6, **L8:** 7.3.2, **L9:** 3.6.4, 3.6.8, **L10:** 3.6.8, **SWYK Review & Expand:** 3.6.4, 7.3.2	RI/RL.2.1, RI.3.2, RI.3.4, RI.2.5, RI.3.5, W.2.3, W.3.4, W.3.5, W.3.8, SL.3.1.a, SL.3.1.b, SL.3.1.c, SL.3.1.d, SL.3.2, SL.3.2.3, SL.3.4, SL.3.6, L.2.1.a, L.3.1.a, L.2.1.g, L.3.1.g, L.2.1.l, L.3.1.l, L.2.1.m, L.3.1.m, L.2.2.h, L.3.2.h, L.2.2.i, L.3.2.i, L.2.2.j, L.3.2.j, L.3.3.a, L.2.4.a, L.3.5.a, L.3.5.b, L.2.6, L.3.6
U11: 0.1.2, 0.1.3, 0.1.5, **L1:** 1.8.1, 7.4.2, **L2:** 1.8.1, **L3:** 1.6.7, 7.3.2, **L4:** 1.5.2, 1.8.1, **L6:** 1.5.1, **L7:** 1.5.1, 1.5.2, 7.3.2, **L8:** 1.5.3, 7.3.2, **L9:** 1.4.2, **L10:** 1.4.2, **SWYK Review & Expand:** 1.5.1, 7.3.2	RI/RL.2.1, RI.3.2, RI.3.4, RI.3.6, W.3.2.a, W.3.2.b, W.3.2.c, W.3.2.d, W.3.4, W.3.5, W.3.8, SL.3.1.a, SL.3.1.b, SL.3.1.c, SL.3.1.d, SL.3.2, SL.3.2.3, SL.3.4, SL.3.6, L.2.1.a, L.3.1.a, L.2.1.g, L.3.1.g, L.2.1.l, L.3.1.l, L.2.1.m, L.3.1.m, L.2.2.h, L.3.2.h, L.2.2.i, L.3.2.i, L.2.2.j, L.3.2.j, L.3.3.a, L.2.4.a, L.3.5.a, L.3.5.b, L.2.6, L.3.6
U12: 0.1.2, 0.1.3, 0.1.5, 0.2.4, **L1:** 5.2.6, 7.4.3, **L4:** 0.1.7, 2.2.1, 2.2.5, **L6:** 2.7.1, 5.5.2, 5.5.3, 5.5.4, **L8:** 5.2.1, **L9:** 5.2.1, 7.4.4, **SWYK Review & Expand:** 0.1.7, 2.2.1, 7.3.2	RI/RL.2.1, RI.3.2, RI.3.4, RI.3.7, RL.3.7, W.3.1.a, W.3.1.b, W.3.1.c, W.3.1.d, W.3.4, W.3.5, W.3.8, SL.3.1.a, SL.3.1.b, SL.3.1.c, SL.3.1.d, SL.3.2, SL.3.2.3, SL.3.4, SL.3.6, L.2.1.a, L.3.1.a, L.2.1.e, L.3.1.e, L.2.1.g, L.3.1.g, L.2.1.h, L.3.1.h, L.2.1.j, L.3.1.j, L.2.1.l, L.3.1.l, L.2.1.m, L.3.1.m, L.2.2.h, L.3.2.h, L.2.2.i, L.3.2.i, L.2.2.j, L.3.2.j, L.3.3.a, L.2.4.a, L.3.5.a, L.3.5.b, L.2.6, L.3.6

About the Series Consultants and Author

SERIES CONSULTANTS

 **Dr. Beatriz B. Díaz** has taught ESL for more than three decades in Miami. She has a master's degree in TESOL and a doctorate in education from Nova Southeastern University. She has given trainings and numerous presentations at international, national, state, and local conferences throughout the United States, the Caribbean, and South America. Dr. Díaz is the district supervisor for the Miami-Dade County Public Schools Adult ESOL Program, one of the largest in the United States.

 **Ronna Magy** has worked as an ESL classroom teacher and teacher-trainer for nearly three decades. Most recently, she has worked as the ESL Teacher Adviser in charge of site-based professional development for the Division of Adult and Career Education of the Los Angeles Unified School District. She has trained teachers of adult English language learners in many areas, including lesson planning, learner persistence and goal setting, and cooperative learning. A frequent presenter at local, state and national, and international conferences, Ms. Magy is the author of adult ESL publications on life skills and test preparation, U.S. citizenship, reading and writing, and workplace English. She holds a master's degree in social welfare from the University of California at Berkeley.

 **Federico Salas-Isnardi** has worked for 20 years in the field of adult education as an ESL and GED instructor, professional development specialist, curriculum writer, and program administrator. He has trained teachers of adult English language learners for over 15 years on topics ranging from language acquisition and communicative competence to classroom management and individualized professional development planning. Mr. Salas-Isnardi has been a contributing writer or consultant for a number of ESL publications, and he has co-authored curriculum for site-based workforce ESL and Spanish classes. He holds a master's degree in applied linguistics from the University of Houston and has completed a number of certificates in educational leadership.

AUTHOR

Irene E. Schoenberg has taught ESL for more than two decades at Hunter College's International English Language Institute and at Columbia University's American Language Program. Ms. Schoenberg holds a master's degree in TESOL from Teachers College, Columbia University. She has trained teachers at Hunter College, Columbia University, and the New School University, and she has given workshops and academic presentations at ESL programs and conferences throughout the world. Ms. Schoenberg is the author or co-author of numerous publications, including *True Colors*; *Speaking of Values 1*; *Topics from A to Z*, Books 1 and 2; and *Focus on Grammar: An Integrated Skills Approach* (levels 1 and 2).

Acknowledgments

The author and publisher would like to extend special thanks to our Series Consultants whose insights, experience, and expertise shaped the course and guided us throughout its development.

Beatriz B. Díaz Miami-Dade County Public Schools, Miami, FL
Ronna Magy Los Angeles Unified School District, Los Angles, CA
Federico Salas-Isnardi Texas LEARNS, Houston, TX

We would also like to express our gratitude to the following individuals. Their kind assistance was indispensable to the creation of this program.

Consultants

Wendy J. Allison Seminole Community College, Sanford, FL
Claudia Carco Westchester Community College, Valhalla, NY
Maria J. Cesnik Ysleta Community Learning Center, El Paso, TX
Edwidge Crevecoeur-Bryant University of Florida, Gainesville, FL
Ann Marie Holzknecht Damrau San Diego Community College, San Diego, CA
Peggy Datz Berkeley Adult School, Berkeley, CA
MaryAnn Florez D.C. Learns, Washington, D.C.
Portia LaFerla Torrance Adult School, Torrance, CA
Eileen McKee Westchester Community College, Valhalla, NY
Julie Meuret Downey Adult School, Downey, CA
Sue Pace Santa Ana College School of Continuing Education, Santa Ana, CA
Howard Pomann Union County College, Elizabeth, NJ
Mary Ray Fairfax County Public Schools, Falls Church, VA
Gema Santos Miami-Dade County Public Schools, Miami, FL
Edith Uber Santa Clara Adult Education, Santa Clara, CA
Theresa Warren East Side Adult Education, San Jose, CA

Piloters

MariCarmen Acosta American High School, Adult ESOL, Hialeah, FL
Resurrección Ángeles Metropolitan Skills Center, Los Angeles, CA
Linda Bolognesi Fairfax County Public Schools, Adult and Community Education, Falls Church, VA
Patricia Boquiren Metropolitan Skills Center, Los Angeles, CA
Paul Buczko Pacoima Skills Center, Pacoima, CA
Matthew Horowitz Metropolitan Skills Center, Los Angeles, CA
Gabriel de la Hoz The English Center, Miami, FL
Cam-Tu Huynh Los Angeles Unified School District, Los Angeles, CA
Jorge Islas Whitewater Unified School District, Adult Education, Whitewater, WI
Lisa Johnson City College of San Francisco, San Francisco, CA
Loreto Kaplan Collier County Public Schools Adult ESOL Program, Naples, FL
Teressa Kitchen Collier County Public Schools Adult ESOL Program, Naples, FL
Anjie Martin Whitewater Unified School District, Adult Education, Whitewater, WI
Elida Matthews College of the Mainland, Texas City, TX
Penny Negron College of the Mainland, Texas City, TX
Manuel Pando Coral Park High School, Miami, FL
Susan Ritter Evans Community Adult School, Los Angeles, CA
Susan Ross Torrance Adult School, Torrance, CA
Beatrice Shields Fairfax County Public Schools, Adult and Community Education, Falls Church, VA
Oscar Solís Coral Park High School, Miami, FL
Wanda W. Weaver Literacy Council of Prince George's County, Hyattsville, MD

Reviewers

Lisa Agao Fresno Adult School, Fresno, CA
Carol Antuñano The English Center, Miami, FL
Euphronia Awakuni Evans Community Adult School, Los Angeles, CA
Jack Bailey Santa Barbara Adult Education, Santa Barbara, CA
Robert Breitbard District School Board of Collier County, Naples, FL
Diane Burke Evans Community Adult School, Los Angeles, CA
José A. Carmona Embry-Riddle Aeronautical University, Daytona Beach, FL
Veronique Colas Los Angeles Technology Center, Los Angles, CA
Carolyn Corrie Metropolitan Skills Center, Los Angeles, CA
Marti Estrin Santa Rosa Junior College, Sebastopol, CA
Sheila Friedman Metropolitan Skills Center, Los Angeles, CA
José Gonzalez Spanish Education Development Center, Washington, D.C.
Allene G. Grognet Vice President (Emeritus), Center for Applied Linguistics
J. Quinn Harmon-Kelley Venice Community Adult School, Los Angeles, CA
Edwina Hoffman Miami-Dade County Public Schools, Coral Gables, FL
Eduardo Honold Far West Project GREAT, El Paso, TX
Leigh Jacoby Los Angeles Community Adult School, Los Angeles, CA
Fayne Johnson Broward County Public Schools, Ft. Lauderdale, FL
Loreto Kaplan, Collier County Public Schools Adult ESOL Program, Naples, FL
Synthia LaFontaine Collier County Public Schools, Naples, FL
Gretchen Lammers-Ghereben Martinez Adult Education, Martinez, CA
Susan Lanzano Editorial Consultant, Briarcliff Manor, NY
Karen Mauer ESL Express, Euless, TX
Rita McSorley North East Independent School District, San Antonio, TX
Alice-Ann Menjivar Carlos Rosario International Public Charter School, Washington, D.C.
Sue Pace Santa Ana College School of Continuing Education, Santa Ana, CA
Isabel Perez American High School, Hialeah, FL
Howard Pomann Union County College, Elizabeth, NJ
Lesly Prudent Miami-Dade County Public Schools, Miami, FL
Valentina Purtell North Orange County Community College District, Anaheim, CA
Mary Ray Fairfax County Adult ESOL, Falls Church, VA
Laurie Shapero Miami-Dade Community College, Miami, FL
Felissa Taylor Nause Austin, TX
Meintje Westerbeek Baltimore City Community College, Baltimore, MD

Thanks also to the following teachers, who contributed their ideas for the Persistence Activities:

MaryAnn Florez D.C. Learners, Washington, D.C.
Lisa Johnson City College of San Francisco, San Francisco, CA

Special thanks to **Sharon Goldstein** for her invaluable contribution to the pronunciation strand.

Pre-Unit

Getting Started

Welcome to Class

1 LEARN ABOUT YOUR BOOK

A CLASS. **Turn to page iii. Answer the questions.**

1. What information is on this page?

2. How many units are in this book?

3. Which two units are about health?

4. Which two units are about work?

B CLASS. **Sometimes you will need to go to the back of the book to do activities. Look at the chart. Find the pages in the book and complete the chart.**

Page	Activity
245	Grammar Review
257	
263	

C PAIRS. **There is additional information for you in the back of the book. Find each section. Write the page number.**

Grammar Reference _____   U.S. and Canadian map _____

Audio Script _____   World map _____

Word List _____   Index _____

D PAIRS. **Look through pages 278–284. What resources are available in the Life Skills Reference? Discuss.**

2 LEARN YOUR CLASSMATES' NAMES

A GROUPS OF 5. **Tell your group your name and repeat the names of the students before you.**

Diana: My name is Diana.
Luis: This is Diana. My name is Luis.
Olga: This is Diana. This is Luis. My name is Olga.
Tran: This is Diana. Excuse me. What's your name again, please?
Luis: Luis.
Tran: OK, thanks. This is Diana. This is Luis. This is Olga. My name is Tran.
Laila: This is Diana. This is Luis. This is Olga. This is Tran. My name is Laila.

B **How many classmates' names do you remember?**

3 FIND THINGS YOU HAVE IN COMMON

A **Read the sentences. Check (✓) all the statements that are true for you.**

☐ I have a small family.
☐ I have a large family.
☐ Most of my family lives in this country.
☐ Most of my family lives in my country.
☐ I live with my family.
☐ I live with friends.

☐ I'm married.
☐ I'm single.
☐ I have children.
☐ I don't have children.
☐ I have a job.
☐ I don't have a job.

B **Complete the statements about things you like.**

My favorite food is _____.

My favorite kind of music is _____.

My favorite free-time activity is _____.

My favorite holiday is _____.

C **Walk around the room. Ask your classmates questions. For example, *Do you have a large family?* Find classmates who have things in common with you. Take notes.**

D CLASS. **Share your results.**

A **Complete the conversations. Use the questions and statement in the box.**

Could you explain that?	I'm sorry. What page?
Did you say a pen?	What's the word for this in English?
Do you mean first we should work alone?	What I mean is that you shouldn't read out loud.

1.

2.

3.

4.

5.

6.

CD1 T2

B 🔘 **Listen and check your answers.**

C ROLE PLAY. PAIRS. **Choose one conversation from Exercise A. Create a new conversation with different information.**

In the Neighborhood

Preview

Where are you from? Where are you living now? What's your neighborhood like?

UNIT GOALS

☐ Make small talk

☐ Talk about life in the U.S.

☐ Talk about holidays and celebrations

☐ Follow a recipe and handle food safely

☐ Compare your life now and in the past

Lesson 1 Vocabulary

1 WHAT DO YOU KNOW?

A CLASS. Which countries on the map do you recognize?

B GROUPS. Match the countries on the map with their names. Write the numbers. If you need help, look at pages 276-277.

Countries

___ Bosnia-Herzegovina

___ Brazil

___ Cambodia

___ China

___ Colombia

___ Ecuador

___ El Salvador

___ Ethiopia

___ South Korea

___ Laos

___ Mexico

___ Peru

___ the Philippines

___ Poland

___ Russia

___ Sudan

___ Ukraine

___ Vietnam

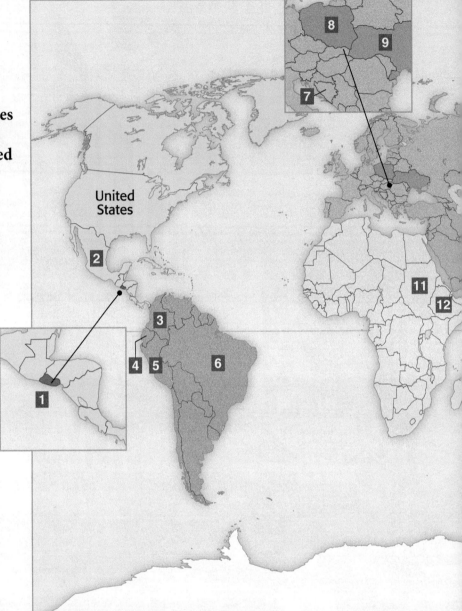

CD1 T3

C Listen and check your answers. Then listen and repeat.

Learning Strategy

Translate words

Make cards for five countries. Write the English name on the front of the card. Write the name in your language on the back.

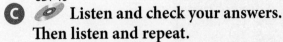

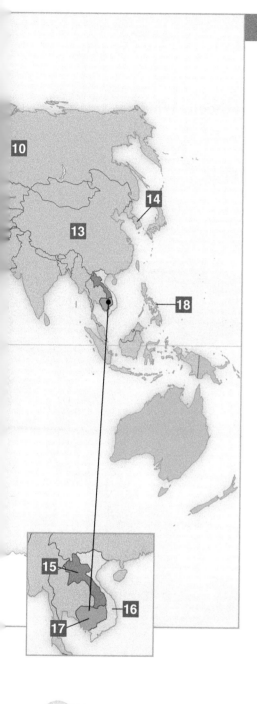

A WORD PLAY. GROUPS. **Match the countries to their most common languages.**

_e_ 1. Brazil   ___ 4. the Philippines

___ 2. China   ___ 5. Poland

___ 3. Peru   ___ 6. Vietnam

a. Polish
b. Spanish
c. Filipino
d. Vietnamese
e. ~~Portuguese~~
f. Mandarin

B GET THE MEANING. **Read the paragraph. Underline the countries. Circle the languages.**

My name is Jamila and my family is from Zanzibar, in Tanzania. We came to the U. S. two years ago. Now we live in Kansas City. We like our neighbors in Kansas City. They are very friendly. We've met many people at a community garden where we grow our own vegetables, like corn, tomatoes, and squash. At our garden, people come from Bosnia, Ethiopia, Sudan, Mexico, and other countries. People speak different languages—like Arabic and Spanish—but everyone speaks at least a little English.

Show what you know!

GROUPS. **Discuss. What country are you from? Did you live in the city or in the countryside? What languages do you speak? Do you like your community now? What do you like about it?**

Listening and Speaking

1 BEFORE YOU LISTEN

A GROUPS. Discuss. Do you know many people in your neighborhood? What are some good ways to meet people?

B Look at the picture. Marco and Edwin are watching a soccer game. Guess their relationship. They are _____.

a. teammates   b. old friends   c. new friends

2 LISTEN

CD1 T4

A Listen to Marco and Edwin's conversation. Was your guess in Before You Listen correct?

CD1 T4

B Read the questions. Then listen again. Circle the correct answers.

1. When does the Atlas soccer league meet?
   a. Saturdays
   b. Sundays
   c. Saturdays and Sundays

2. What happens when it rains?
   a. They play indoors.
   b. They still play.
   c. They don't play.

CD1 T5

C Read the questions. Then listen to the rest of the conversation. Write *T* (true) or *F* (false).

_____ 1. Marco knows many players in Edwin's soccer league.

_____ 2. Marco and Hector are both from Brazil but not from the same town.

_____ 3. Hector is surprised to see Marco.

3 CONVERSATION

A Listen to the words. Then listen and repeat.

Po land   Bra **zil**   Cam **bo** di a   **Chi** na   The U **ni** ted **States**

B Listen to the words. Mark (•) the stressed syllable.

1. La os
2. Ko re a
3. Mex i co

4. Russ ia
5. Vi et nam
6. Co lom bi a

> **Pronunciation Watch**
>
> Words are made up of syllables. In English, one syllable in a word has the strongest stress. It is longer and louder than other syllables.

C Listen and read the conversation.

Marco: Great game. Is this the Atlas soccer league? I've heard about them.

Edwin: Yes. I love to come here and watch them.

Marco: Do they play every Saturday?

Edwin: Yes, unless it rains. By the way, my name's Edwin.

Marco: Hi, I'm Marco. Nice to meet you.

Edwin: Nice to meet you, too. Do you live around here?

Marco: Nearby. I live in Southside. I'm originally from Brazil.

4 PRACTICE

A PAIRS. Practice the conversation.

B MAKE IT PERSONAL. PAIRS. Get to know your partner. Introduce yourself. Ask the questions or your own questions.

Do you live far from school? How do you get here?
Are you a new student in this school?
Why do you want to learn English?

Make small talk

Grammar

Simple present

Affirmative statements		
I You They	**play**	soccer.
He She	**plays**	dominoes.

Negative statements			
We You They	**don't**	**play**	soccer.
He She	**doesn't**	**play**	dominoes.

Yes/No questions			
Do	you	**play**	on a team?
Does	she	**watch**	the games?

Short answers	
Yes, I **do**.	**No**, I **don't**.
Yes, she **does**.	**No**, she **doesn't**.

Grammar Watch

For the third-person singular (*she, he, it*), add *-s* or *-es* to the base form.

1 PRACTICE

A **Read about Zhang's neighborhood. Underline the simple present verbs.**

My family comes from Sichuan province, in China. Now we live in downtown Seattle. People from all parts of Asia live here. My family has an apartment near Hing Hay Park. I like the park a lot. It reminds me of parks in China. Hing Hay Park has benches and tables for Chinese chess. My grandfather plays there with other older men. My grandmother doesn't play chess, but she does tai chi with her friends almost every morning.

B **Look at the paragraph. Circle all of the examples in the third person singular.**

Simple present		
Wh- questions about the subject	Other *wh-* questions	

Who	plays	soccer on Sundays?

How often			**play?**
Where	**do**	you	**meet?**
Who			**play with?**

2   PRACTICE

A **Write questions. Use the simple present and the words in parentheses.**

A: (How / you / spend your spare time) *How do you spend your spare time?*

B: We go to the park almost every weekend. My family loves the park.

A: Oh, yeah? (What / you / do / there) _____

B: We have a barbecue and spend the day together.

A: That's nice. (What kind of food / you / cook) _____

B: We usually eat beef or chicken, rice and beans, and tamales. (you / want to come

with us this weekend) _____

A: Sure, that sounds great.

B **Write questions to a classmate in your notebook. Use the simple present.**

1. What / country / be / you from?   4. What / you / like / about your neighborhood?

2. Where / you live / now?   5. Who / you / live with?

3. you / like / your neighborhood?   6. Who / help you the most / in the U.S.?

Show what you know!   Make small talk

STEP 1. PAIRS. Interview a partner. Ask the questions from Exercise B.
Take notes.

STEP 2. CLASS. Tell the class about your partner.

Jun Park is from Seoul, Korea. Now Jun lives in Koreatown, Los Angeles.

Can you... make small talk? ☐

Reading

1   BEFORE YOU READ

A   **GROUPS.** Do you think it's better to live in a big city or a small city? Why? What are the problems of each? What are the good things about each?

B   Read the words and definitions. Are these words new for you?

> **mayor:** someone who is elected to lead the government of a town or city
>
> **legal advice:** help from a lawyer with problems regarding the law, such as getting a green card

2   READ

CD1 T9

Listen and read the article.

Changing Cities, Changing Lives

When people came to the U.S. from other countries 100 years ago, they went to large cities like New York and Chicago. These days, newcomers are also moving to smaller cities around the country. Why this change? Some reasons are the lower **cost of living**, safer neighborhoods, better schools, and more living space.

Small cities may offer a better **quality of life**, but there can be problems. Big cities like New York and Los Angeles are prepared for new immigrants. Immigrant communities already live there and can help newcomers. But what about small cities? It is sometimes more difficult for immigrants to settle in them.

Green Bay, Wisconsin is an example. When families came from Laos, Mexico, and Central America, Green Bay was not ready for them. The city had jobs, but

Hmong girl in traditional dress

almost no **interpreters**. Very few people spoke Hmong or Spanish. The mayor wanted the city to welcome the new residents. First he met with Hmong and Latino leaders. Then the city hired interpreters to work with schools, hospitals, and the police.

The interpreters helped people get information on health care, education, legal issues, jobs, and housing.

Green Bay found ways to help its newcomers, but the newcomers also found ways to help themselves. Women in the Hmong and Latino community also took steps to build their community. They turned a store into a community center. The store had been selling cigarettes and alcohol to children. The women were angry, so they raised money and bought the store. It is now the Howe Neighborhood Family Resource Center. Every year the center helps 4,000 families with food, rent, and legal advice.

Moving to a smaller city can be difficult but it can create **opportunities**. Many people are making successful lives for themselves in smaller cities throughout the U.S.

3 CHECK YOUR UNDERSTANDING

A Read the article again. What is the main idea? Circle the correct letter.

a. The Howe Neighborhood Family Resource Center helps families with food and rent.

b. Small cities are not able to receive new immigrants.

c. Many immigrants are moving to small U.S. cities to find a better life.

> **Reading Skill:**
> Understanding the main idea
>
> The main idea is the most important idea in an article. The main idea is often found in the first paragraph.

B Read the sentences. Write *T* (true) or *F* (false).

___T___ 1. One hundred years ago, immigrants did not usually move to small U.S. cities.

_____ 2. It's less expensive to live in Green Bay than in New York City.

_____ 3. At first, Green Bay had many interpreters for the new Hmong and Latino families.

_____ 4. The Hmong and Latino families were able to improve their community.

_____ 5. The city bought the Howe Neighborhood Family Resource Center.

4 VOCABULARY IN CONTEXT

Look at the boldfaced words in the article. Guess their meanings. Complete the sentences with the correct words.

1. Small cities often have a better _____ than big cities because they have safer neighborhoods.

2. The _____ in cities like New York is high because housing is expensive.

3. Large cities often offer more job _____ than small cities do.

4. Sometimes it's hard for immigrants to move to small cities because there may not be enough _____ at schools and hospitals who speak their language.

Show what you know!

GROUPS. Discuss. When you moved to the U.S., was it very difficult?

Talk about holidays and celebrations

Listening and Speaking

1 BEFORE YOU LISTEN

A The West Indies is made up of many islands near the U.S. Look at the map. Name two islands.

B GROUPS. Every year, there are many parades that celebrate the cultures from these islands. Do you like parades? Why?

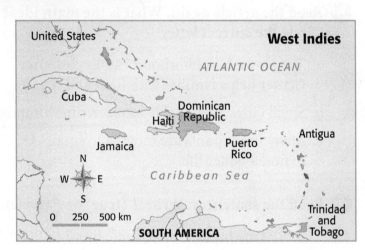

2 LISTEN

CD1 T10

A Listen to a radio announcement about the West Indian–American Day parade. Where is the parade?

CD1 T10

B Read the questions. Then listen again and circle the correct answers. More than one answer is sometimes possible.

1. What can you see at the parade?
   a. costumes   c. dancers
   b. musicians   d. actors

2. What kind of music can you hear?
   a. reggae   c. jazz
   b. rap   d. calypso

3. What can you taste?
   a. fried chicken   c. rice and peas
   b. potatoes   d. eggs

4. What musical instruments can you hear?
   a. pianos   c. guitars
   b. steel drums   d. violins

5. What is free at the parade?
   a. the food   c. parking
   b. tickets   d. music

3 CONVERSATION

CD1 T11

Listen and read the conversation.

Jen: Mmm. This food is great. I brought you some. There are two desserts you must try.

Mei-ling: You're right. They're delicious. They remind me of Chinese New Year. We eat a lot of good food then, too.

Jen: Like what?

Mei-ling: So many things. . . . We eat special dishes, like noodles for long life, spring rolls for wealth, and oranges for luck. We also visit family and friends for the first four days of the holiday.

Jen: Sounds like fun. What else do you do to celebrate?

Dragons at the Chinese New Year Parade

4 PRACTICE

A PAIRS. **Practice the conversation.**

B ROLE PLAY. PAIRS. **Make a similar conversation. Talk about a celebration that you know about.**

A: *My favorite holiday is Ch'usok, the Korean Harvest Moon.*
B: *What do you do on that day?*

Talk about holidays and celebrations

Grammar

Quantifiers

There are	Quantifier	Count noun	
	a few some several a lot of many	desserts	on my plate.
There aren't	many any	desserts	on my plate.

There's	Quantifier	Non-count noun	
	a little some a lot of	fruit juice	in my cup.
There isn't	much any	fruit juice	in my cup.

Grammar Watch

- Quantifiers tell us *how much* or *how many* we have of something.
- Count nouns are things we can count separately (*an orange, two oranges*).
- Non-count nouns are things we can't count separately (*rice, water, information*).
- See page 285 for a list of common non-count nouns.

1 PRACTICE

Read about the holidays and parades. Circle the quantifiers. Underline the nouns they describe.

1. There are (several) parades in New York City each month.

2. Many children dress in costumes on Mexican Independence Day.

3. People carry a lot of flags at the Philippines Independence Day Parade.

4. You can see a few famous stars at the Puerto Rican Day Parade.

5. Food vendors sell a lot of Korean foods on Ch'usok, the Korean Harvest Moon Festival.

6. You can see some traditional dances at the Cinco de Mayo Parade.

7. People set off a lot of firecrackers on Chinese New Year.

8. You can hear several bands playing music like salsa at the Ecuadorian Parade.

A Complete the conversation. Circle the correct words.

A: How did you know about this parade?

B: There were (a few)/ a little announcements on the radio.
But I often look for events on the Internet.

A: Oh, yeah? I've never found **much** / **many** information like that on the Internet.

B: But it's easy. You just google "free events in New York City." Google will show you **a lot of** / **a little** website links. You can click on the links and find **many** / **much** free events. Last year I went to **several** / **a little** street fairs that I found on Google.

B Find and correct six mistakes with quantifiers. The first one is corrected for you.

> My brother and I live in Los Angeles but we don't have ~~many~~ other family
> here. Last year our neighbor invited us for Thanksgiving. We had many
> fun. We ate a lot of turkey with mashed potatoes. We also ate much
> side dishes, like stuffing and squash soup. I liked everything,
> especially the turkey. My neighbor told me it's easy—you just add
> a few onions, a few olive oil, and a little spices. Then you roast
> the turkey. While my neighbor was preparing the meal, her cell
> phone rang a little times. It was her relatives wishing her a "Happy
> Thanksgiving."

any (above "many")

Show what you know! Talk about holidays and celebrations

GROUPS. **Look at the list of U.S. holidays on page 284. Which holidays do you celebrate? How do you celebrate or prepare for them?**

We eat a lot of turkey on Thanksgiving, but we make it with a special sauce, adobo. You make it with tomatoes, a few garlic cloves, and some vinegar.

Can you...talk about holidays and celebrations? ☐

Life Skills

1 FOLLOW A RECIPE

A **GROUPS.** Do you or does someone in your family cook special meals at home for holidays? What kinds of foods? For which holidays?

B **CLASS.** Read the recipe for dirty rice and beans. The box contains rice, beans, and a packet of spices. What other ingredients do you need to make the recipe?

ZARAN'S
A New Orleans Tradition
•
Since 1889

ZARAN'S DIRTY RICE AND BEANS

What you need:

 2 tbs. vegetable oil

 1 lb. ground beef

 2½ cups water

1. Heat the oil in a medium skillet. Cook the meat. Drain.

2. Add the rice, water, and the spice packet. Stir the ingredients and bring to a boil.

3. Lower the heat and cook for 25 minutes.

4. Serve immediately.

Refrigerate any leftovers.

2 PRACTICE

Complete the sentences about the recipe. Circle the correct letters.

1. First, you heat _____.
   a. the rice   b. the meat   c. the vegetable oil

2. You add the rice and spice packet _____ the water boils.
   a. before   b. after   c. while

3. You add _____ of water to the rice.
   a. 2½ tablespoons   b. 2½ ounces   c. 2½ cups

4. You cook the rice mix and meat for _____.
   a. 20 minutes   b. 25 minutes   c. 5 minutes

CLASS. **Read the Safe Food Handling instructions. Discuss any words you don't know.**

Safe Food Handling Instructions

1. Keep meat and poultry in the refrigerator or freezer.

2. Thaw frozen meat and poultry in the refrigerator.

3. Keep raw meat and poultry separate from other foods.

4. Wash hands after touching meat or poultry.

5. Wash any surfaces (plates, counters, utensils) that touch raw meat or poultry.

6. Cook meat thoroughly at high temperatures.

7. Refrigerate leftovers immediately.

4 PRACTICE

A **Read the tips for safe food handling. Complete the sentences. Write the correct letters.**

1. After you buy meat, __b__

2. If you freeze meat, ____

3. After you touch raw meat, ____

4. If raw meat touches surfaces, ____

5. When you are preparing meat, ____

6. After you serve the food, ____

a. you must wash your hands.
b. ~~put it in the refrigerator or freezer.~~
c. refrigerate the leftovers.
d. cook it thoroughly at a high temperature.
e. wash them immediately.
f. thaw it in the refrigerator before cooking.

B **GROUPS. Discuss. What are other food safety tips do you know?**

Can you... follow a recipe and handle food safely? ☐

Compare your life now and in the past

Listening and Speaking

1 BEFORE YOU LISTEN

GROUPS. Discuss. What are things you like to do, but don't have time for? Did you have time for those things in the past?

2 LISTEN

CD1 T12

A 🔘 **Listen to the conversation. Edgar and Lucia are talking. Guess their relationship. They are _____.**

a. cousins

b. husband and wife

c. boyfriend and girlfriend

CD1 T12

B 🔘 **Read the statements. Then listen again. Write *T* (true) or *F* (false).**

___F___ 1. Edgar has no time off at his job.

_____ 2. Lucia and Edgar went dancing when they lived in Mexico.

_____ 3. Lucia and Edgar have known each other for more than ten years.

_____ 4. El Diamante is their favorite restaurant.

_____ 5. Lucia's mother doesn't babysit for Lucia and Edgar.

_____ 6. Lucia is happy at the end of the conversation.

C GROUPS. Discuss the questions.

1. What do you think is a nice way to celebrate a wedding anniversary?

2. Do you have children? If you do, do your relatives ever babysit? Who babysits? When? Do you ever babysit for your relatives' children? When?

3 CONVERSATION

CD1 T13

A  Listen to the pronunciation of *used to*. Then listen and repeat.

I used to play soccer.
We used to go dancing.
We used to go out all the time.

Pronunciation Watch

Used to is usually pronounced "useta." The words are joined together and pronounced as one word.

CD1 T14

B Listen and read the conversation.

Lucia: Edgar, are you working tomorrow?

Edgar: No, I have the weekend off.

Lucia: But you usually work on Saturdays.

Edgar: I do, but I asked for this weekend off.

Lucia: That's great. Let's go out. Why don't we go dancing?

Edgar: Dancing?

Lucia: Yeah! Remember? We used to go out all the time. We went out dancing every weekend.

4 PRACTICE

A PAIRS. Practice the conversation.

B ROLE PLAY. PAIRS. Imagine that you are old friends. You have not gone out together in a long time. Make up a conversation. Use the ideas in the box or your own ideas.

> go out to a nice restaurant
> go to a club
> go to the movies
> go to a soccer match

Compare your life now and in the past

Grammar

Used to:			
I	**used to**	**be**	a wonderful dancer.
We		**dance**	every weekend.

········· **Grammar Watch**

- Use *used to* to talk about past habits.
- We often contrast past habits with present situations. *I used to dance, but I don't anymore.*

1 PRACTICE

A Read the paragraph. Underline *used to* and circle each verb that comes after it.

Last summer I visited my hometown. It's so different from the way it <u>used to</u> (be.) When I lived there, we used to ride bikes or take buses. Now people ride motorbikes. Women used to wear traditional clothes, but now they often wear Western clothes. Back then people used to write letters, but these days everyone uses cell phones and e-mail. Can you guess where I'm from? I'm from Ho Chi Minh City, Vietnam.

B Read the conversation. Complete the sentences with *used to* and the verbs *go, have, make,* or *play.*

Sania: When I was a child, I ___used to go___ to the outdoor market with my mother. I miss that.

Youngju: I miss my grandmother's cooking. She _____ the best *kimchee* in the world. How about you, Jorge? What do you miss about Peru?

Jorge: I _____ more time to play soccer. I _____ soccer every weekend.

Show what you know! Compare your life now with your life in the past

GROUPS. Talk about your life now and in the past. Talk about clothes, food, games, and activities.

Can you...compare your life now with your life in the past? ☐

Write about your life now and in the past

Writing

1 BEFORE YOU WRITE

A Read about Jiitu's life. Then complete the chart with information from the paragraph.

> I grew up in Ethiopia. I'm from Addis Ababa. It has mountains around it and lots of eucalyptus trees. It's warm and pleasant all year. In the winter it was sixty-eight degrees. I used to spend a lot of time outdoors all year. Now I live in Minneapolis, Minnesota. The weather is very cold in the winter, so we stay inside a lot during the winter months. I like Minneapolis, but I miss Ethiopia.

In Ethiopia	In Minneapolis
warm weather	

B How was your life different in the past from the way it is now? Compete the chart.

In my native country	In _____

2 WRITE

Write about your life in your native country. How was your life there different from your life now in the United States?

3 CHECK YOUR WRITING

☐ Does your paragraph talk about life in your native country and the United States?

☐ Does your paragraph end with a feeling or opinion about where you live now?

☐ Did you indent the first line of the paragraph?

1 REVIEW   For your Grammar Review, go to page 245.

2 ACT IT OUT   What do you say?

STEP 1. CLASS. Review the conversation on page 9 (CD1 Track 8).

STEP 2. PAIRS. Make small talk. Tell your partner about yourself.

Student A: Ask these questions:

- What country are you from?
- What languages do you speak?
- Where do you live now?
- What is your neighborhood like?
- Why are you are studying English?

Student B: Answer the questions. Then change roles.

---

3 READ AND REACT   Problem-solving

STEP 1. Read about Wei Jao's problem.

My husband is 70 years old and I'm 65. We came to the United States a year ago to live near our son and daughter. We live in a quiet suburb in Los Angeles with our son. He has a big house, but he and his wife work all day, so we're home alone. You need a car to get anywhere and we don't drive. I miss Shanghai. In Shanghai, we used to spend time with our friends and we miss that. I don't speak English well and I'm bored. My daughter tells us to move to San Francisco. She and her husband live in Chinatown in a small apartment. What should we do?

STEP 2. GROUPS. What is Wei Jao's problem? Give Wei Jao advice. Should she stay in Los Angeles? Should she move to San Francisco? How can she make more friends and find activities?

4 CONNECT   For your Community-building Activity, go to page 257.
For your Team Project, go to page 263.

Which goals can you check off? Go back to page 5.

Dreams and Goals

Preview

What do you dream about for your future? What do you plan for yourself or for your family?

UNIT GOALS

- ☐ Talk about going back to school
- ☐ Talk about future plans
- ☐ Look for a better job
- ☐ Set goals
- ☐ Talk about community services

1 WHAT DO YOU KNOW?

A CLASS. Look at the pictures that describe goals related to work, school, and community. What goals do the pictures show?

B Complete the descriptions of the pictures. Use the words in the box.

> apply   get   take
> enroll   register   volunteer

CD1 T15

C Listen and repeat.

Learning Strategy

Build vocabulary

Make two cards. Write the verbs *get* or *take* on the front of each card. On the back, write three phrases that use the verb. Use a dictionary for help.

> get a degree
> get a job
> get training

_____ a degree

_____ in college

_____ for the semester

_____ at a community center

_____ citizenship classes

2

_____ a certificate

4

_____ for financial aid

6

Congratulations on your promotion to assistant building manager.

_____ a promotion

A WORD PLAY. Look back at the pictures. What kind of goals do they show? Write them in the correct category. Write a check (✓) in the column if they are also your goals.

School goals	Work goals	Community goals
get a degree		

B GET THE MEANING. Read the paragraph about Damir. Underline the new vocabulary.

My dream is to be an electrician. When I lived in Bosnia, I couldn't go to college because of the war. Now I'm planning to go back to school and <u>get an associate's degree</u>. That takes two years to complete. First, I need to enroll in a college or a trade school. Then I'll look at the class schedule and register for the semester. I'm going to sign up for weekend classes and apply for financial aid. I hope that the state will give me some money for tuition. To become an electrician, I will have to work about 4,000 hours under a licensed electrician and pass a test. After that, I can get a certificate and work for myself.

Show what you know!

GROUPS. Talk about your plans. Use the information or your own ideas.

- buy my own home
- get a better job
- graduate from high school or college
- move to a better neighborhood

Talk about going back to school

Listening and Speaking

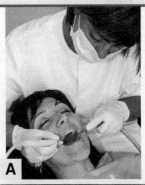

A

1 BEFORE YOU LISTEN

A Match the pictures with the jobs and the training they require. Write the correct letters.

_____ 1. auto body repairer, automative service excellence (ASE) certificate

_____ 2. dental assistant, state license

_____ 3. registered nurse, associate's degree

B

B GROUPS. Discuss. Do you plan to go back to school? Would you like to get a certificate, license, or degree? If you went back to school, what would you study?

2 LISTEN

CD1 T16

A Carmen is talking to Gustavo. Listen to the conversation. What are Carmen's plans? She is going to _____.

a. return to school this summer
b. return to school this fall

C

CD1 T16

B Listen again. Circle the correct answers.

1. When will Carmen take courses?
   a. on weekends   b. at night

2. What will she study?
   a. nursing   b. medical billing

3. What will she do after her basic classes?
   a. apply to a clinical program
   b. get a job at a clinic

CD1 T16

C PAIRS. Read the questions. Listen again. Discuss.

1. How long will it take Carmen to get her degree if she works hard?

2. What does Gustavo give Carmen? Why?

3 CONVERSATION

A 🎧 **Listen to the pronunciation of *will* in each sentence. Then listen and repeat.**

I'll start in the fall.
He'll work part-time.
When will you finish?

We'll help.
You'll study tonight.
What will you study?

> **Pronunciation Watch**
>
> *Will* is often contracted with nouns (*he'll, she'll*) and *wh-*words (*what'll, when'll, where'll how'll*).

B 🎧 **Listen to the sentences. Circle the words you hear.**

1. **I / I'll** work at night.

2. **I / I'll** take classes during the day.

3. **We / We'll** both go to City College.

4. **You / You'll** need a license.

C 🎧 **Listen and read the conversation.**

Carmen: I'm going to take night classes this fall.
Gustavo: Yeah? Where?
Carmen: At Los Angeles City College.
Gustavo: That's great. What will you study?
Carmen: Well, I want to be a nurse. I'd like to get an associate's degree.

4 PRACTICE

A PAIRS. **Practice the conversation.**

B ROLEPLAY. PAIRS. **Make a similar conversation.**

Student A: Talk about going back to school.

Student B: Ask about the certificate or license.
Then change roles. Use the information or your ideas.

Welder
• get a certificate

Real estate agent
• get a license

Medical assistant
• get a certificate

Grammar

Will/will probably/might/won't				
I	**will probably**	not	**go**	to school next fall.
She	**might**		**study**	nursing.

Yes/No questions			
Will	you	**change**	jobs?

Short answers
Yes, I will. / Probably.

Wh– questions				
When	will	you	**take**	classes?
What	will	he	**study?**	

········· **Grammar Watch**

- Use *will* to talk about the future.
- Use *might* to talk about a future possibility.
- Use *will* to ask questions about the future. Do not use *might*.
- *Will + not = won't*
  I will = I'll
  He will = He'll
  (See page 286 for more contractions.)

1   PRACTICE

A   Read about Cam. Underline the examples of *will, won't* and *might* and the verb that follows.

    I'm going to City College this fall. I want to get an associate's degree in computer science. To get the degree, <u>I'll need</u> to take basic classes, like technical mathematics. Then I'll have more choices. I want to learn computer languages. It won't take too long to finish the degree— maybe three years if I work part-time. After I get my degree, I'll work for a while and save money. Then later, if I get financial aid, I might go to a four-year college and get a bachelor's degree. If I have a bachelor's degree, I'll make more money.

B   Complete the sentences with *will, might,* or *won't.*

1. Cam _____ go to college this fall.

2. Cam _____ get a degree next year.

3. Cam _____ get financial aid.

A Complete the conversation between a husband and wife. Circle the correct words.

A: My English class is going to start soon. The first class **will** / **might** meet on Monday at 5:30.

B: I can't take you this Monday because I have to work. How **will** / **might** you get to school?

A: I'm not sure. I**'ll probably** / **'ll** take the bus.

B: OK. I can drive you the following Monday.

A: Well, that Monday is a holiday and the school **will** / **might not** be closed so I **might not** / **won't** need a ride then.

B PAIRS. Read the situations. What do you think these people will do? Discuss and write your answers in your notebook. Use *will, won't, might,* or *will probably.*

1. Jun doesn't have enough money to pay the school tuition.
   I think he'll apply for financial aid. OR *He might get a part-time job.*

2. Soledad can't study full-time because she takes care of her children during the day.

3. Pedro never had time to finish school. His boss is encouraging him to go back.

4. Irina really wants to go to a community college, but she doesn't have a car.

5. Pierre is in his first year of college. He's not getting good grades.

Show what you know! Talk about your future plans

STEP 1. Write three questions with *will* that ask about future plans. Start the questions with *what, where* or *when.*

STEP 2. GROUPS. Ask each other your questions.

1. _____

2. _____

3. _____

Can you...talk about your future plans? ☐

Reading

1 BEFORE YOU READ

Look at the picture and the title of the article. What do you think Ignacio and Eva's goal is?

Reading Skill:
Predicting

Before you read, look at the picture and the title of the article. This can help you predict what the article will be about.

2 READ

CD1 T20

Listen and read. What is Ignacio and Eva's goal? Was your prediction correct?

Dream dreams! Set goals!

Ignacio Moreno and his wife, Eva, have their own bakery, *La Flor del Trigo*, in Little Rock, Arkansas. The bakery was Ignacio's dream. He wanted a bakery like the one his parents had in Mexico. When he and Eva came to the United States, Ignacio thought a lot about the bakery he wanted. His dream became a goal and after fifteen years finally became a **reality**.

What's the difference between a dream and a goal? A dream is something that you hope will happen. It might happen and it might not. A goal is something you can make happen. To reach a goal, you have to make a plan, be patient, and never **give up**.

Ignacio and Eva's **long-term** goal was to open a bakery. To reach this goal, they made several **short-term** goals:

- *Save money*
  Ignacio and Eva were careful with their money. They spent as little as possible and saved for a business.

- *Learn about bakeries in the United States*
  For years Ignacio worked in other people's bakeries and learned the business. Eva learned customer service skills when she worked in a donut shop.

- *Find a place for the business*
  Ignacio found an old building. It was cheap, but it needed a lot of work. The windows were old, and the building needed a new roof.

- *Fix the building and buy equipment*
  Ignacio and Eva first needed to fix the building. They borrowed $167,000 from a bank. They paid a **contractor** to put on a new roof and replace the windows. Finally, they bought **equipment**, like commercial ovens and mixers.

Now Ignacio and Eva are working 12-hour days, but they are happy. And they have a new long-term goal! They want to sell their bread to large supermarkets. Next month, they will start to sell their bread in a supermarket in their neighborhood.

3 CHECK YOUR UNDERSTANDING

A Read the article again. What is the main idea? Circle the correct letter.

a. Ignacio and Eva Moreno have a bakery in Little Rock, Arkansas.
b. To open a business, you need a plan with long-term and short-term goals.
c. Ignacio and Eva are working 12 hours a day at their bakery.

B Read the statements. Write *T* (true) or *F* (false).

_F_ 1. It took Eva and Ignacio ten years to reach their goal.

_____ 2. Ignacio always worked for himself.

_____ 3. The building they bought for the bakery was in good condition.

_____ 4. They borrowed money to buy the equipment for the bakery.

_____ 5. They think having their own bakery is too much work.

4 VOCABULARY IN CONTEXT

Look at the boldfaced words in the article. Guess their meanings. Complete the sentences with the correct words.

1. To make a dream become a _____reality_____ you need to set goals.

2. We need a _____ to fix the walls and put in a new kitchen.

3. It isn't easy to stay in school, but if you keep trying and don't _____, you can finish and get a degree.

4. When you plan for the future, you need _____ goals that you will

   complete soon and _____ goals that will take more time.

5. If you want to work for yourself as a landscaper, you need special

   _____ like lawnmowers.

Show what you know!

GROUPS. Do you ever think about starting a business? What kind of business would you like to have? What would you need to do?

Look for a better job

Listening and Speaking

1 BEFORE YOU LISTEN

GROUPS. How do you look for a job? Do you ask friends or family? Do you look on bulletin boards? Do you look in the newspaper or on the Internet? What are the good things about each way? What are the bad things?

2 LISTEN

CD1 T21

A Listen to the first part of Min and Sheng's conversation. Who is looking for a job?

a. Min

b. Sheng

c. Min and Sheng

CD1 T21

B Read the questions. Then listen again. Circle the correct answers.

1. Why is Min going to look for a new job?
   a. She comes to work late.
   b. Her boss complains about her and keeps her late.
   c. Her bus is late so she never gets home on time.

2. Where is Min going to look for a job?
   a. on the bulletin board at the hospital
   b. on the bulletin board at the community college
   c. on the bulletin board at the community center

3. What advice does Sheng give Min?
   a. stay at her job
   b. go to a temp agency
   c. look for jobs online

CD1 T22

C PAIRS. Listen to the rest of the conversation. Answer the question.

Sheng finds an ad for a job for Min. Is Min going to apply for that job? Why or why not?

3 CONVERSATION

CD1 T23

A 🔘 **Listen to the two pronunciations of *going to*. Then listen and repeat.**

going to ("gonna")   What are you going to do?
                     I'm going to look for a job.

CD1 T24

B 🔘 **Listen and read the conversation.**

Sheng: So, Min, how's work?

Min: Oh, my new boss is terrible. I work hard, but he complains about my work a lot. Then he keeps me late, and I usually miss my bus. I'm going to look for a new job.

Sheng: I'm sorry to hear that. So, are you looking for a job here at the community center?

Min: Yes, there are always good job postings on the bulletin board here.

4 PRACTICE

A PAIRS. Practice the conversation.

B ROLE PLAY. Make up a conversation.

Student A: You don't like your job. Explain why. Use the ideas or your own ideas.
- You need more hours or more money.
- You don't get along with your boss.
- It takes too long to get to work.

Student B: Suggest a place where Student A can find a new job. Use the suggestions or your own ideas.
- Maybe you should look online.
- Maybe you should read the classifieds.
- Maybe you should look for help wanted signs in the neighborhood.

Lesson 6   Look for a better job

Grammar

The future with *be going to*

I	am				
She	is				
You We They	are	(not)	going to	look	for a new job.

Yes / No questions					Short answers	
Are **Is**	you he	going to	look	online?	Yes, I am. Yes, he is.	No, I'm not. No, he's not.

Wh- questions				
When	**are**	you		**begin?**
Where	**is**	he	going to	**study?**

---

1   PRACTICE

A Yuyuan plans to look for a job. What will he do first? Number the steps. Write *1* for the first step.

_____ Then he's going to circle all the ads for a security job.

_____ After that, he's going to answer the ads.

__1__ First, he's going to buy the local newspaper.

_____ Finally, when he's finished, he's going to have a big lunch.

_____ Next, he's going to look at the classified section of the newspaper.

B Look back at Exercise 4. Circle the verbs that follow *be going to*. What form are these verbs?

a. past form   b. base form   c. future form

2 PRACTICE

A Complete the sentences. Use the correct form of *be going to.*

1. Nita and Claudia _are going to_ see what classes the community center has.

2. Pablo works at night. He _____ apply for a job with daytime hours.

3. I saw a help wanted sign at the mall. I _____ apply for the job today.

4. My sister wants help getting a job. She _____ speak to someone at the community center.

5. _____ you _____ go to the library? I'll go with you and we can look on the Internet for jobs.

B Complete the conversation. Use a form of *be going to* and the verb in parentheses.

Ania: Veronica and I _are going to visit_ a temp agency tomorrow.
                                    (visit)

Olga: What's a temp agency?

Ania: It's a place where people help you find jobs for short periods.

I _____ them about a clerical job. Do you want to come?
   (ask)

Olga: Yes, I do. I really need a job. My job _____ next month.
                                                    (end)

Do I need to bring anything?

Ania: I _____ my diploma from Kracow. It's translated into
   (bring)
English. And I think Veronica _____ a letter from her old boss.
                                        (take)

Olga: That's a good idea. I _____ my boss for a letter. I think
                                    (ask)
he likes me. Maybe that will help.

Show what you know! Look for a better job

GROUPS. **You want a better job. Talk about five things you're going to do. Then talk about two things you're not going to do. Give reasons why.**

I'm going to speak to someone at the community center. It has services to help you get a job.

Can you...look for a better job? ☐

Life Skills

1 SET GOALS

A Read about time frames for goals.

When you set a goal, you need to decide on a realistic time frame to reach your goal. For example, if you want to get a certificate and you are studying part-time, you probably won't be able to get it in a year. Instead, a realistic time frame might be a few years.

B PAIRS. Discuss. What makes a time frame realistic or not realistic? What things do you need to think about to set a realistic time frame for your goals?

2 PRACTICE

STEP 1. Complete the chart. What are your goals? Write one or two in each category. By when do you want to complete your goals?

School	By when?

Job	By when?

Community	By when?

Family or personal	By when?

STEP 2. PAIRS. Look at your partner's goals and time frames. Are the time frames realistic for the goals?

STEP 3. PAIRS. Some goals are difficult to reach. Read about Amina. Then answer the questions with a partner.

I grew up in Kabul, Afghanistan. My father was a professor at the University of Kabul. When I turned 18, the Taliban was in power. They didn't want women to go to school, so we had to stay at home. The Taliban also did not let women work as doctors. Now I live and go to college in Queens, New York. My dream is to be a doctor. First, I need to finish my bachelor's degree. Then I'll go to medical school. To reach my goal, I need financial aid and help from my family. Right now my husband works and my family helps take care of my daughter. They want me to go to medical school and they think I can succeed.

1. What is Amina's goal?
2. What are the obstacles to Amina's goal?
3. What are Amina's supports?

Obstacles = things that make a goal difficult to reach (example: not enough time)
Supports = things that help you reach a goal (example: advise or encouragement from a friend)

STEP 4. Think about your most important goal. Is it a difficult goal? If it is, what makes it difficult? What will help you to reach it? Complete the chart.

Goal	What are the obstacles?	What are the supports?

STEP 5. PAIRS. Look at your partner's chart. Can you think of obstacles or supports that your partner did not include? Discuss.

Can you...set goals? ☐

Write about your goals

Writing

1 BEFORE YOU WRITE

A **PAIRS. Read about Amadou. What is his goal?
What steps will he take to meet his goal?**

> I'm from Mauritania, in northwest Africa. Now I live in Philadelphia.
> When I was in Mauritania, I got a pretty good education. I studied Arabic
> and French in high school. But life was hard. We didn't have buses,
> electricity, or running water at our school. I came to the U.S. to have a better
> life, but it wasn't easy at first. I had to work 12-hour days as a taxi driver.
> Now I'm learning English, and I want to go back to school. My goal is to be
> a teacher. I'm going to get a degree and a certificate. Then I'll teach in the
> Philadelphia schools. The U.S. is a competitive country. But if I work hard, I
> know I'll succeed.

B **Complete the chart. Write your most important goal for the future.
Then write the steps you will take to meet this goal.**

Goal	Steps to meet your goal	
	1.	
	2.	
	3.	

2 WRITE

**Write a paragraph about your goal and the steps you will take.
Then say how you feel about your goal. Will it be easy or difficult?
Use the writing model as an example.**

3 CHECK YOUR WRITING

☐ Did you tell your goal in your paragraph?

☐ Did you tell the steps you will take to reach your goal?

☐ Did you tell your feelings at the end of your paragraph?

☐ Did you indent your paragraph?

Listening and Speaking

1   BEFORE YOU LISTEN

GROUPS. Is there a community center in your neighborhood?
What kinds of services and activities does it provide?

2   LISTEN

CD1 T25

A   Listen to a radio announcement
from the Long Beach Community Center.
Does it offer any services you talked
about in Before You Listen?

CD1 T25

B   Listen again. Which services does
the Long Beach Community Center talk
about in the announcement? Check (✓)
the services you hear.

☐ health-care service

☐ food and clothes for families in need

☐ classes for adults

☐ baby-sitting services

☐ neighborhood improvement

CD1 T25

C   Listen again. Match the dates with the events.
Write the correct letters.

_____ 1. Sept.–Aug.   a. English placement test

_____ 2. Oct. 20   b. mural painting

_____ 3. Sept. 8, 9   c. distribute food and clothes

_____ 4. Oct. 1   d. food and clothing drive

_____ 5. Sept. 10   e. English and computer classes

D   **GROUPS.** Write a list of the things your community needs.
Then share your list with the class.

Talk about community services

Grammar

Present continuous for the future

I	am			
He	is	(not)	**helping**	with the food drive this weekend.
You	are			

Are	you	**helping**	with the food drive this weekend?
Is	she		

· · · · · · Grammar Watch

- Use the present continuous for planned events in the future.

- We usually use a future time expression like *tomorrow* or *next week* to indicate the future.

1 PRACTICE

A Read the conversation. Underline the examples of the present continuous for the future.

Jack: Hi. I'm with the Dolores Community Center. We're having a meeting next Saturday night. We're meeting to find volunteers for the neighborhood.

Hugo: Sorry, I'd like to help out, but I don't have time.

Jack: Oh, sure, I understand. But you can come and meet new people if you want. It's at 7:00 P.M. We're having a potluck dinner and giving out prizes. . . .

B Complete the sentences with the present continous for the future.

1. The Dolores Community Center _____ (meet) next week.

2. The community center _____ (offer) free babysitting tomorrow.

3. We _____ (bring) our children to the center tomorrow.

4. _____ (you/go) to the meeting tomorrow night?

A Complete the conversations. Use the present continuous for the future.

1. **A:** _____Are you going_____ to the meeting tomorrow night?
   (you / go)

   B: No, I can't. _____ for my granddaughter.
   (I / babysit)

2. **A:** _____ English classes next semester?
   (your sister / take)

   B: Well, they don't know if they have enough space. They put her on a waiting list.

   Next week _____ her back to let her know.
   (they / call)

3. **A:** _____ at the food drive?
   (you / volunteer)

   B: Yes, I am. _____ there on Saturday morning.
   (I / work)

B PAIRS. Mei Lu is a stay-at-home mother. Look at the calendar.
Ask your partner *yes/no* and *wh-* questions about her plans for next week.

MONDAY	TUESDAY	WEDNESDAY	THURSDAY	FRIDAY
Babysit for Feng 3:30 English class 7:00	Go shopping! Chinese community center — Legal Aid 5:00	Library — kids story time 9:00 English class 7:00	Chinese community center — Mom's group 6:00	Take Jin to clinic 9:00

A: *When is Mei Lu babysitting?*
B: *Monday afternoon at 3:30.*
A: *What is Mei Lu doing on Wednesday?*

Show what you know! Talk about community services

GROUPS. Discuss the questions.

1. What services does your community center or religious organization have this month? How can you find out more? How can you volunteer and help?

2. What are you doing with your family this month? Are you spending time together?

Can you… talk about community services? ☐

1 | REVIEW   For your Grammar Review, go to page 246.

2 | ACT IT OUT   What do you say?

STEP 1. CLASS. Review the conversation on page 29 (CD1 Track 19).

STEP 2. PAIRS. Talk about going back to school. Talk about your real plans to go back to school or make up the plans.

> **Student A:** Tell Student B you are going back to school. Answer Student B's questions.

> **Student B:** Ask Student A these questions:
> - Are you going to get a degree, a certificate, or a license?
> - What are you going to study?
> - What classes will you take?
> - How long will it take?

3 | READ AND REACT   Problem-solving

STEP 1. Read about Jean Paul's problem.

Jean Paul works for a moving company. His boss always pays him late so Jean Paul can't pay his bills on time. He is upset and wants to get a new job. Jean Paul is very friendly and likes people. He is interested in a job in sales, but he doesn't have training.

STEP 2. GROUPS. What is the problem? Give Jean Paul advice. What goals can he set? What are things he can do to look for a better job?

4 | CONNECT   For your Goal-setting Activity, go to page 257.
For your Team Project, go to page 264.

Which goals can you check off? Go back to page 25.

School Days

3

Preview

In the United States, there are elementary schools, middle schools, and high schools. Is this the same or different in other countries?

UNIT GOALS

- ☐ Talk about problems at school

- ☐ Find ways to help children with school

- ☐ Talk about library services

- ☐ Write a letter of request

- ☐ Deal with bullies

- ☐ Read a report card

- ☐ Help children continue their education

1 WHAT DO YOU KNOW?

A Look at the phrases that relate to school. Which phrases do you know?

B Match the pictures with the words. Write the numbers.

School activities

_____ do research

_____ figure out an answer

_____ go online

_____ go over homework

_____ go to a parent-teacher conference

_____ hand in homework

_____ help someone out

_____ look up a word in a dictionary

_____ make up a test

CD1 T26

C Listen and check your answers. Then listen and repeat.

Learning Strategy

Use context

Make cards for five phrases. Write the phrase on the front of the card. Write a sentence on the back of the card about the picture the phrase describes.

2

WORD PLAY. Read the letter. Why is Jen's mother worried about her? What does *drop out* mean?

3/15/10

Dear Mrs. Halter,

I'm writing this letter because I'm worried about my daughter, Jen. She's getting bad grades in your math class. She says she doesn't understand the lessons. When she does her math homework, she has trouble figuring out the answers. I try to go over the homework with her, but I don't always have time. Jen says she doesn't care about school anymore and says she wants to drop out. Could you please call me? My number is 562-555-2665.

Thank you.
Sincerely,
Karin Hirsh

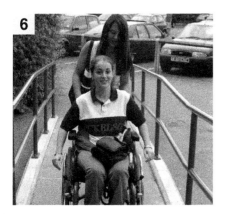

4

7

8

6

Show what you know!

GROUPS. Discuss. Why do children sometimes fall behind in school? Did this ever happen to you? When you were a child at school, were you better in some classes than in others? Which ones?

Talk about problems at school

Listening and Speaking

1 BEFORE YOU LISTEN

A GROUPS. Discuss. What are three ways parents can help their children in school?

B Look at the vocabulary. Do you know these words?

> *discipline*: make children behave
> *get involved*: be a part of something
> *pick on*: be mean to
> *vice principal*: the second in charge
> of a school, after the principal

2 LISTEN

A CD1 T27 Listen to the radio talk show interview about school. Who is Kendra Williams?

a. a principal   b. a parent with children   c. a writer and teacher

B CD1 T28 Read the statements. Then listen again. Write *T* (true) or *F* (false), according to the interview.

_____ 1. Parents should get involved with their child's school.

_____ 2. Parents shouldn't come to school meetings if their English isn't good.

_____ 3. Parents need to go to one parent-teacher conference each year.

_____ 4. Parents should look at their children's homework a few times each month.

_____ 5. Parents should not write to their child's teacher. Teachers are too busy.

_____ 6. Vice principals help make sure students behave well.

C CD1 T28 Listen again. Kendra Williams talks about schoolwork. Then she answers questions about two other problems. What are they? Circle them.

a. Safety outside the school   c. Teachers who pick on students
b. Safety in classrooms   d. Children who pick on other children

3 CONVERSATION

CD1 T29

A Listen to the words. Notice the stress in the first syllable. Then listen and repeat.

Pronunciation Watch
Most two-syllable nouns in English take stress on the first syllable.

- practice
- soccer
- Thursday

CD1 T30

B Listen to the words. Mark the stress.

1. answer
2. college
3. English
4. language
5. letter
6. message
7. music
8. photo
9. problem
10. question
11. science
12. tutor

CD1 T31

C Listen and read the conversation.

Mr. Reyes: Daniel, did you do your homework?
Daniel: Not yet.
Mr. Reyes: When do you have to hand it in?
Daniel: Thursday.
Mr. Reyes: Well, you'd better get started. You don't want to fall behind in class.
Daniel: OK, Dad, but how about after I watch the soccer game? Monterrey is playing against Santos.
Mr. Reyes: How about now? You can watch soccer later, and tomorrow is soccer practice. You don't want to miss that, do you?

4 PRACTICE

A PAIRS. Practice the conversation.

B MAKE IT PERSONAL. GROUPS. What are the biggest school problems in your area? What are ways that parents can help change things that they don't like at their children's schools?

Grammar

Inseparable phrasal verbs

She never	**falls behind.**	
He	**keeps up with**	his schoolwork.

Separable phrasal verbs

Hand in your <u>homework</u>.	**Hand** your <u>homework</u> **in**.	**Hand** <u>it</u> **in** today.
object	object	object pronoun

Grammar Watch

- A **phrasal verb** is made of a verb + a **particle**. Particles are words such as *up, down, on, off, after, by, in,* and *out.*
- For **inseparable phrasal verbs**, the verb and the particle must stay together.
- For **separable phrasal verbs**, the verb and the particle can stay together or be separated.
- Many phrasal verbs take **objects** (nouns or pronouns).
- When the object of a separable phrasal verb is a noun, the object can come before or after the particle.
- When the object is a pronoun, the object must come before the particle.
- Inseparable phrasal verbs sometimes have two particles. For example, *drop out of.*

Inseparable	Separable
drop out of	figure out
fall behind	hand in
go over	make up
keep up with	sign up
make fun of	
miss out on	
pick on	

---

1 PRACTICE

Circle the phrasal verbs in the sign-up sheet.

FREE TUTORS AT THE GREENVILLE PUBLIC LIBRARY!
Monday–Friday 3–5

Are your children having trouble with classes? Don't let them fall behind or drop out of school! At the Greenville Public Library, we have free tutors. Sign up for tutoring today so your children can keep up with their classes. Our tutors can help your children in math, science, social studies, or English. Our tutors will go over homework and answer questions. They can also help your children go online and do research. Don't miss out on this opportunity! Sign up today.

A **Unscramble the sentences. Put the words in the correct order. Write in your notebook.**

1. the children / of / making fun / are / my daughter

   The children are making fun of my daughter.

2. falling / in English class / behind / she / is

3. my nephew / out / dropped / school / of

4. he / his project / in / make sure / hands

5. on / my son's teacher / picks / him

> *make fun of = say something unkind*
> *pick on = be mean to someone*

B **Underline the separable verbs. Draw two lines under the inseparable verbs. Circle the objects.**

1. Did you hand in your (homework?)

2. The girls picked on my daughter.

3. Abdir looked up information online.

4. The teacher went over the homework.

5. Sam figured out the answers.

6. Pol can make up the test next week.

C **Rewrite the sentences in Exercise B. Use object pronouns (*it*, *them*, or *her*).**

The girls picked on her.

Show what you know!   Find ways to help children with school

PROBLEM SOLVE. GROUPS. **Talk about problems that children sometimes have in school. Suggest solutions. Use the phrasal verbs in the box.**

drop out	figure out	hand in	make up	sign up
fall behind	go over	help out	pick on	

Can you... find ways to help children with school? ☐

Reading

1 BEFORE YOU READ

GROUPS. Do you go to the library? If so, how often? If you have children, do they go often?

2 READ

CD1 T32

Listen and read the article. What is the article about? What do you know about the topic?

The Trove

Have you ever seen a children's library that looks like Disneyland? In White Plains, New York, you will. The Trove is a magical place that makes children love going to the library.

What makes The Trove magical? The answer is easy. This library has a beautiful **design** and special places to play in. In one corner of the library, children can sit inside a ship and read their favorite books. At the other end of the library, there is a dollhouse and a play kitchen in the Play Cottage. In the StoryTrove, small children can listen to stories in English and Spanish. There's even a theater for special **performances**, like music.

Are you ready to **check out** books and other materials? At The Trove, children, like adults, can have their own library cards. Librarians help them check out books, DVDs, CD-ROMs, and magazines to take home. They can **return** books when they're done.

Or if they want to keep the books longer, they can **renew** them. They just need to come in or call the library. Sometimes they keep a book too long. Then they have to pay a **fine**! Kids can borrow a lot of things from The Trove at one time. The **limit** is 50 items per card!

Why was The Trove made? In the 1990s, the White Plains public library had a small children's section. The library's director, Sandra Miranda, wanted to make it a more exciting place for children to visit. The city liked her ideas and gave the library money to build The Trove. And children *are* coming. These days after school, you see children meeting their friends at The Trove.

CHECK YOUR UNDERSTANDING

Write *T* (true) or *F* (false).

_T_ 1. There are many different activities for kids at The Trove.

____ 2. At The Trove, children can check out their own books.

____ 3. The Trove does not have storytime in Spanish.

____ 4. Kids don't have to pay if they keep books too long.

____ 5. The library built The Trove with help from the city.

____ 6. Kids in White Plains often go to the White Plains Public Library after school.

4 **VOCABULARY IN CONTEXT**

**Look at the boldfaced words in the article. Guess their meanings.
Then complete the sentences with the correct words.**

1. Tony didn't _____return_____ the book on time. He had to pay a _____.

2. The _____ of The Trove looks like Disneyland.

3. I didn't finish this book. I'd like to _____ it, please.

4. You need to use your library card if you want to _____ a book.

5. You can borrow three DVDs at one time. That's the _____.

6. There will be free music _____ at the library this month on Friday nights.

Show what you know! Talk about library services

**GROUPS. What does your library have or not have? What do you like or not
like about your library? Talk about the ideas in the box or your own ideas.**

after-school tutoring	convenient hours	materials in your language
comfortable seats	ESL classes	performances
computers	good books and videos	story time for small children

Can you... talk about library services? ☐

Write a letter of request

Writing

1 BEFORE YOU WRITE

A GROUPS. Are there any changes you would like to make to your library? What are they? Talk about the ideas from page 53 and your own ideas.

B Read the letter. Why did Ramona Matos write a letter to the library?

February 4, 2010

Ms. Amanda F. Reade
Director of Library Services
Riverside Public Library
100 Main Street
Riverside, FL 33446

Dear Ms. Reade:

My family really likes Riverside library. We especially enjoy story time for our small children and we would like to use the library more often.

We would like to make a request. Our family has time to visit the library only on the weekend but the library is closed on Saturdays after 1 P.M. Could the library stay open on Saturday afternoon? Then we could come more often.

Thank you for your consideration.

Sincerely,

Ramona Matos

Ramona Matos

2 WRITE

Write a letter to your library. Use the format of the letter in Exercise B. Ask for one improvement to the library. Use the ideas from page 53 or your own ideas.

3 CHECK YOUR WRITING

☐ Did you write the date and the name and address of the person the letter is for?

☐ Did you politely ask for one improvement?

Deal with bullies

Listening and Speaking

1 BEFORE YOU LISTEN

GROUPS. Discuss. Sometimes children are mean and bully other children. Sometimes problems happen in class or on the playground. What should parents do if a child picks on their child?

playground

2 LISTEN

CD1 T33

A Listen to the conversation. Rafael is in middle school. He is talking to his mother. How does Rafael feel? He's _____.

a. upset   b. bored   c. confused

CD1 T33

B Listen again. Answer the questions. Write *T* (true) or *F* (false).

_____ 1. Rafael is not doing well in Mr. Meltzer's class.

_____ 2. Two boys are bullying Rafael at school.

_____ 3. The boys took Rafael's lunch money.

_____ 4. Rafael got in a fight far away from the school.

_____ 5. The boys made fun of Rafael's name.

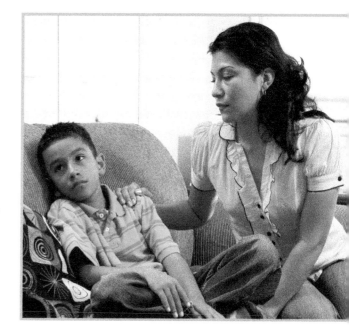

C PAIRS. **Discuss the questions.**

1. Why doesn't Rafael want to talk to his mother about the problem?

2. What does *beat up* someone mean?

3. How do you think Rafael's mother feels?

D MAKE IT PERSONAL. GROUPS. **Discuss. If a bully picks on your son, what do you say? If a bully picks on your daughter, do you say the same thing?**

Deal with bullies

Grammar

Simple past review: Regular and irregular verbs

Affirmative		
She	**called**	the teacher.
He	**hit**	me.
They	**took**	my money.

Negative			
She		**call**	the principal.
I	**didn't**	**hit**	him.
We		**take**	his money.

Yes/No questions		
Did	**you**	tell anyone?

Short answers	
Yes, I did.	**No, I didn't.**

Grammar Watch

- Regular past tense verbs end in *-d* or *-ed*.
- The past of *be* is *was* and *were*.
- See page 285 for a list of irregular verbs.

1 PRACTICE

A Underline all verbs in the simple past.

Last year my son <u>was</u> in the third grade. One day he came home late. He was very upset. Some students in his class made fun of his name. He has a beautiful Vietnamese name, but many Americans can't pronounce it. My son wanted to change his name. At first, I didn't want him to change his name. Finally, I said OK. He decided to call himself Henry. He loves his new name. I'm happy for him, but for me he will always be Hao.

B Complete the conversation with the simple past and the words in parentheses.

A: Monday, Tom _____*beat*_____ me up on the playground.
　　　　　　　　　　　(beat)

B: _____ your mom _____ the vice principal's office?
　　　　　　　　　　　　　　　　　(call)

A: Yes, but the vice principal _____ in the office, so my mom
　　　　　　　　　　　　　　　　　　(not / be)

　　_____ a message.
　　　(leave)

B: _____ Tom _____ into trouble?
　　　　　　　　　　　　(get)

A: Yes, he _____. The vice principal _____ him for three days.
　　　　　　　　　　　　　　　　　　　　　(suspend)

Simple past review: *Wh-* questions

Wh- questions about the subject		Answers
What	happened?	Someone hit me.
Who	hit you?	Tom.

Other *wh-* questions		Answers
Who	**did** you tell?	The teacher.
What	**did** he do?	He called the vice principal.
When	**did** this happen?	Yesterday.
Where	**did** it happen?	On the playground.

· · · · · **Grammar Watch**

Grammar Watch

Wh- questions about the subject do not use *did*.

2 PRACTICE

Complete the conversation. Use the simple past and the words in parentheses.

A: Some kids got into a big fight at school today.

B: Oh? (What / happen) _What happened?_

A: Tom hit a kid and took his baseball cards.

B: (Who / he / hit) _____

A: Angel.

B: (When / he / do) _____ that?

A: In the afternoon. Right after school let out.

B: (Why / Tom / beat up) _____ Angel?

A: They got in an argument in school. Then they went outside and started to fight.

B: (Where / the / fight / happen) _____

A: On the playground next to the school.

Show what you know! Deal with bullies

GROUPS. Talk about a time you (or your child) had a problem in school with bullies, for instance, a time that someone hurt you or a time you got into trouble. What happened?

Can you...deal with bullies? ☐

Read a report card

Life Skills

1 READ A REPORT CARD

A Look at the chart. Which grades are good? Which are bad? Which grade means the student failed the class?

> In the United States, high school students receive letter or number grades on their tests, homework, and papers. Then they get a final grade for the class. The grades are different in different school districts.

Grades

A+	A	B+	B	C+	C	D	F
95–100%	90–94%	85–89%	80–84%	75–79%	70–74%	65–69%	Below 65%

B Students usually get a report card in the fall, winter, spring, and before the summer. Look at the report card. Which class did Joey do best in?

Randolph High School Report Card

Student: Joey Miller   Quarter   Year: 2010–2011

Class	Teacher	Q 1	Q 2	Q 3	Q 4	Final	Comments
Art	Jones	B					Good student.
English	Smith	B–					Needs to spend more time on homework.
Algebra 1	Moyer	A+					Participates well in class.
Phys. Ed.	Cavallo	A					Fine student.
Earth Science	Gold	B+					Good student, but needs to pay more attention in class.
Social Studies	Manzo	C–					Does not complete all assignments. Please call me.
Spanish	Mendez	B					Good in class but missed two quizzes.

2 PRACTICE

PAIRS. **Answer the questions about the report card.**

1. In which classes does Joey need to work harder?

2. In which class did Joey not take some of the tests?

3. In which class does Joey need to listen more to the teacher?

4. Which teacher do Joey's parents need to call?

3 LISTEN TO A TELEPHONE RECORDING

A GROUPS. **Discuss. Why do parents sometimes call their children's school?**

B CD1 T34
🔊 Listen to a telephone message from a high school.
Circle the word or words you hear.

a. main office   b. weather   c. school closing

C CD1 T34
🔊 You are a parent calling the school. Read the statements.
Then listen again and write the correct numbers.

1. You don't know where the school is. You need to press ____.

2. You need to call the main office. Press ____.

3. Your son got sick at school. The school nurse left a message on your cell

   phone. Press ____ to call her back.

4. A boy in school hit your son. Press ____ for the vice principal.

5. Your son Joey is doing badly in Mr. Manzo's class. You want to talk to

   Mr. Manzo. Press ____.

4 PRACTICE

ROLE PLAY. PAIRS. **Pretend Joey's parent is talking to his teacher.**

Student A: You are Joey's teacher. Explain the problem. Joey doesn't hand in his homework and he didn't do the last report. He comes to class late, and his test scores are low. Give Joey's parent advice.

Student B: You are Joey's parent. Ask how Joey can do better.

Help children continue their education

Listening and Speaking

1 BEFORE YOU LISTEN

GROUPS. What things can parents do to help their children continue their education?

School counselors help students with many kinds of problems—problems at school and personal problems. They also help students apply for college.

2 LISTEN

CD1 T35

A 🔘 Listen to a conversation between Mrs. Andrade and a school counselor. Why is Mrs. Andrade talking to the school counselor?

a. She wants to plan for her son's future.

b. Her son is depressed.

c. Her son is having a problem with a teacher.

CD1 T35

B 🔘 Listen again. Circle the answers.

1. Braulio's grades were especially good in _____.
   a. computers and math
   b. math and social studies
   c. math and science

2. Braulio's mother wants Braulio to _____.
   a. attend a community college
   b. attend a four-year college after high school
   c. become a doctor

CD1 T36

C 🔘 Listen to the second part of the conversation. Braulio wants to go to college. How many years of each subject does he need to take?

____1 semester____ computer science

_____ foreign language

_____ math

_____ science

_____ social studies

CD1 T37

A Listen to the phrasal verbs and sentences. Then listen and repeat.

hand it **in**   He hands it in on time.

fall be**hind**   You don't want to fall behind.

keep up with   Try to keep up with the work.

CD1 T38

B Listen and read the conversation.

Counselor: What would you like to see for Braulio's future?

Mrs. Andrade: We really want him to go to a four-year college.

Counselor: Oh, that's great. Well, in that case, we have to make sure he takes the right courses. The four-year colleges want students to take certain classes. That way they are prepared for college.

Mrs. Andrade: What classes does he need?

Counselor: Well, he has to take four years of English. He also needs three years of social studies, math and science, as well as, two years of a foreign language, and a semester of computer science.

4 PRACTICE

A PAIRS. Practice the conversation.

B MAKE IT PERSONAL. GROUPS. Discuss. What things do you think teachers or counselors should do to help children?

Grammar

Should and Have to

Questions with *should*				Answers
Should	he	**talk**	to a counselor?	Yes, he **should**. He should talk to a counselor.
	I	**wait?**		No, you **shouldn't**. You shouldn't wait.

Questions with *have to*				Answers
Do	I			Yes, you **do**. You have to take English.
Does	he	**have to**	**take** English?	No, he **doesn't**.

Grammar Watch

- We use *should* to give advice.
- We use *have to* when it is necessary to do something.
- *Should not* = shouldn't
- *Don't/Doesn't have to* means there is a choice.
- *Should* is followed by the base form of the verb. For example, *he should visit*.

1 PRACTICE

**Julio is talking to his younger brother about his college application.
Read the advice. Check (✓) the statements with the same meaning.**

1. It is a good idea to show your college essay to a few people before you hand it in.

   ☐ a. You have to show it to some people.

   ☐ b. You should show it to some people.

2. This application isn't due until December 31.

   ☐ a. You don't have to send it in before December 31.

   ☐ b. You shouldn't send it in before December 31.

3. Mr. Cooper writes good letters of recommendation and he likes you.
   He gave you an A in English.

   ☐ a. You have to ask him for a letter of recommendation.

   ☐ b. You should ask him for a letter of recommendation.

A Complete the sentences. Use affirmative or negative forms of the verbs in parentheses.

PSAT ENGLISH TEST

1. The test begins at 8:00. You _____ (**have to / be**) in room 201 by 8:00. No one can enter the room after 8:00.

2. You _____ (**should / go**) to bed late on the night before

   the test. You _____ (**should / get**) a good night's sleep.

3. Bring two number 2 pencils. You _____ (**have to / use**) a number two pencil for the test.

4. You _____ (**should / work**) quickly. You only have two hours to complete the questions.

5. You _____ (**should / answer**) all questions.

   You _____ (**should / leave**) any blanks.

B Read the questions and answers. Circle the correct word.

1. **Q:** Does my daughter need algebra to graduate from high school?

   A: Yes, she **should / has to** take algebra. She can't graduate without it.

2. **Q:** My son needs help with science. What can I do?

   A: He **should / has to** ask classmates who are good in science for help.

3. **Q:** We want my daughter to go to college next year. How can we find out about financial aid?

   A: You **should / have to** apply to the college first to find out about financial aid.

Show what you know!   Help children continue their education

GROUPS. Should children continue their education after they finish high school? Why or why not?

Can you...help children continue their education? ☐

1 REVIEW

For your Grammar Review, go to page 247.

2 ACT IT OUT What do you say?

STEP 1. CLASS. Listen to the conversation on page 61 (CD1 Track 38).

STEP 2. PAIRS. Role-play a conversation between a parent and a school counselor. Talk about a problem with bullies. Use the situation.

> **Student A:** You have a child in middle school. Your child used to get good grades and enjoy school. Now there are two bullies in his or her class. They pick on your child. In the mornings, your child refuses to go to school. Complain to the counselor.

> **Student B:** You are the counselor. Discuss action that the school and the parent can take:
> • talking to the teacher
> • talking to the vice principal
> • talking to the child

3 READ AND REACT Problem-solving

STEP 1. Tanya is from Russia. She and her son moved to the U.S. two years ago. Read Tanya's problem.

My son Alex is in eleventh grade. In the past he was a good student. Now his grades are dropping. He's never at home. He goes out at night even when he doesn't have permission. He looks terrible. I'm worried about him, and I don't like his new friends.

STEP 2. GROUPS. Discuss. What is Tanya's problem? Give Tanya advice. What can she do to help her son Alex succeed in school? How can she keep him out of trouble?

4 CONNECT

For your Goal-setting Activity, go to page 258.
For your Team Project, go to page 265.

Which goals can you check off? Go back to page 45.

Getting a Job

Preview

Do you have a job now? Are you looking for a job?

UNIT GOALS

- [ ] Talk about your work experience
- [ ] Read and complete a job application
- [ ] Describe your work history
- [ ] Learn job interview skills
- [ ] Write a thank-you letter
- [ ] Talk about positive work behavior

1   WHAT DO YOU KNOW?

A   CLASS. Look at the vocabulary. These words describe qualities that employers look for in employees. Which words do you know?

B   Complete the descriptions of the pictures. Use the words in the box. More than one answer is sometimes possible.

Qualities of employees
cooperative
dependable
efficient
hardworking
motivated
organized
pleasant
punctual

Learning Strategy

Make connections

Make cards for five new words. Write a quality on the front of the card. Write a job that needs that quality on the back.

C   PAIRS. Compare answers.

CD1 T39

D   Listen and repeat.

1

Carmella is _____ and takes good care of her patients.

3

Alisa keeps her desk neat and _____.

4

Bill always comes to work on time. He's very _____.

6

Mai is _____ and works well with her co-workers.

7

These men are strong and _____.

John is fast and _____.

Carlos is always friendly and

_____ to customers.

Yusef sells wallpaper. He is

very _____ and works

hard so he'll get a promotion.

A WORD PLAY. Sometimes former employers write a letter of recommendation. This letter tells a new employer good things about the employee. Read the letter.

To Whom It May Concern:

I would like to recommend Omar Ramos as a sales associate for your car dealership. Omar has worked at my car dealership for five years. We'll miss him when he moves to Los Angeles.

Omar is a very good salesman. He is always friendly and pleasant. He knows how to speak with customers and make them comfortable. Omar is sincere. Customers feel like they can buy a good car from him. He's also hardworking and almost never misses work. Please call me at 312-555-6571 if you have any questions.

Sincerely yours,

Sam Banks

Sam Banks
Manager

B Answer the questions about the letter. Write *T* (true) or *F* (false).

_____ 1. Omar is leaving his current job.

_____ 2. Customers feel that Omar is honest.

_____ 3. Omar's employer thinks Omar needs to work harder.

_____ 4. This is a good letter of recommendation.

Show what you know!

GROUPS. What kind of a job would you most like to have? Did you have this job in your native country?

Listening and Speaking

1 BEFORE YOU LISTEN

A PAIRS. Technicians are people who fix things. Do you know any technicians? What do they fix?

B PAIRS. Match the specialties with the pictures. Write the correct letters.

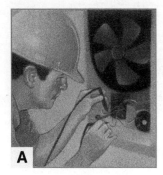
A

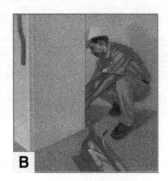
B

C

D

___ 1. refrigeration   ___ 2. automotive   ___ 3. air-conditioning   ___ 4. electronics

2 LISTEN

CD1 T40

A Listen to a radio commercial for a technical school. Why does the commercial say that it is a good idea to be a technician?

a. There are always jobs.

b. Technicians make good money.

c. Technicians decide their own hours.

CD1 T40

B Read the statements. Then listen again. Write *T* (true) or *F* (false).

_____ 1. ACME has programs in refrigeration.

_____ 2. ACME has classes at night but not on weekends.

_____ 3. ACME has part-time and full-time programs.

_____ 4. Financial aid is not available at ACME.

_____ 5. ACME helps students find a job when they finish the program.

3 CONVERSATION

CD1 T41

A 🎧 Listen to each word. Then listen and repeat.

/s/	/z/	/ɪz/
electronics	programs	classes

Pronunciation Watch

When a word ends in -s, the -s has an /s/, /z/, or /ɪz/ sound.

CD1 T42

B 🎧 Listen to each word. What ending sound do you hear? Write /s/, /z/, or /ɪz/.

1. technicians _____
2. things _____
3. nights _____
4. schools _____
5. services _____
6. computers _____
7. employers _____
8. offices _____

CD1 T43

C 🎧 Joe Kelly is at a job interview for an HVAC technician job. Listen and read the conversation.

Mr. Murphy: Can you tell me about your experience?

Joe: Sure. I started out five years ago. My uncle is a manager for an apartment building. I used to help him fix the heating and air-conditioning equipment. So then last year I got a certificate in HVAC from the ACME school.

HVAC = heating, ventilation, and air-conditioning

Mr. Murphy: Umhmm. And what kinds of equipment did they train you on?

Joe: We worked on all kinds of air conditioners, heaters, and ventillation systems.

Mr. Murphy: What about walk-in refrigerators? Have you ever worked on those?

Joe: Yes, I've repaired walk-in refrigerators and freezers in a few restaurants.

4 PRACTICE

A PAIRS. Practice the conversation.

B MAKE IT PERSONAL. STEP 1. Think of a job. Write a list of questions that you think an employer would ask at a job interview. Then write your answers.

STEP 2. PAIRS. ROLE PLAY. Give your list of questions to your partner. Then role-play a job interview.

UNIT 4　69

Grammar

Present perfect: Yes/No questions with *ever* and *never*

Have/Has	Subject	Ever	Past participle	
Has	he/she			
Have	you we they	**ever**	**worked**	at night?

	Affirmative			Negative	
Yes,	he/she	**has.**	**No**	he/she	**hasn't.**
	I you they	**have.**		I you they	**haven't.** / **have never worked** at night.

Grammar Watch

- Use the present perfect with *ever* to ask about any time up until now.
- Use the simple past to talk about a specific time in the past.
- See Page 287 for a list of irregular past participles.

1 PRACTICE

A Underline the examples of the present perfect. Circle the simple past.

A: Have you ever driven a truck? There's a job here for a driver with Safe Way Moving Company in Los Altos.

B: No. I've driven a taxi, but I've never driven a truck.

A: Where did you drive a taxi?

B: In Los Angeles. My brother and I shared the cab. The money was OK until gas became so expensive.

B Complete the sentences. Write the past participle form of the verbs in parentheses.

1. Have you ever _____ in an office?
   (work)
2. Have you ever _____ a taxi?
   (drive)
3. Have you ever _____ a commercial license?
   (get)
4. Have you ever _____ automobiles?
   (sell)
5. Have you ever _____ problems on the job?
   (solve)

A Complete the conversations. Use the present perfect or the simple past and the verbs in parentheses.

1. **A:** _____Have_____ you ever _____had_____ (**have**) your own business?

   B: Yes, I _____. My husband and I _____ (**own**) a small grocery store in Guatemala ten years ago.

2. **A:** _____ you ever _____ (**work**) at a bank?

   B: No, I _____, but my wife _____ (**be**) a bank teller from 1990 to 2005.

3. **A:** _____ you ever _____ (**answer**) phones for an office?

   B: No, I _____. But I _____ (**make**) copies and _____ (**send**) faxes in an office last year.

B Write questions in the present perfect with *ever*. Use the words in parentheses.

1. you / take care of patients _____Have you ever taken care of patients?_____

2. you / volunteer or work in a hospital _____

3. you / teach at a school _____

4. you / do office work _____

5. you/ repair a car _____

6. you / fix computers _____

7. you / own a business _____

8. you / operate heavy machinery _____

Show what you know! Talk about your work experience

PAIRS. Ask and answer the questions in Exercise B. If the answer is *yes*, explain. Use *No, never* for negative answers.

A: *Have you ever taken care of patients?*
B: *Yes, I have. I was a nurse in the Philippines. Have you ever done office work?*
A: *No, never.*

Can you...talk about your work experience? ☐

Read and complete a job application

Life Skills

1 READ A JOB APPLICATION

When you apply for a job, sometimes you send a résumé with a cover letter. See pages 278–279 for an example. Some jobs require only a job application.

A **CLASS. Read the job application. Talk about any words that you don't understand.**

CARUSO'S APPLICATION FOR EMPLOYMENT
PLEASE PRINT CLEARLY

NAME	ADDRESS	PHONE
Chiu, Li	342 Sycamore Street Alhambra, CA 91803	(520) 555-9832

If hired, can you show proof of eligibility to work in the U.S. within 3 days of hiring? ☒ YES ☐ NO

Are you 18 years of age or older? ☒ YES ☐ NO

POSITION APPLYING FOR: *Inventory Supervisor*   ☒ FT ☐ PT

AVAILABILITY: ☐ M–F DAY ☒ M–F EVE. ☐ WEEKENDS

Have you ever been fired from a job? ☐ YES ☒ NO   IF YES, what was the reason?

EDUCATION	NAME/ADDRESS	GRADUATED YES/NO	DIPLOMA OR DEGREE	YEAR	MAJOR
COLLEGE	East Los Angeles College, CA	No	No		Business
HIGH SCHOOL	Iloilo Sun Yat Sen H.S.	Yes	Yes	2004	NA

B **Answer the questions about the application. Write T (true) or F (false).**

_____ 1. Li is looking for a part-time job.

_____ 2. Li wants to be a store manager.

_____ 3. If Li gets the job, he needs to prove that he can work in the United States.

_____ 4. Li was fired from his last job.

A Read the second part of the job application.

EMPLOYMENT HISTORY

CURRENT OR LAST EMPLOYER

EMPLOYER	ADDRESS
IWS	3500 E. Sunrise Drive Monterey Park, CA 91754

SUPERVISOR	PHONE #	May we contact? [X] YES [ ] NO
Hector Borado	(520) 555-8100	

STARTING POSITION	ENDING POSITION
Inventory Associate	Inventory Associate

DATES WORKED TO	JOB DUTIES
05/20/08 - present	count stock, help organize warehouse inventory

SALARY/WAGE	REASON FOR LEAVING
$8.00/hr	want promotion and better salary

PREVIOUS EMPLOYER

EMPLOYER	ADDRESS
Koll's	2200 E. Elm Street Monterey Park, CA 91754

SUPERVISOR	PHONE #	May we contact? [X] YES [ ] NO
Victor Santoro	(520) 555-9875	

STARTING POSITION	ENDING POSITION
Clerk	Clerk

DATES WORKED TO	JOB DUTIES
03/15/08 - 04/28/10	worked cash register, customer service

SALARY/WAGE	REASON FOR LEAVING
$6.75/hr	wanted more hours

APPLICANT SIGNATURE: _Li Chiu_   DATE: _October 14, 2010_

B PAIRS. Answer the questions about the second part of the job application.

1. Where does Li work now? Where did he work before?

2. Why does he want to leave his job?

3. Is it OK for Caruso's to call Koll's?

C Apply for the same job. Complete the job application on page 280.
Use your own information or made-up information.

Can you...read and complete a job application?   ☐

Describe your work history

Listening and Speaking

1 BEFORE YOU LISTEN

CLASS. Read the online job advertisement. Talk about any words you don't know. What questions do you think the employer will ask?

> **Chef needed.** Small busy restaurant. Must be fast, efficient, dependable, and able to work under pressure. Minimum 5 years experience. Management experience necessary. Full-time position. Some night hours. Health benefits available. References necessary. E-mail JMorgan@PJs.com or call (520) 555-9786.

2 LISTEN

CD1 T44

A Listen. James Morgan is interviewing Luis Garcia for a chef position. How did Luis find out about the job?

a. He saw the advertisement.

b. A friend told him.

c. A worker at Giovanni's told him.

CD1 T44

B Read the statements. Then listen to the interview. Write *T* (true) or *F* (false).

_____ 1. Luis is a line cook at El Norte.

_____ 2. Luis owned a restaurant in Mexico City.

_____ 3. Luis is unhappy at El Norte.

_____ 4. Luis wants to be a manager at PJs.

CD1 T45

C Listen to the second part of the conversation. What skills does James ask Luis about? Check (✓) the skills you hear.

☐ managing employees

☐ planning menus

☐ preparing meals

☐ using kitchen equipment

3 CONVERSATION

Pronunciation Watch

When words end in *-sion* or *-tion*, we stress the syllable before the last syllable.

CD1 T46

A Listen to each word. Notice the stress. Then listen and repeat.

reputation   situation   tradition

CD1 T47

B Mark the stressed syllable.

1. permission   2. conversation   3. discussion   4. direction

CD1 T48

C Listen and read the conversation.

James: So, I'm looking for a chef. Can you tell me about your restaurant experience?

Luis: Sure. I've been a line cook at El Norte restaurant for the last five years. I also owned my own café in Mexico City. And before that, I worked in a couple of restaurants in Mexico for several years.

James: So, why do you want to leave El Norte?

Luis: Well, I've worked there for five years. It's a very good restaurant, but I'm ready for a change. And your restaurant has a great reputation.

4 PRACTICE

A PAIRS. Practice the conversation.

B ROLE PLAY. PAIRS. Imagine that you are at a job interview. Make a similar conversation. Use the information or your own ideas. Then change roles.

Student A: You own a Singular cell phone store. You are interviewing Student B for a job as a store manager. Ask questions.

Student B: You have been an assistant manager in a Horizon cell phone store for six years. Before that you were a sales associate at the Horizon store for two years.

Describe your work history

Grammar

.... **Grammar Watch**

Present perfect: Statements with *for* and *since*

Subject	*Have/Has*	Past participle		*For/Since*	Time expression
He	**has**	**been**	a line cook	**for**	four years.
We	**have**	**lived**	here	**since**	January.

Grammar Watch

Use the present perfect with *for* or *since* to describe an activity that began in the past and continues into the present.

1 PRACTICE

A Read the conversation. Write *T* (true) or *F* (false). Change false statements to true ones.

Alex: I haven't seen Akim for a long time. Is he still living in East Hollywood?

Sergey: Yes, he is but in a different apartment building. You probably haven't seen him because he's been working a lot of hours. He's a manager at Embassy Limousine Warehouse.

Alex: No kidding? I thought he was just driving for them. How long has he been a manager?

Sergey: For six months. He was a driver for two years and then they promoted him to manager. So, he's making more money and moved to a better building a month ago.

_____ 1. Akim became a manager six months ago.

_____ 2. Akim is working a lot of hours right now.

_____ 3. Alex has seen Akim recently.

_____ 4. Akim has been in his new apartment for one month.

B Complete the sentences. Use *for* or *since*.

1. Mark has worked at H&B Electronics ___for___ six months.

2. I haven't heard from them _____ May.

3. We've been out of town _____ three weeks.

4. Soo Jin has been a sales manager _____ many years.

5. They have helped us _____ the beginning of the year.

6. We haven't taken a vacation _____ 2005.

A **Complete the sentences. Use the present perfect and the verbs in parentheses.**

1. Awa ___has waited on___ tables in a restaurant for the last year.
   (wait on)

2. Edgar _____ a living in construction since 2005.
   (make)

3. Jean Paul _____ as computer programmer for the last year.
   (work)

4. You _____ for a car service for two years, right?
   (drive)

5. I _____ a vacation since 2006.
   (not / take)

6. Mi Hee _____ at St. Vincent Hospital for the last year.
   (help out)

B **Look at part of Luis Garcia's résumé. Write four questions in your notebook. Use the present perfect or the simple past.**

1. How long has Luis been a caterer?

C **PAIRS. Ask and answer your questions from Exercise B.**

Work Experience

2005–present	Line cook El Norte restaurant Tucson, Arizona
2005–present	Caterer: Part-time Tucson, Arizona
1998–2005	Owner Luis's Café Mexico City, (sold business and moved to the United States in 2005)
1991–1998	Line cook Casa Hidalgo restaurant Mexico City

Show what you know! Describe your work history

PAIRS. ROLE PLAY. **Imagine you are at a job interview. Use your own résumé or the résumé on page 73.**

Student A: Interview Student B for a job. Ask questions.
Student B: Answer the questions based on your résumé. Then change roles.

Can you...describe your work history? ☐

Reading

1 BEFORE YOU READ

GROUPS. Have you ever had a job interview? What happened? Did you get the job? What do you think are good and bad things to do at a job interview?

2 READ

CD1 T49

Listen and read the article. Did you guess any of the advice in the article?

Making a Good Impression

When you interview for a job, it's natural to be a little nervous. You're meeting an employer for the first time. To **make a good impression** on the employer, here are some suggestions:

Arrive on time. Plan to come early. That way if something happens, such as a traffic jam, you will still be on time for the interview. If you know you are going to be late, call the interviewer.

Dress appropriately. Wear simple **conservative** clothes and dress shoes. In the United States, people often wear colors like gray, blue, or brown at work, instead of very bright colors.

Make eye contact. In some cultures, it can be rude to look directly at a person of authority. However, in the United States, it's important to look at the interviewer when you're speaking.

Watch your body language. When you meet the interviewer, shake hands firmly. A firm handshake shows that you are **confident** and not afraid. Stand about three feet away. In the United States, people are not **comfortable** if others stand too close to them.

Speak up. Make sure that you speak loudly enough when you answer the interviewer's questions. It's also OK to ask the interviewer to repeat a question if you don't hear or understand it.

During the interview, try to be yourself and show **enthusiasm.** Make it clear that you want the job and that you will work hard. Interviewers look for employees who are enthusiastic and hardworking.

3 CHECK YOUR UNDERSTANDING

A Read the article again. What is the main idea. Circle the correct letter.

a. It is important to speak up at a job interview.
b. Dressing well will help get you the job.
c. You need to make a good impression at the job interview.

Reading Skill:
Making inferences

In an article, some ideas are not stated directly. Readers often guess or *infer* these ideas as they read.

B Read the article again. What inferences can you make? Read the statements. Write *T* (true) or *F* (false).

_____ 1. Many Americans don't think bright colors are a good choice for the workplace.

_____ 2. In the United States, employers don't mind if you are not punctual.

_____ 3. People from some cultures do not feel it is OK to look at employers.

_____ 4. People stand closer to each other in some countries than in the U.S.

_____ 5. It's rude to ask an employer to repeat a question.

4 VOCABULARY IN CONTEXT

Look at the boldfaced words in the article. Guess their meanings. Complete the sentences with the correct words.

1. At a job interview, show you're _____ about your skills.

2. People often wear _____ clothes like a jacket and tie in offices.

3. Employers like employees who like their job and show _____.

4. Come early to a job interview, so you'll _____ on the employer.

5. Employees who get along feel _____ in the workplace.

Show what you know!

GROUPS. The article talks about making a good impression at job interviews in the U.S. Is it the same or different in your country? How?

Writing

1 BEFORE YOU WRITE

A GROUPS. What should you say in a thank you letter after a job interview?

B Luis Garcia had a job interview at PJs restaurant. Read the thank you letter. Which of your ideas from Exercise A are included in the letter?

2 WRITE

Write a thank you letter for a job interview. Make up an employer and a job situation. Use the letter as a model.

3 CHECK YOUR WRITING

- ☐ Did you thank the employer?
- ☐ Did you remind the employer about your qualifications?
- ☐ Did you use the correct letter format?
- ☐ Did you spell the employer's name correctly?
- ☐ Did you check your spelling and grammar?

> The day after you interview for a job, send a thank-you letter or an e-mail to the employer. Make sure to always check your grammar and spelling.

Luis Garcia
509 North Grande Avenue
Tucson, AZ 85745

September 10, 2010

James Morgan, Manager
PJ's
434 North Fourth Avenue
Tucson, Arizona 85701

Dear Mr. Morgan:

Thank you for the interview for your chef position yesterday. I enjoyed meeting you and learning more about PJ's.

As I mentioned at the interview, I have experience managing a kitchen in a fast-paced restaurant.

I think I would be a good addition to your staff. Please call me at (646) 555-2877 if you have any more questions about my qualifications. I look forward to speaking with you soon.

Sincerely,

Luis Garcia

Luis Garcia

Learn about illegal interview questions

Listening and Speaking

1 BEFORE YOU LISTEN

GROUPS. What kinds of questions do you think might be illegal at a job interview? Guess. Write a list of ideas.

> The United States has many laws that protect employees in the workplace. Some questions are illegal (against the law) for employers to ask at a job interview.

2 LISTEN

CD1 T50

A 🔘 Listen to Leon Vasquez, a career counselor, talk about illegal questions at job interviews. Did you guess some of the questions?

CD1 T51

B 🔘 Read the questions. Then listen again to the first part of the interview. Check (✓) the questions that are illegal.

☐ 1. How old are you?

☐ 2. Do you have children?

☐ 3. Why do you want to leave your job?

☐ 4. Have you ever been fired?

CD1 T52

C 🔘 Listen again to the second part of the interview. Check (✓) the other things that Leon says are illegal for an employer to ask about?

_____ religion _____ race _____ money problems _____ national origin

D PROBLEM SOLVING. **GROUPS.** Discuss. What would you do if an employer asked you an illegal question? Would you refuse to answer? Would you change the subject?

Talk about positive work behavior

Grammar

It + Be + Adjective + Infinitive and It + Be + Noun Phrase + Infinitive

It	Be	Adjective or Noun phrase	(Preposition + object)	Infinitive	
It	is	important	(for you)	to know	your rights.
	was	a good idea		to arrive	early.

1 PRACTICE

A Circle the examples of *It* + *be* + the adjective and *It* + *be* + noun phrase.

It's hard for me to say much about my new job. I've only been there a week. But one thing I know: It's important to be on time. It's a requirement to call if you can't come to work. One of my co-workers didn't show up for his shift and didn't call. My boss was really angry.

B Complete the sentences. Put the words in the correct order.

1. It's important for employers to be polite.
   (important / employers / to be polite / for / it's)

2. _____
   (sometimes / to / it's / difficult / me / come / for / to / work on time)

3. _____
   (necessary / it's / employees / to / problem-solve / for)

4. _____
   (it's / to argue / not / with your manager / a good idea)

5. _____
   (very important / to / report problems / it's / to your manager)

6. _____
   (for employees and employers / to discuss problems early on / important / it's)

Write sentences with *It is* + adjective + infinitive. Use the words in parentheses.

1. Kar Wai needs to take off two days in January.

   It's a good idea for him to ask his boss _____ in advance.
   (good idea / him / ask / his boss)

2. Jun doesn't know what to do when he doesn't understand his boss.

   _____ because he's shy.
   (difficult / him / ask / questions)

3. Some of my co-workers are not polite to me.

   _____ each other.
   (important / employees / respect)

4. Our boss doesn't want us to speak our language.

   _____ at work.
   (important / us / speak / English)

Show what you know! Talk about positive work behavior

STEP 1. **Answer the questions.**

1. Is it difficult for you to understand instructions at work?

2. Is it easy for you to get along with your co-workers?

3. Is it hard for you to ask for time off or get time off?

4. Do you think it is a good idea to ask questions when you don't understand something?

5. Do you think it is OK to tell your boss if someone does something wrong?

STEP 2. GROUPS. **Share your answers.**

Can you...talk about positive work behavior? ☐

1 REVIEW

For your Grammar Review, go to page 248.

2 ACT IT OUT   What do you say?

STEP 1. CLASS. Review the conversations on pages 75 and 81 (CD1 Tracks 48 and 50).

STEP 2. PAIRS. Role-play a job interview. Make up the information.
Student A: You are interviewing for a job.
Student B: You are the employer.

> **Student A:** Answer Student B's questions.

> **Student B:** Ask Student A questions such as:
> - Do you have experience?
> - Can you tell me about your past jobs?
> - Do you know how to . . . ?
> - Why do you want to leave your current job?

3 READ AND REACT   Problem-solving

STEP 1. Sofia is filling out a job application for the Halton Hotel. Read Sofia's problem.

Sofia worked for four years at a small hotel. The manager liked her a lot, but the hotel closed. Sofia got a different job at the Aluvia Hotel. She got into a fight with the manager and he fired her. She doesn't know what to write on her job application. She doesn't want the new employer to call that job.

STEP 2. GROUPS. Discuss. What is Sofia's problem? Give Sofia advice. Should she write the Aluvia Hotel on her job application? What should she tell the new employer?

4 CONNECT

For your Goal-setting Activity, go to page 258.
For your Team Project, go to page 266.

Which goals can you check off? Go back to page 65.

Traveling

5

Preview

How often do you take buses, trains, or planes? Where do you go?

UNIT GOALS

- ☐ Follow instructions at an airport
- ☐ Talk about airline travel
- ☐ Read screen instructions and maps
- ☐ Make travel arrangements
- ☐ Identify personal belongings
- ☐ Make polite requests and ask for permission

1 WHAT DO YOU KNOW?

A CLASS. Look at the vocabulary. The words describe things at an airport or terminal. Which words do you know?

B Match the words with people and things in the terminal. Write the numbers.

Travel

___ arrivals and departures

___ bins

___ boarding pass

___ carry-on bag

___ gate

___ kiosk

___ luggage

___ luggage tags

___ metal detector

___ passenger

___ round-trip ticket

___ security

___ ticket agent

___ X-ray machine

Learning Strategy

Use pictures

Make cards for five words. Write the word on the front of the card. Print a picture of the word from the Internet. Cut it out and paste it to the back of the card.

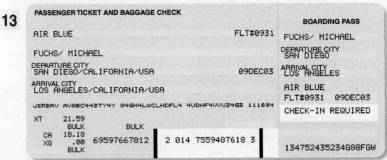

CD2 T1

C Listen and check your answers. Then listen and repeat.

A WORD PLAY. PAIRS. Look at the picture and the vocabulary on page 86. Discuss. What are the people doing?

A: *What is the ticket agent doing?*
B: *She's taking the passenger's boarding pass.*

B GET THE MEANING. Complete the sentences with ten travel words from page 86.

1. To go through airport ___security___ you need to walk through a _____.

2. We need _____ for our suitcases.

3. A _____ often costs less than two one-way tickets.

4. The airline lost his _____ .

5. Check the _____ to find out which _____ your plane leaves from.

6. You need a _____ to board the plane.

7. Buy your ticket at the _____.

8. You need to take off your shoes and put them in the _____. Then they will go through the _____.

Show what you know! Talk about product defects

GROUPS. Discuss. Have you ever had problems when you traveled on trains, subways, or in airports? What happened?

Can you...talk product defects? ☐

Listening and Speaking

1 BEFORE YOU LISTEN

A GROUPS. Discuss. What kinds of announcements do you hear at airports?

B PAIRS. Match the pictures with the words. Write the correct letters.

A

B

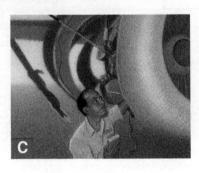
C

___ 1. board   ___ 2. mechanical problem   ___ 3. pre-board

2 LISTEN

CD2 T2

A Listen to four announcements at an airport. After each announcement, answer the question.

Announcement 1

What is the situation with Flight 385?
a. It's boarding.   b. It's taking off.   c. It's landing.

Announcement 2

What is the situation with Flight 289?
a. It's pre-boarding.   b. It has been delayed.   c. It has been canceled.

Announcement 3

Which gate is Flight 870 to Caracas departing from?
a. Gate 2   b. Gate 8   c. Gate 22

Announcement 4

What is the problem with Flight 901?
a. a mechanical problem   b. a cancellation   c. a gate change

B PAIRS. Compare answers.

3 CONVERSATION

Pronunciation Watch

Can usually has a weak pronunciation "c'n," with a short quiet vowel sound, when another word comes after it. *Can't* never has a weak pronunciation. It always has a clear vowel sound.

A CD2 T3 🔘 **Listen to the pronunciation of *can* and *can't* in these sentences. Then listen and repeat.**

You can check it.
You can buy a drink on the plane.
Why can't I take it on the plane?
You can't take this through security.

B CD2 T4 🔘 **Listen to the sentences. Circle the words you hear.**

1. You **can / can't** park here.
2. We **can / can't** take a bus there.
3. We **can / can't** board the plane now.

4. You **can / can't** use your cell phone.
5. I **can / can't** take this bag.
6. I **can / can't** get another flight.

C CD2 T5 🔘 **Listen and read the conversation.**

Security screener: Excuse me. Could you please step over to the side?
Passenger: Is there a problem?
Security screener: Something in your bag is showing up on the X-ray machine. Could you please open your bag? Hmm. You can't take this bottle of water. You either have to drink it all now or throw it away.

4 PRACTICE

A PAIRS. **Practice the conversation.**

B ROLE PLAY. PAIRS. **Pretend a passenger is going through airport security.**

Student A: You are the passenger. The security agent has found a problem with an item in your bag.

Student B: You are the security agent. Explain the problem to the passenger. Use one of the items from the box.

moisturizer   jar of peanut butter   yogurt

Grammar

Can/Could: Affirmative and negative

We	can/can't	take	the water bottle.
I	could/couldn't	hear	the announcement.

Be able to: Affirmative and negative

She	was/wasn't			
They	were/weren't	able to	fly	home.
We	will be/won't be			

Grammar Watch

- Use *can* for present ability and present or future possibility.
- Use *could* for past ability.
- Use *will be able to* for future ability.
- Use *was/were able to* for past ability.
- *Am/Is/Are able to* are not used often.

1 PRACTICE

A **Read and match the sentences. Write the correct letters.**

__d__ 1. You won't be able to reach him.

_____ 2. Vic didn't have his passport.

_____ 3. You can't take that bag on board.

_____ 4. My brother missed the flight.

a. You have to check it.

b. He won't be able to get a refund.

c. He couldn't get through security.

d. His cell phone is turned off.

B **Complete the sentences. Circle the correct words.**

1. You **can't / couldn't** bring that moisturizer in your carry-on.

2. My flight was canceled so I **couldn't / was able to** go to my uncle's funeral.

3. I **can't / couldn't** hear the announcement. There was too much noise.

4. Flight 380 **will be able to / wasn't able to** land due to bad weather.

5. Our flight **will be able to / won't be able to** take off for another ten minutes.

6. We **wasn't able to / weren't able to** catch our flight.

7. You **won't be able to / weren't able to** use your cell phone until the plane lands.

2 PRACTICE

A **Complete the paragraph. Use the correct form of the verb in parentheses.**

We had a lot of problems when my family flew to San Diego. First, at the airport, I ___couldn't___ (**not / can**) find my passport. I had to drive back home and get it, so we missed our plane. We _____ (**be able to**) get onto another plane, but it was very full. There was almost no room for our carry-ons, but finally the airline attendant _____ (**be able to**) fit them in the overhead compartment. Then we sat in the plane and waited. There was a storm, so the plane _____ (**not / can**) take off. After a half hour, the airline attendant announced, "Due to bad weather, we _____ (**not / be able to**) leave the runway. All passengers must exit the plane and wait at the terminal." We got off the plane. We _____ (**not / can**) believe our bad luck!

B **Write five sentences about how travel is different today from in the past. Use the pictures and your ideas. Use _can_ and _be able to_.**

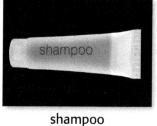

shampoo

scissors   e-ticket

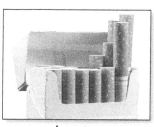

cigarettes

In the past, you could smoke on airplanes.
Now you can't smoke on airplanes or in airports.

Show what you know!   Talk about airline travel

GROUPS. Discuss. What are other ways that travel today is different from the way it was in the past?

Can you... talk about airline travel? ☐

Life Skills

1 READ SCREEN INSTRUCTIONS

A GROUPS. **Do you ever have problems following directions or reading maps when you travel? Do you have problems buying your ticket?**

B **Read the screen instructions on the ticket machine.**

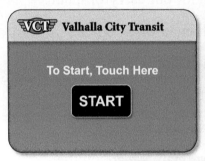

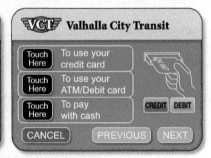

2 PRACTICE

Read the questions. Circle the correct answer. More than one answer is sometimes possible.

1. You want to buy a Monthly Ticket. You pressed One-Way Ticket by mistake. Which button should you press?
   a. Cancel   b. Previous   c. Next

2. You want to buy a ticket, but you realize you don't have enough money. Which button should you press?
   a. Cancel   b. Previous   c. Next

3. Which instruction tells you to put money in the machine?
   a. Purchase a Monthly Ticket   b. To use your ATM/Debit card   c. Insert Cash

4. You bought your ticket. You do not want any more tickets. The machine printed your ticket. Which button do you press?
   a. Cancel   b. Previous   c. More Tickets

CLASS. **Look at the map of North Bus Terminal and the symbols.**

North Bus Terminal

⬆⬇	Elevators
🎫	Ticket Booths
$	ATM
🚌	Bus Gates
🚺	Women's Restrooms
🚹	Men's Restrooms
☎	Phones
🛡	Security/Police

A **You are looking for something in the bus terminal. Match each question with the correct answer. Write the correct letter.**

1. Someone stole my wallet. Where is security? __b__

2. Where is a newsstand? _____

3. Excuse me, where are the elevators? _____

4. I need to find an ATM. _____

5. Where is Information? _____

6. I need to find a telephone. _____

a. Go to the middle of the terminal. You'll see it there.

b. Next to the newsstand.

c. Next to the women's room.

d. There's one near the entrance.

e. Next to the ticket booths.

f. There's one next to the men's room.

B **ROLE PLAY. PAIRS. Look at the map. You are next to the newsstand. Ask and give directions to four places.**

Can you...read screen instructions and maps? ☐

Listening and Speaking

1 BEFORE YOU LISTEN

GROUPS. Do you have public transportation in your city?
What kinds? Is the public transportation good or bad?

2 LISTEN

CD2 T6

A Ken is calling his friend Amy from the BART train.
Why is Ken late?

a. He missed the earlier train.   b. The BART train was delayed.

> BART = (Bay Area
> Rapid Transit) a train
> system in the San
> Francisco Bay Area

CD2 T6

B Listen again to the conversation. Write *T* (true) or *F* (false).

_____ 1. Ken expects to arrive around 3:30.

_____ 2. Amy is meeting Ken at 24th Street.

_____ 3. Amy is driving Ken home in her car.

_____ 4. Amy can't park her car outside the station.

CD2 T7

C Listen to the second part of the conversation. What is Ken's problem?

a. He took the wrong train.

b. He got off at the wrong station.

c. He took the wrong bag.

Pronunciation Watch

We stress the important words in a sentence. Stressed words are longer and sound louder than other words.

CD2 T8

A Listen to the sentences. Notice the stressed words. Then listen and repeat.

•   •
I **missed** the **bus**.

•   •
When are you ar**ri**ving?

•   •
I'll m**eet** you at the **ter**minal.

•   •   •
Are you **ta**king me **home** in your **car**?

CD2 T9

B Listen to the sentences. Mark (•) the stressed syllables.

1. I'm taking the bus.
2. It leaves at seven.
3. It arrives at eight fifteen.
4. Can you pick me up?
5. See you soon.
6. Call me when you get there.

CD2 T10

C Listen and read the conversation.

Ken: Hey, Amy. It's me, Ken. I'm on BART.
Sorry, I'm running late. There was a 30-minute delay. A train got stuck at 24th Street.

Amy: That's too bad. So, what time are you arriving then?

Ken: I think about 3:30. Which station should I get off at?

Amy: The Lake Merritt station. Call me when you get there. I'll park and wait for you. Oh, I forgot to tell you. My car isn't running, but my mom will let me borrow hers. I'll be in a red Toyota Corolla.

Ken: Great. See you soon.

4 PRACTICE

A PAIRS. Practice the conversation.

B GROUPS. Discuss. Have you ever visited a friend who lived in a different city? In the U.S. or in your native country? How did you get there? What was the experience like?

Grammar

Possessive adjectives and possessive pronouns	
Possessive adjective	Possessive pronoun
This is **my** bag.	This is **mine**.
That is **your** bag.	That is **yours**.
Is this **his** luggage?	No. **His** is on the bus.
Is that **her** book bag?	No. **Hers** is at home.
This is not **our** car.	**Ours** is on the second level.
That's not **their** car.	**Theirs** is in the shop.

Grammar Watch

- A noun never follows a possessive pronoun.
- The verb after a possessive pronoun agrees with the noun it replaces.

  *Her bag is heavy. = Hers **is** heavy.*
  *Her bags **are** heavy. = Hers **are** heavy.*

1 PRACTICE

A Circle the possessive pronouns.

Yesterday, I took a bus to Dallas. I left my cell phone on the bus. Luckily, the bus driver found it. We were leaving the gate when the driver ran up with the phone and asked if it was (ours.) One passenger thought it was hers. But then I felt in my jacket and my cell phone was missing. I told the bus driver I thought I had lost mine, so he showed it to us. We knew it was mine, not hers, because it had all my relatives' and friends' names in it.

B Circle the correct words.

1. We almost left **our / ours** tickets at home.

2. That's not my suitcase. **My / Mine** is bigger.

3. Aren't these **your / yours** keys?

4. His car is parked on this level, but **her / hers** must be on a different level.

5. The keys don't fit this car because it's not **our / our car**.

6. Is that my soda or y**ours / your**?

A Change the underlined words to possessive pronouns.

1. **A:** Did you leave this water bottle on the seat?

   B: No. ~~My water bottle~~ *Mine* is in my bag.

2. **A:** Is that her suitcase?

   B: No, it's his suitcase. Her suitcase is in the overhead compartment.

3. **A:** Who left this bag?

   B: It's his bag. I'm watching it for him while he gets some coffee.

4. **A:** Are these your boarding passes?

   B: No. They're not. I have our boarding passes in my pocket.

5. **A:** Is that their bus?

   B: No. Their bus is at the next gate.

B Complete the sentences. Write *is* or *are*.

1. These are my bags. His _____ over there.

2. Whose ticket is this? _____ it yours?

3. Is that our gate or _____ ours gate 12?

4. Dan, my ticket is missing. _____ yours, too?

5. My relatives are here. _____ yours, too?

6. These boarding passes _____ hers.

Show what you know!   Identify personal belongings

GROUPS OF 3. ROLE PLAY. **You are at a lost and found at a bus terminal. Students A and B, tell Student C, the clerk, what you lost. Use possessive pronouns.**

Student A: You lost a pair of leather gloves and a cell phone.

Student B: You lost a cell phone and an umbrella.

Student C: Ask questions. You see a silver Alexis phone, a pair of brown gloves, a T-moby cell phone, and a blue umbrella.

Can you...identify personal belongings? ☐

Reading

1 BEFORE YOU READ

A Have you ever had problems with your luggage when you were traveling? What can people do to make traveling easier?

B Read the first paragraph of the article. Guess. What does *restrictions* mean?

Reading Skill:
Getting meaning from context

You can sometimes guess the meaning of a word from the words or sentences around it.

2 READ

CD2 T11
Listen and read the article.

SAFE TRAVELING

When people travel, their luggage can be lost or stolen. Heavy suitcases can make travel difficult. How can you protect your luggage and make traveling easier? Here are a few tips.

LEARN ABOUT BAGGAGE RESTRICTIONS.

Many things aren't allowed in suitcases or carry-ons. For example, sharp metal objects like scissors are usually **prohibited**. Don't put these in your bags or they will be taken away. Also, make sure that your luggage isn't too heavy or large. You need to follow the size and weight limits or you will pay fees. Check the website of your bus or airline to find out restrictions.

CHECK LUGGAGE SAFELY.

Don't check any luggage with money, important documents, or expensive items in it. Carry these items with you in a safe carry-on bag. Keep this bag close to you at all times. Remember to keep your claim check. You may need to show this when you pick up your luggage.

TRANSFER YOUR BAGS ON THE BUS.

When you travel by bus, you are **responsible** for your baggage. You will need to pick up your bags at each **transfer** location and carry them to your **connecting** bus. Remember this when you pack. Don't let your suitcases get too heavy.

MARK YOUR BAGS CLEARLY.

Make sure you put your name and address on luggage tags outside and inside of your luggage in case it gets lost. To help identify your luggage easily, put something "special" on it, for example, a purple ribbon.

Follow these tips, and your luggage will be less likely to get lost or stolen.

3 CHECK YOUR UNDERSTANDING

A What is the main idea of the article? Circle the correct letter.

   a. Passengers are often careless and lose their luggage.

   b. Passengers should not travel with heavy items.

   c. Passengers can keep their luggage safe by following the tips.

B Read the statements. Circle the correct answer.

   1. When you travel, you should keep _____ with you.
     a. luggage tags   b. heavy suitcases   c. expensive items

   2. You usually can't take this in carry-on: _____.
     a. your claim check   b. luggage that weighs 15 pounds   c. sharp metal objects

   3. You have to pay fees at the airport if your suitcase _____.
     a. sets off the metal detector   b. is lost   c. is too big or heavy

   4. When you change buses, you need to put this onto the second bus: _____.
     a. your claim check   b. your checked luggage   c. your luggage tags

4 VOCABULARY IN CONTEXT

Look at boldfaced words in the article. Guess their meanings.
Complete the sentences with the correct words.

   1. When you travel, you are _____ for your luggage. You need
     to know where your luggage is at all times.

   2. Large bottles of shampoo are _____ in carry-on luggage
     when you fly. You need to pack them in your suitcase.

   3. Lu Yi is flying from New York. His plane stops in Chicago. Then he has to

     _____ to a _____ flight that will take him to San Francisco.

Show what you know!

GROUPS. Imagine someone is going to visit your country for the first time and
does not speak the language. What tips would you give them to travel safely?

Write about a traveling problem

Writing

1 BEFORE YOU WRITE

A **Read the paragraph about Dipak's trip to Bangladesh.**

> Last year I went to Bangladesh with my 12-year-old son, Karan, and my father. Before we traveled, Karan and I got a shot for typhoid fever. It's a serious disease in Bangladesh. I told my father he needed the shot. But he said, "I can't get this disease because I lived most of my life in Bangladesh." When they got to Bangladesh, Karan and I were fine, but my father got sick with typhoid fever. He went to the hospital. He finally got better, but when I go to Bangladesh next time, I will make sure everyone gets shots.

B GROUPS. **Discuss. Talk about a problem you had when you traveled. Was it a problem you could not change, like the weather, a delay, or a canceled flight? Or was it something you did not prepare for?**

2 WRITE

Write a paragraph about a problem you had when you traveled.

- Explain the problem.
- Tell what happened or what you did.
- Will you do anything differently the next time you travel?

3 CHECK YOUR WRITING

☐ Did you describe the problem?

☐ Did you explain what happened?

☐ Did you say something you might do differently next time?

☐ Did you indent your paragraph?

Talk about delays and cancellations

Listening and Speaking

1 BEFORE YOU LISTEN

GROUPS. Were you ever at a bus station or airport when your trip was delayed or canceled? What was the reason? How long did you have to wait? How did you feel?

2 LISTEN

CD2 T12

A Listen to the announcement at a bus station. The announcement is about a bus that was _____.

   a. delayed   b. canceled   c. repaired

CD2 T13

B Listen again to the announcement. Then listen to Carlos and his mother. Answer the questions.

1. Who is the announcement for? People going to _____.
   a. Miami   b. Jacksonville   c. Georgia

2. What time is the next bus leaving?
   a. at 9:08   b. at 3:24   c. at 3:30

3. What's the number of the next bus?
   a. 908   b. 980   c. 918

CD2 T14

C Listen again. Carlos tells his mother he has bad news and good news.

What is the bad news? _____

What is the good news? _____

Grammar

Polite requests with *would / could / will / can*			
Would Will Could Can	**you** (please)	**do**	me a favor?

Answers
Sure. Of course. No problem.

Requests for permission			
Could Can **May**	**I** (please)	**sit**	here?

Answers
Yes, you can. / Sure. No, you can't. Yes, you may. No, you may not.

• • • • • • **Grammar Watch**

• To say *no* to a request, we usually say "Sorry" and give a reason.

• We do not use *could* in short answers. We use *can*.

• We usually do not use *may* for requests. *May* is very formal.

---

1 **PRACTICE**

A **Underline the requests.**

A: Hi, could you tell me when bus #20 leaves?

B: Sure. It leaves in ten minutes.

A: Thanks. Can I bring food on the bus?

B: Yes, you can.

B **Circle the best response to each request.**

1. **A:** Could I look at your bus schedule?

   B: **Yes, you can. / Yes, you could**.

2. **A:** May I please have a transfer?

   B: **Yes, I would. / Sure**.

3. **A:** Could you change seats with me?

   B: **No. I'm glad to do it. / No problem**.

4. **A:** Would you please move to the back of the bus?

   B: **No, you may not. / Sure**.

A Complete the conversation. Use the words in the box and *can*, *could*, *may*, or *would*. There may be more than one correct answer.

get   give   have   help   put   ~~watch~~

Ali: Hey, Bob. ____Can____ you ___watch___ my things? I'm getting a drink.

Bob: No problem. Hey, _____ you _____ me a cola.

Ali: Sure. I'll be right back.

Counterman: _____ I _____ you?

Ali: Thanks. _____ I _____ a large orange juice and a cola?

Counterman: Here you go.

Ali: Oh. _____ you also _____ me a small bag of pretzels and an apple?

Counterman: OK. Anything else?

Ali: No, thanks. But _____ you _____ everything in a bag?

B Rewrite the requests in your notebook. Use the words in parentheses.

1. Is it OK to bring food on the bus? (May)
   May I bring food on the bus?

2. Please watch my luggage. (Could)

3. Is it OK to smoke on the bus? (Can)

4. Is it OK to sit here? (Can)

Show what you know!   Make polite requests and ask for permission

PAIRS. ROLE PLAY. You are traveling. Make polite requests and ask for permission. Use the ideas in the box or your own ideas.

get a bus schedule   move that bag off the seat
get a transfer   move to the back of the bus

Student A: You are a passenger.
Student B: You are the bus driver.

Can you...make polite requests and ask for permission? ☐

REVIEW & EXPAND — Show what you know!

1 REVIEW For your Grammar Review, go to page 249.

2 ACT IT OUT What do you say?

STEP 1. CLASS. Review the conversation on page 95 (CD2 Track 10).

STEP 2. PAIRS. ROLE PLAY. Make travel arrangements.

> **Student A:** Call Student B on the phone. You missed your flight. Tell Student B when you are coming.

> **Student B:** You are picking up Student A at the airport. You want to meet Student A outside Terminal A. There is easy parking near Terminal A.
>
> Talk about:
> • where you will meet
> • what time you will meet
> • how you will get home

3 READ AND REACT Problem-solving

STEP 1. Read the problem.

Cam is going to Vietnam for her sister's wedding. Her flight on American Airlines (AA) has been canceled. There is another flight, but it takes much longer. It has two connecting flights. Cam does not want to miss the wedding.

STEP 2. GROUPS. What is the problem? Give Cam advice. What should she do? For example:

• Take the long flight. It has two connecting flights, but it will still get there in time.
• Ask the ticket agent if there is another AA flight soon.
• Ask about other airline flights to Vietnam.

4 CONNECT
For your Community-building Activity, go to page 259.
For your Team Project, go to page 267.

Which goals can you check off? Go back to page 85.

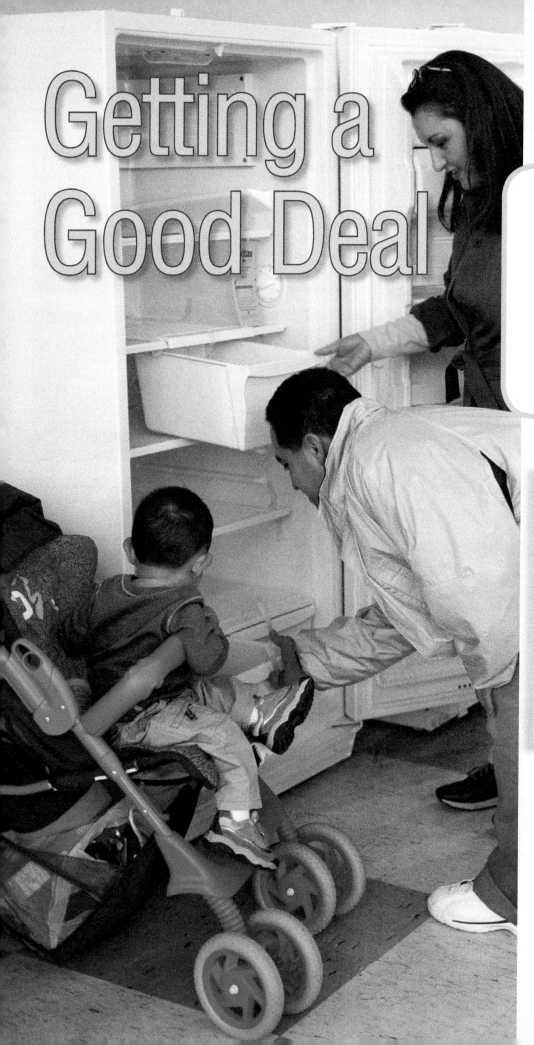

Getting a Good Deal

Preview

When you buy appliances, electronics, or a cable or cell phone plan, what is most difficult? Getting a good price? Getting a refund? Making a decision?

UNIT GOALS

- [ ] Talk about product defects
- [ ] Get a good deal
- [ ] Compare price and quality
- [ ] Read sales ads and rebates
- [ ] Compare shopping experiences

1 WHAT DO YOU KNOW?

A Look at the vocabulary. The words describe problems with purchases (things you buy). Which words do you know?

CD2 T15

B Look at the pictures and listen. Listen again and repeat.

problems with purchases

1. bent
2. broken
3. cracked
4. damaged
5. dented
6. defective
7. frayed
8. leaking
9. scratched

Learning Strategy

Make connections

Make cards for five words. Write the problem on the front of the card. Write two things that you buy that can have the problem on the back of the card.

leaking—air conditioner
refrigerator

WORD PLAY. **Match each sentence with the correct response. Write the letter.**

1. You got a package but it's dented. __c__
2. There's something wrong with this DVD. ____
3. Why did that company ask us to send back the toy? ____
4. What's wrong with the refrigerator? ____
5. You can't plug in this cord. It's frayed. ____
6. Why are you returning this TV? ____

a. I know. It's scratched.
b. I'm not sure, but it's leaking out the bottom.
c. Look inside and see if the merchandise is broken.
d. It's defective and dangerous for children.
e. The remote control is broken.
f. You're right. It could start a fire.

Show what you know!

When you buy a product, it sometimes comes with a *warranty*. This is a written guarantee. If the product is defective, the company will fix or replace it under certain conditions.

STEP 1. GROUPS. Read the warranty. How long does this warranty last?

CANA **Digital Camera™ Limited Warranty** USA, Canada only

This Cana digital camera is under warranty for 1 year from the date of purchase. NOTE the following conditions:

• Cameras must be in new condition at time of purchase.
• Cana will replace a defective camera with new parts or a new camera.
• This warranty does not cover cameras scratched or dented from everyday, regular use.

STEP 2. GROUPS. Which kinds of products is it most important to get a warranty for? Do you have a warranty for any products you own? What are they?

Talk about product defects

Listening and Speaking

1 BEFORE YOU LISTEN

A GROUPS. What do you do if your appliances don't work?

B Match the pictures with the words. Write the letters.

A

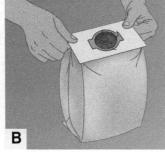
B

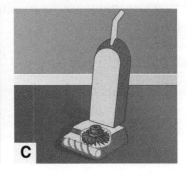
C

_____ 1. vacuum bag   _____ 2. motor   _____ 3. plug

2 LISTEN

CD2 T16

A Listen. Emilio and Ana are talking about their broken vacuum cleaner. What will they do?

a. Try to fix it.

b. Call service repair.

c. Buy a new vacuum.

CD2 T16

B Read the questions. Then listen again. Write *T* (true) or *F* (false).

_____ 1. Emilio thinks that there is something wrong with the plug.

_____ 2. Ana changed the bag.

_____ 3. The warranty on the vacuum is still good.

_____ 4. The vacuum is less than five years old.

_____ 5. Ana is unhappy that the vacuum is damaged.

CD2 T17

A Listen to the words and sentences. Notice the voiced or voiceless *th-* sound. Then listen and repeat.

this	When did we buy this?
the	What's the matter?
think	I think it's broken.
three	The model number is 3223.

There are two *th* sounds in English. To say the voiced *th* sound in the word *this*, put your tongue between your teeth and use your voice. To say the voiceless *th* sound in the word *think*, put your tongue between your teeth but do not use your voice.

CD2 T18

B Listen to the words. Is the sound voiced or voiceless? Check (✓) the correct column.

	Voiced (this)	Voiceless (think)
1. thing		
2. then		
3. that		
4. throw		

CD2 T19

C Listen and read the conversation.

Emilio: Ana. Pull out the plug.

Ana: What's the matter?

Emilio: I think something is burning.

Ana: Oh, no. What do you think is wrong?

Emilio: Maybe it's the motor, or maybe the bag is full. Did you change the bag?

Ana: Of course I changed the bag. The vacuum is just old.

4 PRACTICE

A PAIRS. Practice the conversation.

B ROLE PLAY. PAIRS. Make a similar conversation.

Student A: Tell Student B to turn off the air conditioner. You smell something burning. You think either the air conditioner is dirty or broken. Ask Student B if he or she changed the air filter.

Student B: You changed the air filter. You think the air conditioner is just broken.

Talk about product defects

Grammar

Noun clauses

I guess I think	**that**	**there's something wrong with it.**
I don't think		**I can fix it.**
Do you think		**it's broken?**

I'm sure	**that**	**it's broken.**
Are you sure		**you can't find the receipt?**

Grammar Watch

- We often leave out *that* when speaking.

- We often say *I think so* or *I don't think so* to answer a *Yes/No* question.
  Can you fix this?
  I don't think so.

- We can use many expressions with noun clauses, including *I'm afraid, I'm angry, I'm happy, I'm upset, I'm worried.*

1 PRACTICE

A Read the conversation. Underline the noun clauses.

A: Continental customer service. May I help you?

B: Yes. I think that my refrigerator is broken.

A: What seems to be the problem?

B: Well, the refrigerator isn't cold inside, and the freezer is making a strange noise. I don't think it ever made this sound before.

A: Give me the model and serial number, please.

B: The model number is RM3062, and the serial number is 64003130.

A: Do you have the proof of purchase?

B: Umm . . . yeah, I'm sure I have it somewhere. . . . Here it is.

A: OK. We may need to send out a technician. Hold on.

B PAIRS. Compare answers. Then practice the conversation.

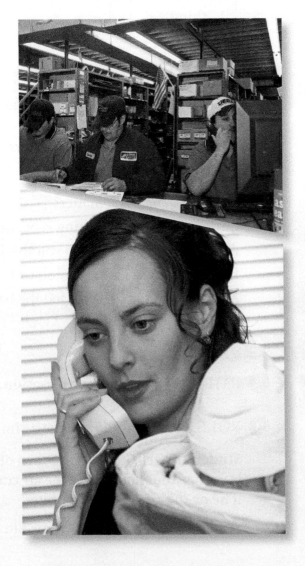

A Unscramble the sentences. Put the words in the correct order.

1. I guess / is damaged / the vacuum cord / that

   <u>I guess that the vacuum cord is damaged.</u>

2. the repairman never came / I'm angry / to fix my oven / that

   _____

3. the pilot light / Are you sure / is not coming on / that

   _____

4. I think / there's a delivery charge / I'm picking up the air conditioner / because

   _____

5. that / I'm upset / this broken phone / the cell phone company won't replace

   _____

B Read the situations. Then write sentences with noun clauses in your notebook. Start with a phrase from the box. More than one answer is possible.

> You're afraid   You're worried   You think   You don't think

1. Water is leaking from your refrigerator. (refrigerator / broken)

2. Your vacuum plug is cracked. (need / buy / new vacuum)

3. Your oven is broken. The repair service is five hours late. (repair service / come)

4. Your freezer is making a loud noise. (need / call / repair service)

5. Your toaster is not working well. (need / clean / toaster)

Show what you know!   Talk about product defects

GROUPS. Do you ever try to fix your own appliances? Which ones do you think are safe to fix? Which ones do you think might be dangerous to fix?

Can you...talk product defects?   ☐

Reading

1 BEFORE YOU READ

A GROUPS. When you buy a major appliance or electronic item, what do you do to get a good deal?

B Look quickly at the article. Read the words and sentences in color. What are five tips to shop smart?

> **Reading Skill:**
> Formatting clues
>
> Authors sometimes use formatting such as boldface type, bullets, and color to help readers find the main points.

2 READ

CD2 T20

Listen and read the article.

Shop Smart

Have you ever needed to buy an appliance or electronics, such as a TV, but you weren't sure where to begin? These days making a decision can be difficult because there are so many choices. How can you find the best price and **value**? Here are some easy tips for shopping smart.

Do research. Compare prices and **features**. There are several ways. The fastest way is to look online at the store websites. You can also look at newspaper ads and sale **flyers**. Write down the prices and features of each model.

Get recommendations. Talk to friends and co-workers. What **brand** do they recommend? Why? Where did they buy their TV?

Measure your space. Before you shop, make sure you know exactly how much room you have for the TV.

Shop at the right times and go to several stores. There are big sales on appliances in September and October. Go to at least two stores and write down prices and features to compare.

Ask the store to price match. When you go into a store, you might see a refrigerator you want. If you saw it for a lower price at a different store, you can ask the manager if he or she will match the lower price.

Following these tips may sound like a lot of work—just to buy a TV. But when you see your savings, you'll be glad that you made the effort.

> Before you make your final decision, check for these things to get better value:
> - Does the product have a warranty?
> - How long does the warranty last? One year? Five years?
> - Does the store offer free delivery? Usually, if you buy a large appliance like a refrigerator, the store will bring it free to your home.
> - Does the store offer free **installation** or do you need to pay for that service?

A **Read the article again. What is the main idea? Circle the correct letter.**

a. Use recommendations when you shop for appliances.

b. Shop at the right times and stores.

c. Comparison shop to find the best deal.

B **Read the article again. Answer the questions. Write *T* (true) or *F* (false).**

_____ 1. The fastest way to research an appliance is to visit a store.

_____ 2. You should visit more than two stores before you buy an appliance.

_____ 3. You may need to speak to a store manager to get a lower price on an appliance.

_____ 4. The store manager can always match the price of a sale item at another store.

4 VOCABULARY IN CONTEXT

Look at the boldfaced words in the article. Guess their meanings. Then complete the sentences with the correct words.

1. Oh no, this TV doesn't fit on the table. Didn't you ____*measure*____ the space?

2. In my Sunday newspaper I saw some _____ for a sale at Kolls.

3. I shop at Di-mart store because the quality is better. You get a better _____.

4. I'm thinking about buying a Whirltool stove. It's a good _____.

5. This oven has different _____. It's both an oven and a microwave.

6. The store offers free _____ for this refrigerator, so you don't need to pay someone to connect it.

Show what you know! Get a good deal

The article talks about ways to get a good deal. Which ways have you tried? Which would you like to try? What information in this article do you think is the most useful?

Can you…get a good deal? ☐

Talk about problems with cell phone service

Listening and Speaking

1 BEFORE YOU LISTEN

GROUPS. Have you ever gotten a bill for a cell phone or cable that was much higher than you had expected? What did you do?

2 LISTEN

CD2 T21

A 🔘 **Listen. Luis is complaining about a cell phone bill to his friend Manuel. What does Manuel do?**

a. He listens but doesn't have advice.

b. He doesn't understand Luis's problem.

c. He listens and gives advice.

CD2 T22

B 🔘 **Listen again to the first part. Circle the correct answers.**

1. Luis's bill was _____.
   a. $90   b. $653   c. $99

2. The salesperson told Luis that on nights and weekends he has _____.
   a. limited minutes   b. unlimited minutes

3. The cell phone company charged Luis for _____.
   a. long-distance   b. night and weekend minutes

> **carrier**: a telecommunications company
>
> **long distance (call)**: a call to a far-away place
>
> **unlimited minutes**: as many minutes to talk as you want

CD2 T23

C 🔘 **Listen again to the second part. Write *T* (true) or *F* (false).**

_____ 1. Luis has a contract with Sunphone.

_____ 2. Luis called the Sunphone company to complain about his bill.

_____ 3. The Sunphone company said Luis has to pay only part of the bill.

_____ 4. If Luis doesn't pay, the Sunphone company will shut off his phone.

CONVERSATION

Listen and read the conversation.

Manuel: What's wrong, Luis?

Luis: I just got my cell phone bill. It was $653!

Manuel: What? How did that happen?

Luis: Last month I signed up for a cheaper plan with Sunphone. The plan said 900 minutes for $99. The salesperson said I could talk for 900 minutes during the day and unlimited minutes on nights and weekends.

Manuel: So what happened?

Luis: Look at this bill. They charged me for both nights and weekends.

4 **PRACTICE**

A PAIRS. **Practice the conversation.**

B PROBLEM-SOLVE. GROUPS. **Read the situations and the possible solutions. Discuss. Which of the solutions will work best?**

Situation 1

Vera bought a prepaid phone card for $10 to call Brazil. The phone card promised 1000 minutes. She used only 600 minutes, and now her card doesn't work any more.

Situation 2

Sergio just signed a contract with the cell phone company. He found out that he lives on a street where the cell phone company has bad cell phone reception. When he makes or gets a call, the signal often fails.

Possible Solutions:

- ask the company for a refund
- cancel the plan
- change cell phone providers
- file a complaint against the company
- find someone to take over your plan

Grammar

Comparison of adjectives

My new phone plan is	cheaper	than my old plan.
	more convenient	
	less convenient	

······· **Grammar Watch**

- Use the comparative form of an adjective + *than* to compare two people, places, or things.
- The comparison forms of *good, bad,* and *far* are irregular: *good–better, bad–worse, far–farther.*
- See page 288 for rules with comparison adjectives.

1 PRACTICE

A **Look at the ad. Circle the adjectives of comparison.**

CALL INTO FALL

PACIFIC
The cell phone provider you've been looking for.

Are you tired of expensive monthly fees?
Poor reception?
Bad customer service?

$99

Sign up with Pacific today. We offer cheaper monthly rates, no hidden fees, clearer reception, and faster, more efficient customer service. We can also bundle your cell phone, Internet and cable at a great low rate. Make your life more convenient and save money. Call Pacific today and get your first 1,000 minutes free.

B **Read the paragraph. Write the correct form of the adjectives.**

My family used to have a phone with the T-M cell phone company. We

signed up for the plan because we thought the T-M had a ___lower___ price.
                                                        (low)

But there were also monthly fees, so the plan wasn't really _____. We
                                                              (cheap)

had bad reception, too. We often lost the cell phone signal on our phones. And

our night minutes didn't start until 9:00 P.M. Now we have a Pacific plan. Night

minutes start at 7:00 P.M., so it's _____ than my old plan. The reception
                                    (convenient)

is also _____. We have no problem calling our family in Florida. We're
        (clear)

_____ with Pacific. It's a much _____ cell phone provider.
(happy)   (good)

A Read the ads. Compare the TVs. Write the correct form of the adjectives.

1. The Viza color is ___brighter___ than the Polara color. (bright)

2. The Viza is _____ than the Polara. (clear)

3. The Viza screen is _____ than the Polara screen. (big)

4. The Viza is _____ than the Polara. (expensive)

B Read the ads. Compare the vacuum cleaners. Write sentences in your notebook. Use the adjectives *cheap*, *expensive*, *good*, *heavy*, and *powerful*.

Example: The Dirt Angel is lighter than the Haber vacuum.

Show what you know! Compare price and quality

ROLE PLAY. PAIRS. You are both shopping for a new cell phone. Compare two cell phone plans, the Sunphone plan and the TCP plan. Which has more minutes, cheaper service, better phones, etc? Make up the information.

Can you...compare price and quality? ☐

Life Skills

1   READ A NEWSPAPER SALES AD

CLASS. Look at the newspaper sales ad. Talk about words you don't know. What is the rebate for?

Valley Appliance Store

ALL REFRIGERATORS ON SALE

$75 CASH BACK
AFTER YOU RETURN THE MAIL-IN REBATE WHEN YOU BUY 1 APPLIANCE OF $399 OR MORE

SALE
$399.99
SAVE $90

KENVORE
18.2 CU.FT.
#65812 Reg. 489.99
While quantities last

OFFER VALID FROM JULY 22 THROUGH JULY 28

Sometimes when a customer buys something, the manufacturer (company) or the store will give the customer money back. This is called a *rebate.*

2   PRACTICE

Read the statements. Write *T* (true) or *F* (false). Correct the false statements.

_____ 1. The sale price of the refrigerator is $489.99.

_____ 2. You get back $110 if you mail in the rebate.

_____ 3. You can buy this refrigerator for the sale price in August.

_____ 4. You buy an appliance for $399. You can get a rebate for $75.

_____ 5. Kenvore has no more refrigerators. They can't order more on sale for you.

3 COMPLETE A REBATE FORM

To get a rebate, you need to fill out a form. Read the form and the label below. Complete the form. Write the model and serial numbers.

Kenvore Refrigerator Rebate   Expires 8/1/10

1. Complete the information below. Include model and serial number.

2. Include a copy of the sales receipt (photocopy OK). The copy must show the model number and date of purchase. Keep a copy of the sales receipt and rebate form for your records.

3. Mail this form and the sales receipt before August 1, 2010 to:

   Rebate Department
   P.O. Box 34987
   El Paso, TX 88554

(last) _Hernandez_   (first) _Andrew_   _10 Gaviota Avenue_
Customer Name   **Address**

Long Beach   _CA_   _90813_   _562 555-2098_
City   **State**   **Zip**   **Phone**

_____   _____   Offer void where prohibited. Please allow 6–8 weeks for processing.
Model Number   **Serial Number**

MODEL Number

SERIAL Number

6 9 9 7 8 3 4   5 6 7 8 4 5
General Energy Company
MOD: **WPSR412023W**
SER: **DZ162112G**

4 PRACTICE

A PAIRS. Discuss the questions.

1. What does Andrew need to send with this form to get a rebate?

2. Can he send this form in September?

3. How long will it take him to get the rebate?

4. What does Andrew need to make a copy of?

B GROUPS. Stores sometimes give people rebates to get their business. What are other ways stores get more business?

Can you... read sales ads and rebates?   ☐

Make an exchange

Listening and Speaking

1 BEFORE YOU LISTEN

Look at the picture of the electronics store. What is the customer doing?
Guess: The customer is _____.

a. getting a cash refund   b. making an exchange   c. getting a store credit

2 LISTEN

CD2 T25

A 🎵 **Listen to the conversation between the store clerk and the customer.**
Was your guess correct?

CD2 T25

B 🎵 **Read the questions. Then listen again. Circle the correct answers.**

1. What is the customer returning?
   a. a cell phone   b. an iPod   c. an MP3 player

2. Why is the customer returning the merchandise?
   a. It's broken.   b. It's not easy to use.   c. It's the wrong color.

3. Why doesn't the customer want the Simsung phone?
   a. It's too expensive.   b. It's defective.   c. It's the wrong color.

4. Why doesn't the customer like the Moondisk phone?
   a. It's not expensive.   b. It's too expensive.   c. It's the wrong color.

5. What does the customer ask the clerk to do?
   a. Show her more MP3s.   b. Call another store.   c. Call the manager.

3 CONVERSATION

A Listen to the sentences. Notice how we link a consonant sound to a vowel sound. Then listen and repeat.

Do you have any in silver?

We're all out of silver.

This isn't as expensive.

Can you exchange it for another?

Is there anything wrong with it?

Pronunciation Watch

We link words in a phrase together. We do not stop between each word. We usually link a consonant sound at the end of a word to a vowel sound at the beginning of the next word.

CD2 T27

B Listen and read the conversation.

Store clerk: May I help you?

Rahel: Yes, I want to return this phone.

Store clerk: Sure . . . Is there anything wrong with it?

Rahel: The volume doesn't work very well.

Store clerk: OK. Will that be a refund or an exchange?

Rahel: I'd like an exchange, please.

Store clerk: All right. Do you have your sales receipt?

Rahel: Yes, here it is. Could I exchange it for this Simsung?

Store clerk: Sure, but that's $30 more.

Rahel: How about this Moondisk?

Store clerk: That isn't quite as expensive. . . . Let's see, it's $55.

4 PRACTICE

A PAIRS. Practice the conversation with a partner.

B ROLE PLAY. PAIRS. Pretend you are a customer and a sales clerk. Make a similar conversation.

Student A: You're returning a Moondisk cell phone. It's hard to take pictures with the phone. You want to exchange it for a T-Moby cell phone.

Student B: You are the clerk. The T-Moby costs $50 more. You think the Simsung cell phone is a great phone. It's not as expensive.

Grammar

As ... as with adjectives

	As	Adjective	As	
This store is
This store isn't	**as**	clean	**as**	that store.

· · · · · · · · · · · **Grammar Watch**

Grammar Watch

Use *as ... as* to say how two things, places, or people are like each other.

- Use *not as ... as* to say how two things, places, or people are not like each other.

- We can leave out the second part of an *as ... as* phrase when the meaning is clear from the context.

That TV isn't as wide (as this TV).

1 PRACTICE

A Read the statements about two stores. Write *T* (true) or *F* (false).

The Trego store is as clean as the Archway store.
The Archway store is not as big as the Trego store.
The lines at Archway are shorter.

_____ 1. The Archway store is cleaner.

_____ 2. The Trego store is bigger.

_____ 3. The lines at Archway are not as long.

B Complete the sentences about Internet stores.

1. Customer service __is not as good__ at aro.com as it is at acb.com.
   (not / good)

2. Delivery _____ as it is at acb.com.
   (not / fast)

3. The merchandise _____ at aro.com as it is at acb.com.
   (good)

4. Shopping on aro.com _____ as it is on acb.com.
   (easy)

5. Prices _____ at aro.com as they are on acb.com.
   (not / high)

Show what you know! Compare shopping experiences

GROUPS. Compare shopping for large purchases in your country to shopping in the U.S. Are items the same price? Are they the same quality?

Can you...compare shopping experiences? ☐

Writing

1 BEFORE YOU WRITE

A GROUPS. Compare two stores that sell the same type of merchandise, for example, electronics. Or compare large "box" stores that sell everything. What do you like and dislike about them?

B Read the paragraph. What are three reasons the writer likes the Arcadia store?

> There are two big stores in my neighborhood, Dollarmart and Arcadia. I prefer Arcadia for many reasons. For one thing, the employees are friendlier. It's more organized, too, so you can find things right away. The merchandise is also much better quality. Dollarmart says its prices are lower. But I've shopped there and their prices are only a few cents lower. Their store is not as clean, either. The employees are less helpful, and they don't know where things are. Arcadia is a much better store. I prefer to shop there.

2 WRITE

Write a paragraph about two stores you know. Compare them and tell which you like better and why. Use the ideas in the box or your own ideas. Use adjectives of comparison and (*not*) *as . . . as*.

big parking lots	fast service	good quality
bright lighting	friendly employees	organized
clean	good discounts	short lines
convenient hours	good prices	wide selection

3 CHECK YOUR WRITING

☐ Did you compare two stores in your paragraph?

☐ Did you use adjectives of comparison?

☐ Did you use (*not*) *as . . . as*?

☐ Did you tell which store you prefer and why?

REVIEW & EXPAND Show what you know!

1 REVIEW For your Grammar Review, go to page 250.

2 ACT IT OUT What do you say?

STEP 1. **CLASS. Review the conversation on page 121 (CD2 Track 27).**

STEP 2. **PAIRS. Role-play an exchange between a customer and a sales person.**

> **Student A:** You bought a Simsung TV. The color looked good in the store, but the sound system is not very good. You want to exchange it, but you don't want to spend more money.

> **Student B:** Ask if Student A wants a refund or exchange. Ask what the problem is. Suggest that Student A buy a Sundisk TV. It costs more than the Simsung, but it is not as expensive as the Universe TV.

3 READ AND REACT Problem-solving

STEP 1. **Read the problem.**

The Sanchez family moved to a new apartment. The kitchen is small, and there is no refrigerator in the apartment. They need to buy a new one. They went to one store and the salesman tried to sell them a very big, expensive refrigerator with a lot of features. He said it was a good price, but they're not sure.

STEP 2. **Give the Sanchez family advice. What can they do to get a good deal on a refrigerator?**

4 CONNECT For your Self-monitoring Activity, go to page 259.
For your Team Project, go to page 268.

Which goals can you check off? Go back to page 105.

Getting There Safely

Preview

Is it important to have a car where you live? What problems do car owners have?

UNIT GOALS

- ☐ Talk about car maintenance
- ☐ Identify parts of a car
- ☐ Talk about traffic accidents
- ☐ Write a letter to a city official
- ☐ Talk about driving costs

1 WHAT DO YOU KNOW?

A Look at the picture and the words. We use these words to talk about traffic. Which words do you know?

B Match the pictures with the words. Write the numbers.

On the road

_____ construction

_____ entrance ramp/on ramp

_____ exit

_____ freeway/highway

_____ lane

_____ overpass

_____ shoulder

_____ toll booth

_____ tow truck

_____ traffic jam

_____ vehicle

CD2 T28

C Listen and check your answers. Then listen and repeat.

Learning Strategy

Translate words

Make cards for five words. Write the English word on the front of the card. Write the word in your language on the back.

TOLL BOOTH

3

6

FREEWAY ENTRANCE

85 SOUTH CALIFORNIA

7

8

A 🎧 CD2 T29 **WORD PLAY. Listen to the first part of a traffic report. What city is this traffic report for?**

B 🎧 CD2 T30 **Listen to the entire traffic report. Circle the correct answers.**

1. On the 110 South, there has just been _____.
   a. construction
   b. a major accident
   c. a traffic jam

2. On Slauson Avenue East, there is _____.
   a. a traffic jam
   b. a delay of 25 minutes
   c. construction

3. On the 105 East _____.
   a. there are no delays
   b. there is construction
   c. there is a blocked vehicle

4. On the 405 South _____.
   a. the right lane is closed
   b. an accident has just happened
   c. an accident is almost cleared

Show what you know!

GROUPS. Compare traffic where you live now to traffic in your native country. Is the traffic better or worse? Are the roads safer or less safe? Discuss.

Talk about car maintenance

Listening and Speaking

1 BEFORE YOU LISTEN

A GROUPS. What are common car problems? What can you do to keep a car in good condition?

B Look at the pictures. Match the pictures with the words.

A **B** **C**

_____ 1. change the oil   _____ 2. replace the brakes   _____ 3. rotate the tires

2 LISTEN

CD2 T31

A Listen to the first part of the conversation. Why is Li talking to a mechanic? He wants _____.

a. an oil change   b. a new tire   c. new brakes

CD2 T32

B Read the statements. Then listen to the whole conversation. Write *T* (true) or *F* (false).

__F__ 1. An oil change costs $25.

_____ 2. An oil change takes 15 minutes.

_____ 3. Li needs new brakes.

_____ 4. Li needs new front tires.

_____ 5. The mechanic is going to rotate Li's tires.

_____ 6. Li is going to fix the dent in his car.

3 CONVERSATION

CD2 T33

A 🎧 **Listen to the phrases and sentences. Notice the weak pronunciation of *a*, *an*, and *the*. Then listen and repeat.**

a new battery   You need a new battery.

an oil change   I'd like an oil change.

the tires   We should rotate the tires.

CD2 T34

B 🎧 **Listen and read the conversation.**

Mechanic: So, what can I do for you?

Li: I'd like an oil change.

Mechanic: No problem.

Li: How much will that be?

Mechanic: $29.95.

Li: OK. How long will that take?

Mechanic: About half an hour.

4 PRACTICE

A PAIRS. **Practice the conversation.**

B ROLE PLAY. PAIRS. **Look at the information below and make a similar conversation.**

Student A: You are a car owner. Tell the mechanic what you need. Ask how much it will cost.

Student B: You are a mechanic. Answer the questions.

You need a new battery.
Cost: $75
Time to fix: 15 minutes

You need a new tire.
Cost: $120
Time to replace:
15 minutes

The air conditioner in your car isn't working. You need coolant.
Cost: $15
Time to put in: 2 minutes

Grammar

A, An, The
The car needs **a** battery and **an** air filter.
The battery is weak and **the** air filter is dirty.

Grammar Watch

- Use *a* or *an* the first time you talk about something. Use *a* before consonant sounds. Use *an* before vowel sounds.

- Use *the* when you talk about something for the second time.

- Use *the* for things that are known to both you and the listener.

- Use *the* when there is only one of something.

1 PRACTICE

A **Read the correct sentences. Circle the correct article in the second sentence.**

1. Alex told Claudia about a used car he liked. Claudia asked:

   Did you buy **a / the** car?

2. Alex told Claudia that he bought the car. Claudia asked:

   Does it have **a / the** warranty?

3. Claudia asked if the car needed a lot of repairs. Alex answered:

   No. But **a / the** turn signal wasn't working.

4. Claudia then asked what Alex did. He told her:

   I bought **a / the** new light bulb and installed it. Now **a / the** turn signal light works.

B **Complete the sentences. Use *a*, *an*, or *the*.**

Two months ago I bought ___an___ old car for very little money. _____ car had

problems. _____ air conditioner and _____ heater didn't work well. I also had to

buy _____ air filter. There was _____ noise coming from _____ engine. There

was also _____ hole on _____ floor of _____ car. I covered _____ hole and

got used to _____ noise. _____ car gets me to work, and that saves me time. I hope

_____ car lasts until _____ summer. Then I'll have enough money for _____

better car.

A Complete the conversations with *a*, *an*, or *the*.

1. **A:** My car won't start. ___The___ battery must be dead.

   B: Let me jump-start your car. I have jumper cables in my car.

2. **A:** I think there's _____ oil leak under _____ car.

   B: I'll take _____ look.

3. **A:** After the accident he called for _____ tow truck.

   B: Did it take long for _____ tow truck to come?

   A: It finally came after _____ hour.

4. **A:** We have _____ flat tire.

   B: Oh no. I hope we have _____ spare tire in the trunk.

5. **A:** Is there _____ good auto repair shop nearby?

   B: I always go to _____ garage on East 4th Street. _____ mechanics there are excellent, and _____ prices are fair.

6. **A:** What's _____ problem with your car?

   B: There's _____ noise in the engine.

   A: Is it _____ same noise you complained about last month?

   B: No. It's _____ different noise.

jumper cables

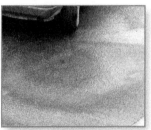

oil leak

flat tire

spare tire

CD2 T35

B 🖭 **Listen and check your answers.**

C PAIRS. **Practice the conversations.**

Show what you know! Talk about car maintenance

GROUPS. **Discuss. Talk about an experience or problem you have had with a car, a mechanic, or getting to work or school.**

Can you... talk about car maintenance? ☐

Life Skills

1 IDENTIFY CAR PARTS

A Look at the picture and the words in the box. Which parts of the car do you know?

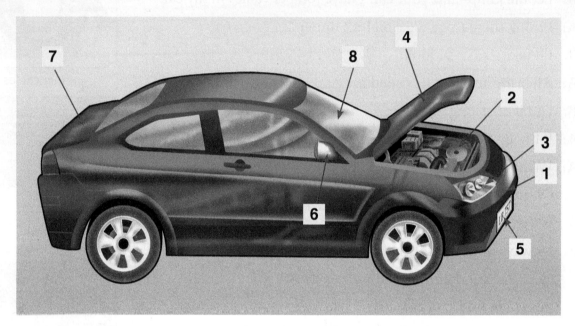

| 1 bumper | 3 headlights | 5 license plate | 7 trunk |
| 2 engine | 4 hood | 6 sideview mirror | 8 windshield |

B PAIRS. Complete the sentences with the words from Exercise A.

1. You always need to have a ___license plate___ on the back of your car.

2. _____ help the driver see the road at night.

3. It's a good idea to keep a spare tire in the _____ of your car.

4. Check the _____ before you change lanes.

5. Window wipers help you see through the _____ when it rains.

6. The _____ protects your car if you have a small accident.

7. The _____ is located under the _____ of the car.

A Look at the picture and the words in the box. Which parts of the car do you know?

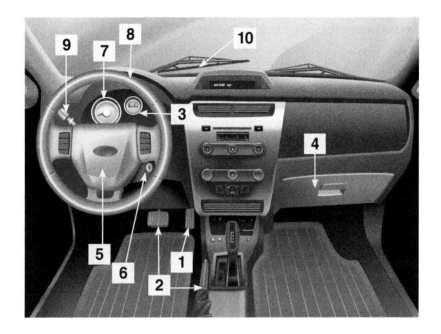

1 accelerator/	3 gas gauge	6 ignition	9 turn signal
gas pedal	4 glove compartment	7 speedometer	10 wipers
2 brakes	5 horn	8 steering wheel	

B Write the name of the correct car part next to each instruction.

1. Turn this to move the car to the right or left: _____

2. Step on this to go faster: _____

3. Keep your insurance card inside this: _____

4. Step on this to stop the car: _____

5. Put the key in this to start the car: _____

6. Turn these on when it rains: _____

Can you...identify parts of a car? ☐

Talk about traffic accidents

Listening and Speaking

1 **BEFORE YOU LISTEN**

CLASS. **What are common causes of traffic accidents?**

2 **LISTEN**

CD2 T36

A 🔘 **Listen. A police officer is interviewing two drivers after an accident. What do you think caused the accident?**

a. speeding and cell phone use
b. broken traffic light
c. tired driver

CD2 T37

B 🔘 **Read the statements. Then listen again to the first conversation. Write *T* (true) or *F* (false).**

_____ 1. Mr. Desmond needs an ambulance.

_____ 2. Mr. Desmond has a serious injury.

_____ 3. Mr. Desmond thinks the other car was going too fast.

_____ 4. Mr. Desmond was talking on his cell phone.

CD2 T38

C 🔘 **Read the questions. Listen again to the second conversation. Circle the correct answers.**

1. The officer asks to see Ms. Yu's license, registration, and _____.
   a. car insurance   b. social security card

2. Ms. Yu was driving in the _____.
   a. left-hand lane   b. right-hand lane

3. The police officer asks if Ms. Yu was _____.
   a. talking on a cell phone
   b. text-messaging on her cell phone

4. Talking on a cell phone in California is _____.
   a. legal   b. illegal

CD2 T39

A Listen to the words. Notice the sound of the unstressed vowels. Then listen and repeat.

> In words with more than one syllable, one syllable is stressed. Other syllables are unstressed. The vowel in an unstressed syllable often has a very short, quiet sound.

• hap**pen** • **in**surance • **ac**cident • construc**tion**

CD2 T40

B Listen to the words. Put a dot over the stressed syllable. Underline the unstressed vowels.

1. license   2. about   3. statement   4. engine   5. ambulance

CD2 T41

C Listen and read the conversation.

Officer: Are you hurt, Ma'am?

Ms. Yu: No, I'm all right, officer.

Officer: Okay. May I see your license, registration, and insurance please? . . . Well, Ms. Yu, can you explain what happened?

Ms. Yu: Yes, Officer. I was driving in the right-hand lane. There was nothing in front of me. Suddenly, this car came out of nowhere—I think it came from the left lane. It was slowing down in front of me to turn onto Martine Avenue. There wasn't time for me to stop.

4 PRACTICE

A PAIRS. Practice the conversation.

B ROLE PLAY. PAIRS. Make a similar conversation.

Student A: You are the officer. Ask questions.

Student B: You are the driver. You were exiting the freeway on the off ramp. It was raining. You lost control and hit the car in front of you.

Grammar

Past Continuous

Subject	Was/were	Not	Verb + -ing	
I He/She	was			
You We They	were	(not)	driving	fast.

Grammar Watch

- Use the past continuous for activities that were happening at a specific time in the past.
- was not = **wasn't**
- were not = **weren't**

1 PRACTICE

A Underline four more examples of the past continuous.

> There was an accident on Route 4 just before the bridge yesterday afternoon. It <u>was raining</u> and a car hit the car in front. The driver of the car in front was slightly injured. He wasn't wearing a seat belt. Cars were slowing down to see what happened. They weren't driving at the regular speed. They were "rubbernecking." As a result, there was a big traffic jam.

B Unscramble the sentences. Write the words in the correct order.

1. the men / crossing / against the light / were

   _____

2. the child / wearing / not / was / a seat belt

   _____

3. was / the woman / speeding / on the highway

   _____

4. the drivers / were / paying attention / not

   _____

5. talking on the phone and / the people / driving / were

   _____

2 PRACTICE

A **Complete the sentences with the past continuous form of the verbs.**

They _____ construction on the highway, so we drove through the
            1 (do)

city. It took a long time because it _____ and traffic was heavy. It often
                                        2 (rain)

floods on that highway, but we were lucky. It _____ that day. Then my
                                                3 (not / flood)

car broke down on 14th Street. Fortunately, by then it _____ anymore.
                                                            4 (not / rain)

The sun _____ and it _____ warm. I _____
            5 (shine)   6 (get)   7 (get)

impatient, but at last the tow truck arrived.

B **Complete the letter. Use the past continuous.**

Dear Mayor Gordon:

I'm writing to you to tell my concern about traffic accidents in our city. There

aren't enough traffic lights downtown. This week there was another accident on

West Adams Street and North 19th Avenue. I (sit) _____ on a bench

on 19th Avenue. I (wait) _____ for the Number 4 bus and I saw the

accident. A taxi (drive) _____ down 19th Avenue when a bus hit it.

The bus driver didn't see the taxi coming. Fortunately, the drivers (not/speed)

_____, and they (wear) _____ their seat belts. No one was

hurt, but we need a traffic light at that intersection.

Thank you for your attention.

Mary Ann Watson

Show what you know!   Talk about traffic accidents

GROUPS. **Talk about an accident you were in, saw, or heard about.**

Can you... talk about traffic accidents?   ☐

Identify causes of car accidents

1 BEFORE YOU READ

GROUPS. Discuss. Do you know anyone who is a dangerous driver? What things do drivers do that are unsafe?

2 READ

CD2 T42

Listen and read the article. Does it talk about your ideas from Before You Read?

Dangerous Drivers

Did you know that about *75 percent of accidents* on U.S. highways are caused by driver errors? That means most accidents wouldn't happen if people drove more carefully! Here are common mistakes:

Speeding: Most people think speeding only means driving over the speed limit. But it also means driving too fast in rainy or snowy weather. When roads are wet and **slippery**, driving at the speed limit can be dangerous.

Tailgating: Cars need enough space between them to be safe. Drivers always need at least three seconds to slow down if the car in front stops **suddenly**.

Unsafe lane changes: Many accidents occur because drivers drive into another lane or off the road. Drivers need to be careful to stay in their lane and always signal before changing lanes.

Ignoring traffic signs and traffic lights: Drivers should come to a complete stop at red lights and stop signs. They need to look carefully for cars and **pedestrians** who are crossing the street. It's also important to **obey** "slow" signs near schools or hospitals.

Driving under the influence (DUI): Most people know that DUI means driving after drinking alcohol. But DUI also means driving after you take medications that make you sleepy. Be careful. Never drive under the influence.

You can be a safer driver. Don't make these mistakes. **Think ahead.** Watch out for dangerous drivers on the road. You never know what they will do next!

Three top causes of accidents	Number of injuries
Failure to keep in proper lane	16,551
Speeding	11,803
Driving under the influence (DUI)	7,441

Source: 2005, FARS, NHTSA, DOT

3 AFTER YOU READ

A Read the article again. What is the main idea? Most accidents _____.

a. are from DUI   b. can be prevented   c. cause injuries

B Write *T* (true) or *F* (false). Correct the false statements.

> **Reading Skill:**
> Interpreting charts
>
> Charts show important information in an article.

_F_ 1. Safe drivers should drive at the speed limit in bad weather.

____ 2. If you are six seconds behind another car, you are tailgating.

____ 3. At a stop sign, you can stop or just slow down.

____ 4. DUI means driving under the influence of alcohol or some medications.

____ 5. If someone is tailgating you should move to a different lane.

C Look at the chart on page 138. Write the cause of accident with the most injuries:

_____

4 VOCABULARY IN CONTEXT

Look at the boldfaced words in the article. Guess their meanings. Then circle the correct ending for each sentence.

1. On a slippery road, it is **easy to stop / difficult to stop**.

2. When a car stops suddenly, it stops **slowly / quickly**.

3. A pedestrian is someone who is **walking / driving**.

4. When you obey a traffic sign, you **do what it says / don't pay attention**.

5. When you think ahead, you think about the **past / future**.

Show what you know!

GROUPS. Discuss. What are other causes of car accidents? What are some tips for avoiding them?

Write a letter to a city official

Writing

1 BEFORE YOU WRITE

A GROUPS. Discuss the traffic problems in the box. Why are these problems for drivers or pedestrians? Are these problems for your city or neighborhood?

> dangerous intersections   vehicles that double-park
> not enough sidewalks   walk signals that are too short

B Read the letter.

September 10, 2010

Mayor Tom Leppert
Dallas City Hall
1500 Marilla Street, Room 5EN
Dallas, TX 75201-6390

Dear Mayor Leppert:

I am writing about a traffic problem in the Fair Oaks neighborhood. There is a dangerous intersection at Hemlock Lane and Ridgecrest Road. Trucks often stand at this intersection to unload. As a result, drivers turning right can't see pedestrians. This has caused many accidents. We need a "no standing" sign at this intersection. Then cars and pedestrians will be safer.

Thank you for your attention.

Sincerely,

Marison Jimenez

Marison Jimenez

2 WRITE

Write a letter to the mayor of your city about a traffic problem. Use a problem on this page or your own idea.

3 CHECK YOUR WRITING

☐ Did you use the correct letter format?

☐ Did you explain the problem?

☐ Did you suggest a solution?

Identify steps to take after an accident

Listening and Speaking

1 BEFORE YOU LISTEN

GROUPS. **What should you do after a car accident with another moving car?**

2 LISTEN

CD2 T43

A 🔘 Listen to a radio show that talks about what to do after a car accident. Does the show mention your ideas from Before You Listen?

CD2 T44

B 🔘 Read the statements. Listen again to the first part. Write *T* (true) or *F* (false).

_____ 1. You should stop after you have an accident with a moving car, parked car, or a pedestrian.

_____ 2. It is a felony to hit and run

felony: a serious crime

_____ 3. If you hit something and don't stop, you can go to jail.

_____ 4. If you hit something and don't stop, you can lose your license.

_____ 5. If you hit a parked car and you can't find the owner, you do not need to report the accident.

CD2 T45

C 🔘 Read the statements. Listen again to the second part. Circle the correct answers.

1. If someone is hurt in an accident, you should _____.
   a. move the person
   b. call 911 for an ambulance

2. After a car accident, get the other driver's name, address, driver's license number, license plate number, and _____.
   a. e-mail address
   b. insurance information

3. When the police come, they will want to see proof of insurance and your _____.
   a. driver's license
   b. proof of citizenship

Talk about driving costs

Grammar

Present time clauses

Time clause	Main clause
Before you buy a car,	you should compare prices at different dealers.
When you have a car,	you need car insurance.
After you get an oil change,	you get better gas milage.

Grammar Watch

- For present time clauses, use a present form in both the time clause and a simple present verb, a present modal, or an imperative in the main clause.

- The main clause can come before the time clause. When the main clause comes first, do not use a comma.

  You need car insurance when you have a car.

1 PRACTICE

A Circle the main clause in each sentence. Underline the time clause.

1. When you drive a car, you need a license, registration, and insurance.

2. Before you buy car insurance, you should compare rates of different companies.

3. People pay more for car insurance when they have a bad driving record.

4. Drivers break the law when they drive without car insurance.

5. When people drive without car insurance, they can get a fine, lose their license, or go to jail.

B Write sentences in your notebook. Use the words and add commas where necessary. More than one answer is possible.

1. when you / read the Sunday newspapers / look for coupons for auto service specialists.

2. before you / make a list of all its problems / take your car to the garage

3. describe any car problems to the mechanic / bring your car in / when you

4. a mechanic works on your car / before / you should ask how much it will cost

5. after / take your car for a test drive / the mechanic works on your car

C **Complete the paragraph. Write the correct form of the verbs.**

When you _____go_____ to Tom's Automative, you _____
                    (go)   (get)
great service. Tom is very honest. Before he _____ on your car,
                                              (work)
he _____ you a written estimate. When Tom _____ problems,
   (give)   (find)
he always _____ you exactly what the problem is. Tom only charges
          (show)
you for work he does. After he _____ a car part, he always _____
                                (replace)   (return)
the old part so you know the work is done.

D **Combine the sentences into one sentence. Use the words in parentheses.**

1. You fill up your car with gas. Don't fill it to the top. (when)

    When you fill up your car with gas, don't fill it to the top.

2. You save gas. You get regular tune-ups. (when)

    _____

3. Buy gas. Check the Internet for good deals. (before)

    _____

4. Buy gas. Find the stations with the lowest prices. (before)

    _____

5. You buy gas. Check your tire pressure so your tires will last longer. (when)

    _____

Show what you know! Talk about driving costs

GROUPS. **Look at the tips on pages 142-143. Which tips do you follow?
What are other ways to save money on gas and cars?**

Can you...talk about driving costs? ☐

1 REVIEW For your Grammar Review, go to page 251.

2 ACT IT OUT What do you say?

STEP 1. CLASS. Review the conversation on page 135 (CD2 Track 41).

STEP 2. ROLE PLAY. PAIRS. Read the situation. Then role-play.

Student A: You were driving on a busy street when a truck pulled out in front of you. You had to stop suddenly. The driver in the car behind you wasn't paying attention, and she hit the back of your car.

Student B: You are a police officer. Ask the driver if he or she is hurt. Ask for his or her license and registration. Ask questions about the accident.

3 READ AND REACT Problem-solving

STEP 1. Read about Julia.

Julia was shopping at the supermarket. When she finished her shopping, she got in her car and backed out of her parking space. But she didn't look where she was going, and she hit a parked car. She smashed one of the car's headlights. There was no one in the car. Julia is afraid that her car insurance costs will go up if she reports the accident.

STEP 2. PAIRS. What is the problem? Talk about Julia's problem. What should Julia do?

4 CONNECT For your Self-evaluation Activity, go to page 260.
For your Team Project, go to page 269.

Which goals can you check off? Go back to page 125.

Staying Healthy

Preview

What foods do you eat every day? What did you eat in your native country? Do you have healthy eating habits?

UNIT GOALS

- ☐ Talk about eating habits
- ☐ Read a nutritional label
- ☐ Talk about diets
- ☐ Talk about family health
- ☐ Talk about dental health

1   WHAT DO YOU KNOW?

A   Look at the pictures and phrases. They describe eating habits and food shopping habits. Which words do you know?

CD2 T46

B   Look at the pictures and phrases. Listen. Listen again and repeat.

have a snack

drink sugary beverages

eat fast food

eat fatty foods

buy junk food

be on a diet

get takeout

cook home-made meals

buy frozen dinners

buy fresh fruits and vegetables

2 PRACTICE

WORD PLAY. Look at the phrases on pages 146–147. Are the habits healthy or unhealthy? Can they be either? Write them in the diagram.

Healthy   **Either**   **Unhealthy**

Show what you know!

GROUPS. Compare your answers from Word Play. If the habit can be healthy or unhealthy, give examples.

Talk about eating habits

Listening and Speaking

1 BEFORE YOU LISTEN

Do you ever skip meals? If you do, which meals do you skip? Why? How do you feel if you skip meals?

> skip meals = not eat one or more meals (breakfast, lunch, or dinner)

2 LISTEN

CD2 T47

A Listen to the radio show "Our Nation's Health." Complete the sentence. Circle the correct word.

Most U.S. workers have _____ eating habits.

a. healthy   b. unhealthy

CD2 T47

B Read the statements. Then listen again. Circle the correct answers.

1. Skipping meals is _____ for your health.
   a. good
   b. bad
   c. neither good nor bad

2. In the U.S., _____ percent of workers eat snacks.
   a. 33
   b. 55
   c. 89

3. Most U.S. workers eat _____ for snacks.
   a. fruit
   b. donuts
   c. junk food

4. U.S. workers eat snacks because they're hungry, stressed and _____.
   a. bored
   b. thirsty
   c. they need energy

3 CONVERSATION

A Listen to the sentences. Then listen and repeat.

What do they eat for lunch?

Do you ("d'ya") have a snack?

What do you ("d'ya") usually have?

Pronunciation Watch

The word *do* usually has a weak pronunciation with a short, quiet vowel sound when another word comes after it. *Do you* is often pronounced "d'ya."

B Listen and read the conversation.

Tanesha: Do you ever skip meals?

Mike: Well, sometimes I skip breakfast if I'm late to work.

Tanesha: And do you ever snack between meals?

Mike: Sure. Doesn't everyone?

Tanesha: I guess so. So, what kind of snack do you usually have at work? Fruit? Crackers?

Mike: No, I usually get something from the vending machines, like chips or cookies.

4 PRACTICE

A PAIRS. Practice the conversation.

B MAKE IT PERSONAL. GROUPS. Look at the eating habits. What can happen if you have these eating habits?

- eat late at night
- eat in front of the TV
- not eat many fruits or vegetables
- eat fatty foods
- eat salty foods
- skip meals

Talk about eating habits

Grammar

Adverbs of Frequency

Subject	Adverb	Verb	
We	**always**	**eat**	a big breakfast.

Subject	*Be*	Adverb	
I	**am**	**usually**	hungry by noon.

Adverbs of Frequency

always	100%
usually	
often	
sometimes	
rarely	
never	0%

Grammar Watch

- *Sometimes* and *usually* can also start a sentence.
- We also use expressions like *once in a while* and *once a year*. They can start or end a sentence.

1 PRACTICE

A Underline the adverbs or expressions of frequency. Circle the verb that the adverb describes.

Jorge <u>often</u> (goes) to bed late and he wakes up late. He doesn't want to get to work late, so he sometimes skips breakfast. It's OK to skip breakfast once in a while, but not every day. People who skip breakfast usually eat more during the day and increase their risk for heart disease.

B Unscramble the sentences. More than one answer is sometimes possible.

1. never / has / meals / between / snacks / he
   He never has meals between snacks.

2. we / once in a while / get / food / take-out

3. rarely / Camelita / eats / frozen / dinners

4. get / twice a week / we / food / take-out

5. adds / her husband / salt / to his food / almost always

A Add adverbs of frequency to the sentences. Draw arrows.

1. I make rice mixed with vegetables for my children. (sometimes)

2. I cook with olive oil. They say it's good for the heart. (always)

3. My husband loves butter. He adds it to vegetables. (often)

4. I used to use peanut oil, but now I cook with canola oil. (usually)

5. In my native country, we ate a big meal at noon. (always)

B Read the paragraph. Find and correct four mistakes.

I'm from El Salvador. People drink (often) coffee and eat tortillas for breakfast. Usually we eat tortillas for lunch. Lunch almost always is the biggest meal. For dinner, we have often a lighter meal. Now I live in the U.S. I often eat the same foods that I ate in El Salvador, but I have usually a big dinner, and I have a small lunch often.

Show what you know!   Talk about eating habits

STEP 1. GROUPS. Write two questions about eating habits in the chart. Start the questions with *How often . . .*

Questions	Once a week	Every day	Almost never	Not sure
How often do you eat fast food?				

STEP 2. Survey five classmates. Write their names or initials in the chart.

STEP 3. Report your results to the class.

Can you...talk about eating habits? ☐

Read a nutritional label and talk about diets

Life Skills

1 READ A NUTRITIONAL LABEL

All packages of food and snacks have nutritional labels. The label includes important information, such as the number of *calories* for each *serving*, and the amount of fat, *cholesterol*, *sodium* (salt), and the *ingredients*.

A GROUPS. When you buy food, do you look at the nutritional labels?

A CLASS. Look at the two labels for corn chips. How are they the same? How are they different?

Fiesta chips

Nutrition Facts
Serving Size 1 oz. (28g/About 32 chips)
Servings Per Container 3

Amount Per Serving	
Calories 160	Calories from Fat 90

	% Daily Value
Total Fat 10g	16%
Saturated Fat 1.5g	7%
Trans Fat 0g	0%
Cholesterol 0mg	0%
Sodium 170mg	7%
Total Carbohydrate 15g	5%
Dietary Fiber 1g	4%
Sugars less than 1g	
Protein 2g	

Ingredients: Corn, corn oil, and salt. No preservatives. May contain traces of peanuts.

Fritter chips

Nutrition Facts
Serving Size 1 oz. (28g/About 32 chips)
Servings Per Container Approximately 4

Amount Per Serving	
Calories 130	Calories from Fat 45

	% Daily Value
Total Fat 5g	8%
Saturated Fat 1g	2%
Trans Fat 0g	0%
Cholesterol 0mg	0%
Sodium 150 mg	6%
Total Carbohydrate 18g	6%
Dietary Fiber 1g	4%
Sugars 0g	
Protein 2g	

Ingredients: Corn meal, rice, rice and/or sunflower oil, aged cheddar cheese (nonfat milk, salt, cheese cultures, enzymes), whey, and lowfat buttermilk. Contains dairy ingredients.

2 PRACTICE

Complete the statements about the chips. Write with the correct word or number.

1. There are _____ servings in Fiesta chips and _____ servings in Fritter chips.

2. Fiesta chips has _____ calories per serving. Fritter chips has _____ calories.

3. Fiesta chips has _____ more calories than Fritter chips.

4. _____ chips contains more fat than _____ chips.

5. _____ chips contains more sodium than _____ chips.

3 TALK ABOUT DIETS

A PAIRS. Sometimes people can't eat certain foods because they are allergic or must follow a special diet. Read the situations. Are the snacks from page 152 OK for the people? Check (✓) the best answer. Then discuss why.

Situation	Fiesta chips	Fritter chips	Neither
1. Marta needs to reduce the amount of fat in her diet.			
2. Calvin has high blood pressure. He's on a salt-restricted diet.			
3. Eric has type 2 diabetes. He is not supposed to have any sugar.			
4. Liu is allergic to milk.			
5. Mei Lei is allergic to peanuts.			

4 LEARN ABOUT DIABETES

A CD2 T50
Listen to the announcement about diabetes. Why is it a very serious disease?

B CD2 T50
Read the statements. Then listen again. Write *T* (true) or *F* (false).

___T___ 1. There are two types of diabetes.

_____ 2. Diabetes can damage your eyes, cause heart disease, and cause other serious problems.

_____ 3. Diabetes goes away if you eat healthy foods.

_____ 4. Watching your diet helps control diabetes.

_____ 5. Exercising does not help control diabetes.

_____ 6. Children can get diabetes.

Can you...read nutritional labels and talk about diets? ☐

Talk about family health

Listening and Speaking

1 BEFORE YOU LISTEN

GROUPS. Discuss. What can parents do to help their children have a healthy lifestyle?

2 LISTEN

CD2 T51

A 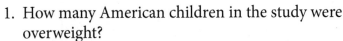 Listen to the information on the radio about family health. Does it mention your ideas from Before You Listen?

CD2 T52

B Read the questions. Then listen again to the first part. Circle the correct answers.

1. How many American children in the study were overweight?
   a. about 17 percent
   b. about 19 percent
   c. about 10 percent

2. What can overweight and obesity cause?
   a. heart problems
   b. type 2 diabetes
   c. both a and b

3. Why are so many children overweight?
   a. family health history
   b. fast food and takeout
   c. bad eating habits and lack of exercise

CD2 T53

C 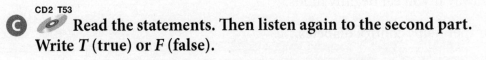 Read the statements. Then listen again to the second part. Write *T* (true) or *F* (false).

_____ 1. You should give children whole grains like wheat bread.

_____ 2. Children should eat high-fat dairy products.

_____ 3. Children need 60 minutes of activity once a week.

_____ 4. The eating habits and physical activity of parents is important for children to have a healthy lifestyle.

CONVERSATION

CD2 T54

A Listen and read the conversation.

Maya: The doctor said that my son needs to lose weight.
What can I do to help him? He doesn't like dieting.

Ana: Well, you can change the way you cook.

Maya: What do you mean?

Ana: You can use low-fat ingredients. For example, get low-fat milk instead
of whole milk. It has less fat and still tastes as good.

4 **PRACTICE**

A PAIRS. Practice the conversation.

B ROLE PLAY. PAIRS. Make similar conversations.

Student A: Someone in your family needs to go on a diet.

Student B: Talk about healthy substitutes. Use the ideas
in the boxes or your own ideas.

lard = white fat from pigs
that is used in cooking

C MAKE IT PERSONAL. GROUPS. Discuss. Make a list of other foods
or cooking ingredients that you think are not healthy and a list of healthy
substitutes. Then compare ideas with a different group.

Talk about family health

Grammar

Verb + Gerund as Object			
He	**enjoys**	**buying**	candy from vending machines.
They	**like**	**eating**	buttered popcorn at the movies.

·····**Grammar Watch**

These verbs can also be followed by a gerund: *can't stand, consider, dislike, don't mind, keep, practice, think about* and *try.*

1 PRACTICE

A Underline the examples of verb + gerund in the paragraph.

Lu Yi is sixty-five years old and lives in Cleveland, Ohio. His doctor told him to exercise. Lu Yi doesn't like exercising too much, but he does like Tai Chi. He used to do it outdoors in China. The problem is Cleveland is too cold in the winter to do Tai Chi outside. Then Lu Yi learned that the Senior Center near his home has a free Tai Chi class. He goes twice a week and enjoys exercising all winter.

Tai Chi, a martial art

B Complete the sentences with the gerund form of the verbs in the box.

> buy   cook   dance   exercise
> give   ~~practice~~   watch

1. For exercise, try ____practicing____ martial arts or _____.

2. When you eat dinner, try _____ your children whole grains.

3. At the supermarket, avoid _____ white bread and potato chips.

4. When you prepare meals, think about _____ more fish and lean meat.

5. Spend time _____ outside with your children.

6. Stop _____ TV and do other activities instead.

2 PRACTICE

Complete the conversations. Use the correct form of verbs in parentheses.

1. **A:** My children just want to sit around and watch TV.

   B: _____Try taking_____ them to the park on weekends. They'll probably _____
   (Try / take)   (start / run)
   around and forget about TV.

2. **A:** My doctor told me to exercise, but I don't have time or extra money.

   B: There are ways to exercise that don't take too much time and are free.

   _____ fast around the mall.
   (Try / walk)

3. **A:** My son _____ vegetables.
   (can't stand / eat)

   B: Give him raw carrots and peppers. Many children _____ them.
   (don't mind / eat)

4. **A:** We eat a lot of canned soups.

   B: We eat a lot of soups, too, but I _____ my own soup. It has a lot less salt.
   (prefer / make)

5. **A:** How can I get my family to eat more fruit?

   B: _____ your children smoothies. Most children _____ them.
   (Try / make)   (love / drink)
   You just mix up fruit, yogurt, juice, and ice in the blender.

Show what you know! Talk about family health

PROBLEM-SOLVING. GROUPS. Talk about how habits can make a family's lifestyle healthy or unhealthy. Discuss the topics in the box. Make suggestions for a healthy lifestyle. Use gerunds.

> food choices   physical activity
> meal portion size   TV/computer habits

A: *My children love eating junk food. I can't get them to stop.*
B: *Stop buying junk food, like potato chips. You can try making them low-fat snacks like low-fat dip and carrots.*

Can you... talk about family health? ☐

Reading

1 | BEFORE YOU READ

GROUPS. Discuss. What kinds of foods do children eat for lunch in your native country? If you have children, what do they eat for lunch here? Is it healthy?

2 | READ

CD2 T55

Listen and read the article. What is the problem with school lunches?

SCHOOL LUNCHES

Most people know that a hungry child can't learn well. The U.S. Government has a National School Lunch Program to help. This program serves free or low-cost lunches to over 30 million children each school day. The lunches are usually hot cooked meals. The program costs the federal government eight billion dollars per year. **School districts** also pay part of the cost.

The program has been successful in some ways. It feeds millions of children safe food. However, some people are not **satisfied**. They think many of the lunches are not **nutritious**. Schools often serve foods like pizza, french fries, and hamburgers. These foods are high in fat, sugar, salt, carbohydrates, and cholesterol. They can make children gain too much weight. Overweight children have a bigger risk for health problems like type 2 diabetes. By 2004, 17.1 percent of U.S. children, or 12.5 million, were overweight.

School districts and state governments are working together to pass laws to solve the problem. For example, California school districts have new rules for fat and sugar levels in foods and beverages. But healthy lunches are not enough. Schools also have to give students food that they will eat. In Minneapolis, Minnesota, school **administrators** ask students what they want in their lunch. Some of the students' answers are: *food that tastes good, food that is good for me, food that is fresh and clean, international cuisine, food that tastes homemade, food that is not too expensive, food that is convenient and fast when I'm in a hurry.* The new lunches should be nutritious, **affordable**, and **appetizing**. Then everyone will be happy!

Some schools have new ideas to make school lunches healthy, affordable, and delicious. In the Chicago Public City schools, three schools have organic gardens. They grow fruits and vegetables for the school lunches. Gardeners, students, and families help take care of the gardens. These schools also teach the community about healthy eating.

3 CHECK YOUR UNDERSTANDING

A PAIRS. Read the article again. Then discuss. What is the main idea?

B Read the statements based on the article. Are they facts or opinions? Write *fact* or *opinion*.

___*fact*___ 1. Thirty million children receive a free or low-cost lunch each school day.

_____ 2. The federal government pays part of the cost of school lunches.

_____ 3. School lunches need to be healthier.

_____ 4. French fries and hamburgers are high in salt and fat.

4 VOCABULARY IN CONTEXT

Look at the boldfaced words in the article. Guess their meanings. Match the words with the correct definitions.

____ 1. school district

____ 2. satisfied

____ 3. nutritious

____ 4. administrators

____ 5. affordable

____ 6. appetizing

a. tasting or smelling good

b. healthy to eat

c. not too expensive

d. the area in which you live where children go to public school

e. pleased (happy) about something because it happened the way you want

f. people who help run a school, company or other institution

Show what you know!

GROUPS. What foods should schools serve (or not) to students? Who should decide? School officials? Governments? Parents? Students?

Talk about dental health

Listening and Speaking

1 BEFORE YOU LISTEN

Match the words with the pictures. Write the letters.

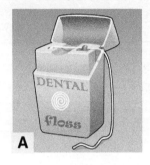
A

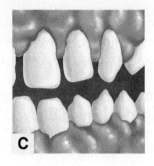
B

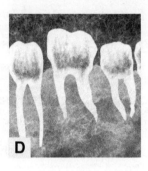
C

D

___ 1. cavity   ___ 2. x-ray   ___ 3. floss   ___ 4. gum disease

2 LISTEN

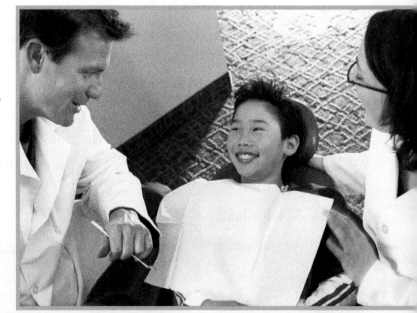

A   CD2 T56   **Listen. Ho is at the dentist's office. He just got a cleaning. What are Ho and the dentist talking about?**

a. checkups

b. flossing and brushing

c. x-rays

B   CD2 T56   **Read the questions. Then listen again. Write *T* (true) or *F* (false).**

__F__ 1. Ho flosses often.

____ 2. Ho does not brush his teeth often.

____ 3. The dentist says flossing is more important then brushing.

____ 4. If you don't floss enough, you can get cavities or gum disease.

____ 5. The dentist says a soft toothbrush is better for teeth than a hard toothbrush.

____ 6. Ho will probably brush and floss more carefully in the future.

3 CONVERSATION

CD2 T57

A 🔘 **Listen to the sentences. Then listen and repeat.**

Do you floss every day? ↗

Is it important? ↗

How often do you floss? ↘

What is a cavity? ↘

CD2 T58

B 🔘 **Listen and read the questions. Does the voice go up or down at the end? Draw arrows, ↗, or ↘, over the last word.**

1. How often do I need to get a checkup?
2. How long should I brush my teeth?
3. What is fluoride?
4. Is it important to use fluoride?

CD2 T59

C 🔘 **Listen and read the conversation.**

Dentist: You probably need to floss more. Do you floss?

Ho: Well, not that much.

Dentist: Try to floss more. Flossing keeps your gums healthy.

Ho: Isn't brushing my teeth enough?

Dentist: Brushing after every meal is important, too. But you can't always get your teeth clean unless you floss.

4 PRACTICE

PAIRS. Practice the conversation.

MAKE IT PERSONAL. PAIRS. Look at the questions in Exercise B. Quiz yourself. What do you think the answers are? Discuss. Then look at the answers below.

Answers: 1. Twice a year. 2. Two minutes. 3. a chemical in toothpaste 4. Yes it is. It stops cavities.

Talk about dental health

Grammar

Gerunds

Flossing	your teeth	is important.
Brushing		prevents cavities.

1 PRACTICE

A **Read about dental care for children. Underline the gerunds.**

For children to have healthy teeth, dental care needs to start at a very early age. Even babies get bacteria in their mouth from milk. Wiping babies' gums with a soft, damp cloth will help keep their mouths clean. Make sure not to leave a baby with a bottle in the crib, since this can damage teeth. Later, when children are pre-school age, help them to brush their teeth. Showing them how to brush their teeth is important. Brush each tooth in circles, one at a time. Giving your children more milk and serving them less juice will also keep their teeth strong.

B **Rewrite each sentence in your notebook. Start with a gerund.**

1. It's bad for your teeth to eat candy or drink soda.
   Eating candy or drinking soda is bad for your teeth.
2. It's important to brush your teeth after meals. _____
3. It's hard to get some kids to brush and floss. _____
4. It's a good idea to get a cleaning twice a year. _____
5. It's important to use toothpaste with fluoride. _____

Show what you know! Talk about dental health

GROUPS. **Talk about how to keep your teeth healthy. What things should you do? What things should you not do? Use gerunds.**

Can you... talk about dental health? ☐

Describe your eating habits

Writing

1 BEFORE YOU WRITE

A GROUPS. Is your diet different from the way it was in your native country? In what ways? Is it better or worse?

B Read Vera's description of her diet before and after coming to the United States.

> I'm from Mexico. My eating habits are different here, especially the things I eat for breakfast. Very early in the morning we always used to eat a light breakfast with sweet bread (*pan dulce*) and coffee. Later in the morning, we had a bigger breakfast, usually an egg dish. Now I eat only one breakfast—usually cereal from the box with some milk. I can't find *pan dulce* here so I hardly ever eat it—I eat white bread instead. And I eat eggs less often. The problem is, the boxed cereals have a lot of calories and white bread is not so good for you.

2 WRITE

Write a paragraph about your diet now and in your native country. Has your diet changed? What did you eat then? Now? Give examples. How do you feel about your diet now?

3 CHECK YOUR WRITING

☐ Did you give examples of your diet in your native country?

☐ Did you give examples of your diet in the United States?

☐ Did you say how you feel about your diet now?

☐ Did you check your paragraph for spelling errors?

1 REVIEW For your Grammar Review, go to page 252.

2 ACT IT OUT What do you say?

STEP 1. CLASS. **Review the conversation on page 155 (CD2 Track 54).**

STEP 2. ROLE PLAY. PAIRS. **Role play a conversation between a parent and a doctor.**

> **Student A:** You are the parent. The doctor said your children are overweight.

> **Student B:** You are the doctor. Talk about ways that Student A can get the children to be active and lead a healthy lifestyle. Talk about:
> - walking or biking to school
> - walking around the mall
> - playing outside after school on the playground
> - watching less TV
> - eating healthier snacks

3 READ AND REACT Problem-solving

STEP 1. **Read about Ana.**

Ana Mendez has two children, Kristina, who is five years old, and Daniel, who is three. Ana took Kristina to the dentist a week ago. The dentist found a cavity. Now Ana is worried about Kristina's and Daniel's teeth. Kristina drinks soda a few times a week and has dessert most evenings. Daniel likes to drink a bottle of milk in his crib. It's hard to brush their teeth because Daniel doesn't like to brush and fights hard. Kristina says she will brush her teeth if she can have a special toothbrush.

STEP 2. GROUPS. **Discuss. What is the problem? Talk about Ana's problem. What should she do? What should she stop doing?**

4 CONNECT For your Self-evaluation Activity, go to page 260.
For your Team Project, go to page 270.

Which goals can you check off? Go back to page 145.

On the Job

9

UNIT GOALS

- [ ] Ask for clarification
- [ ] Talk about health in the workplace
- [ ] Talk about expectations on the job
- [ ] Identify safety hazards at work
- [ ] Follow instructions

1   WHAT DO YOU KNOW?

A Look at the pictures and the phrases that describe job skills. Which phrases do you know?

CD3 T1

B Listen to the phrases. Listen again and repeat.

C GROUPS. What are the people doing in the pictures? Match the phrases with the pictures. Write the numbers and discuss your reasons. More than one answer is possible.

Job skills

_____ be part of a team

_____ be responsible for something

_____ deal with complaints

_____ follow instructions

_____ attend a training session

_____ give someone feedback

_____ discuss a problem

_____ train other employees

_____ give instructions

Learning Strategy

Give examples

Make five cards for job skills. Write the job skill on the front of the card. Write a job that uses that skill on the back. Example: be part of a team/fire-fighter

1

5

9

10

WORD PLAY. Look at the job skills on page 166. Then think about yourself. How good are your skills in these areas? Write next to the phrases. Write *1* for excellent, *2* for good, or *3* for needs work.

Show what you know!

STEP 1. GROUPS. Talk about your best job skills. Give examples.

I work part-time at Blooms. I think I'm good at dealing with customers, even when they complain. I know how to talk to them.

STEP 2. PROBLEM-SOLVE. What are your biggest problems on the job? Which job skills do you need to improve? How can you improve them? Ask your group for suggestions.

Listening and Speaking

1 BEFORE YOU LISTEN

A **GROUPS.** What can you do if you have trouble understanding an employer's instructions?

B Look at the words and definitions. Do you know any of these words?

inventory: a list of all the things in a place

quantity: how much you have of something

supplies: something you use for daily life or work, like paper, tape, or boxes

vendor: a person who sells something

2 LISTEN

A CD3 T2 Listen. Margo is training her assistant, Jason, to order supplies for the office kitchen. Does Jason understand Margo's instructions?

B CD3 T3 Listen again. Write *T* (true) or *F* (false).

cabinet

___T___ 1. Jason needs to do inventory before he orders supplies.

_____ 2. Doing inventory means to throw out old supplies.

_____ 3. Jason needs to use an inventory sheet to order supplies.

_____ 4. Jason needs to mail the inventory sheet.

_____ 5. Jason needs to call the vendor and talk about the order.

_____ 6. Jason does not need to check the quantity in a box.

3 CONVERSATION

We use stress to clarify which thing(s) we are talking about.

A CD3 T4 🔘 **Listen to the conversation. Then listen and repeat.**

A: Please lift this **box**.

B: **Which** box? **This** one?

A: No, **that** one. The **green** one.

B CD3 T5 🔘 **Listen and read the conversation.**

Margo: OK, you need to be sure there are enough supplies in the kitchen. First you do inventory. Start with the things on the counter. See if there are enough paper cups and paper towels. If something is missing, check in the cabinets and drawers.

Jason: OK.

Margo: If we don't have enough, you need to order more.

Jason: How do I do that?

Margo: You fill out an inventory sheet. Write down what you need under *item*. Then write the quantity or amount.

Jason: Which box shows quantity?

Margo: This one.

Jason: OK. Then what do I do?

4 PRACTICE

A PAIRS. **Practice the conversation.**

B ROLE PLAY. PAIRS. **Make up a conversation.**

Student A: You are a new school bus driver. Ask what you should do if no parent is home when you come to drop off a child.

Student B: You are the supervisor. Tell Student A steps to take:
- Never leave a child at home alone without the written permission of a parent.
- Don't drop off the child. Call the transportation office and drop off all the other children.
- If the child's parent still is not at home, take the child to the transportation office.

Grammar

One/Ones

A: Please lift this box.	**A:** Please help me move those boxes.
B: Which one? This one?	**B:** Which ones? These?
A: No, **that one**. The green **one**.	**A:** No, **those**. The big **ones**.

- Use *one* in place of a singular count noun. Use *ones* in place of plural count nouns.
- Use *one* after *this* or *that*. Do not use *ones* after *these* or *those*.
- Use *one* or *ones* after *which*.

1   PRACTICE

A   Read the conversation between a sales associate and a customer. Underline the examples of *ones*, *this one*, *those*, and *which one*.

Sales Associate:	Hi, may I help you?
Customer:	I'm looking for a T-Moby phone. Which one do you recommend?
Sales Associate:	They're all good, but this one has a lot more features.
Customer:	Are those silver phones on sale?
Sales Associate:	No, the black ones are.
Customer:	I'll take this one then.

B   Complete the conversation between a manager and an employee. Circle the correct words.

Manager:	Could you please take those DVD players out of the boxes?
Clerk:	Which **one** / (**ones**)?
Manager:	The 10-inch **one** / **ones**. We need to display them.
Clerk:	OK. Where should I put them?
Manager:	Up front near the cash register.
Clerk:	Sure. Oh, wait, Tony. This **one** / **ones** is scratched.
Manager:	Which **one** / **ones**? Show me. Oh, you're right. OK. Put it back in the box. We'll send it back. But put the other **one** / **ones** out. And put up the sale sign.
Clerk:	Which **one** / **ones** are on sale?
Manager:	The 10-inch Sonic players, but not the Panasony.

A Cross out the underlined words and write *one* or *ones*.

1. We have three orders. Which ~~order~~ *(one)* should I start with?

2. All of those customers are waiting for a table. Which <u>customers</u> should I seat first?

3. I need some mixing bowls. Would you give me the big <u>mixing bowls</u>?

4. Excuse me, this glass is dirty. Can you give me a new <u>glass</u>?

5. This towel is wet. Can you give me a dry <u>towel</u>?

6. I need two more cups. This <u>cup</u> is broken and that <u>cup</u> has lipstick on it.

B Read these sentences. Underline the correct words.

1. There are a lot of CSV pharmacies in Atlanta. I work at the **one / ones** on Buford Highway.

2. We keep batteries next to the cash register so that people can grab **the one / the ones** they need when they are checking out.

3. There are so many batteries to choose from. People ask me **which one / which ones** are the best.

4. People also want to know **which one / which ones** last longer.

5. Some batteries can be recycled. The closest recycling center is **the one / the ones** on Adamson Street.

Show what you know!   Ask for clarification

Student A: You are a supermarket manager. You received new inventory. Tell your employee where to put the boxes. Use *this, that, these,* or *those* in your request.

Student B: You are the employee. Ask questions. Find out which boxes go in which aisles.

4 Del Mante boxes	1 Downey box	5 V-9 boxes	1 Sea Spray box

A: *Put those boxes in Aisle 5.*
B: *Which ones?*
A: *The ones that say Del Mante.*

Can you...ask for clarification? ☐

Reading

1 BEFORE YOU READ

Skim the article. What do you think the article will be about?

> **Reading Skill:**
> Skimming
>
> Skimming means to look quickly over an article. Skimming helps you guess what the article will be about.

2 READ

CD3 T6

Listen and read the article.

http://www.baltimoretimes.com

| Home | Local News | National News | International News | Health Matters | Business | About Us |

Working the Late Shift

Jack sorts newspapers for a newspaper company. He has to work at night. "I have a two-year-old son, Dylan," Jack says. "When I come home, my wife has to go to work, so I stay awake all day to take care of my son. But I don't get enough sleep. I'm **exhausted** all the time."

More people than ever before work late or **irregular** shifts. They work evenings and nights in places like hospitals, restaurants, and factories. Working such hours can **harm** people's health. They become overtired or sick. It can also **interfere** with family life. But there are some ways to help **cope** with the situation:

- *Make sure your sleep is not interrupted and that you sleep at least seven hours a night.* Sleep in a dark room with the windows covered.

- *Watch what you eat and drink.* Don't drink too much caffeine at work and don't drink alcohol or eat heavy foods before you go to bed. These things make it difficult to sleep.

- *Make as much time as you can for your family.* Eat meals together whenever possible.

These days, Jack sleeps more. A relative now comes for five hours a day, and his wife changed her hours, so Jack can sleep seven hours a day. Jack spends time with his family on the weekends and at dinnertime. He **balances** his job and family life better, and everyone is happier.

A Read the article again. Circle the best main idea.

   a. Shift work is becoming a big problem in our society.

   b. Shift work has serious effects on people's health and family life.

   c. Shift work can harm your health and family life, but there are ways
      to improve the situation.

B Write *T* (true) or *F* (false). Correct the false statements.

   _____ 1. Shift work means you work irregular hours, night hours, or
              very long hours.

   _____ 2. Shift workers get sick more often than daytime workers do.

   _____ 3. Sleeping in a dark room makes it easier to rest.

   _____ 4. Shift workers should drink a lot of coffee at work to stay awake.

   _____ 5. Eating a big meal is good for a good night's sleep.

4 **VOCABULARY IN CONTEXT**

Look at the boldfaced words in the article. Guess their meanings.
Then match the words with the correct definitions.

   _____ 1. exhausted   a. to be stopped in the middle

   _____ 2. irregular   b. to not be normal; unusual

   _____ 3. harm   c. to be very tired

   _____ 4. interfere   d. to manage something, deal with something

   _____ 5. cope   e. to hurt someone or something

   _____ 6. interrupted   f. to arrange something, like your life, so it's calm

   _____ 7. balance   g. to stop something from happening in the way
                                  that is normal or planned

Show what you know! Talk about health in the workplace

PROBLEM-SOLVE. GROUPS. **Discuss. What other situations in work places
can cause stress or harm your health? What can you do?**

Can you...talk about health in the workplace? ☐

Writing

1 BEFORE YOU WRITE

GROUPS. Talk about a job. It could be your job now, a job you had in the past, or the job of a family member. What is good or bad about the job? Talk about the issues in the box or your own ideas.

> hours   job duties   manager   pay   pressure   safety/work conditions

> I work in a supermarket, in the deli section. I like my job, but I don't like my manager. He is not understanding. He always tries to make me work late hours, but I can't because I have to pick up my children from school. Last week, he asked me to work late. When I told him that I couldn't, he started to yell at me. While he was yelling, other workers were watching, and I felt very bad.

2 WRITE

Write a paragraph about the job you discussed. What is good or bad about the job?

3 CHECK YOUR WRITING

- ☐ Did you tell what the job is?
- ☐ Did you explain what is good or bad about the job?
- ☐ Did you write your feelings about the job?
- ☐ Did you indent your paragraph?
- ☐ Did you check the spelling and grammar?

Talk about expectations on the job

Listening and Speaking

1 BEFORE YOU LISTEN

CLASS. **What do employers expect from employees? What do employees expect? What is most important to you at a job?**

2 LISTEN

CD3 T7

A Listen. Carl works in real estate. His boss gets information about buildings and gives it to banks. Do you think Carl and his boss have a good relationship? Why or why not?

CD3 T7

B Read the questions. Then listen again. Write *T* (true) or *F* (false).

_____ 1. Tony didn't have time to finish a job.

_____ 2. Carl can't get to the building.

_____ 3. Tony will take photographs of a building.

_____ 4. Carl is going to finish Tony's report.

_____ 5. The report is due on Friday.

CD3 T7

C Read the questions. Then listen again. Circle the correct answers.

1. What does Carl want to do next Friday?
   a. Take the day off.   b. Leave early.

2. Why does Carl make the request?
   a. It's his son's birthday.   b. It's his son's graduation.

3. What does Bill mean when he says, "I don't see why not"?
   a. It's OK.   b. It's not OK.

D MAKE IT PERSONAL. GROUPS. **Discuss. In the United States many employers want employees to call them by their first name. Is it the same in your country, or different? Which way is more comfortable for you?**

Grammar

Verb + Object + Infinitive				
Subject	**Verb**	**Object**	**Infinitive**	
Bill	needs	Carl	to do	this job.
He	would like	me	to finish	the job today.
She	expects	us	not to come	late.

········· **Grammar Watch**

• With verb + object + infinitive, the object can be a noun or pronoun.

1 PRACTICE

A Read the conversation. Then answer the questions. Write *T* (true) or *F* (false).

Fei Yen: John, do you think you can work late tonight? Of course you'll get paid overtime.

John: I think so. Can I make a phone call first?

_____ 1. Fei Yen wants John to work overtime.

_____ 2. Fei Yen wants to know if John can pay her overtime.

_____ 3. John expects Fei Yen to pay him overtime.

B Complete the conversation. Unscramble the sentences.

A: Joe, I need to ask you a favor. _____ for
(to work / someone / need / I)
me June 14th. My sister is getting married. Can you work then?

B: Sure. _____ for you any other day?
(do / me / to cover / need / you)

A: Just then. _____ for you sometime?
(to work / like / me / you / would)

B: How about Friday the 21st? I want to go away for the weekend?

Can you work then?

A: Oh no, I'm sorry, I can't. _____ her parents
(to pick up / needs / me / my wife)
from the airport that day.

Read the complaints from restaurant servers. Then complete the sentences.

Tanya: We have to wear a uniform in my restaurant. I hate the uniform, but my boss says we all have to look alike. Do you have to wear one?

Renata: No, but we sing when it's a customer's birthday. I have a terrible voice, and I really don't like to sing.

Rob: We have to work on holidays because that's when the restaurant is the busiest.

Ardiana: I have to work on Friday and Saturday nights.

1. Tanya's boss expects _____

2. Renata's boss wants _____

3. Rob's boss expects _____

4. Ardiana's boss requires _____

Show what you know! Talk about expectations on the job

PROBLEM-SOLVE. GROUPS. **Discuss the situations. What should the people do?**

1. My employer expects me to stay late almost every day. He doesn't pay me for the overtime. When I complain, he seems annoyed.

2. My employer expects us to work as a team. I'm better and faster than the other employees. I don't want to work with a team. I want to work alone. Should I tell my employer?

Can you...talk about expectations on the job? ☐

Life Skills

1 READ SAFETY INSTRUCTIONS

CLASS. Read the safety poster. Talk about words you don't know.

Safety is very important on the job. Companies often display safety rules for their employees.

Blackman Company Safety Rules

Attention employees: Be aware of safety hazards. Follow the safety procedures.

Prevent Slips, Trips, and Falls.
- Always clean up the work area.
- Make sure wires and equipment are kept out of the way.
- Use caution when walking on wet or slippery floors.
- Wear non-slip shoes.

Operate Machinery Carefully.
- Turn off machinery before cleaning or repairing.
- Turn off machinery when not in use.
- Wear eye protection (goggles) or a face shield.
- Keep hands at a safe distance from machinery.
- Do not wear loose fitting clothes or long sleeves when operating machines.

2 PRACTICE

A PAIRS. What is the main idea of the safety poster?

a. Be careful of machinery.
b. Put away all equipment.
c. Prevent accidents and injuries.

B Answer the questions. Write *T* (true) or *F* (false).

_____ 1. Workers can wear most kinds of shoes.

_____ 2. When workers take breaks, they should not turn off machinery.

_____ 3. Machines need to be turned off when you clean them.

_____ 4. Workers need to protect their eyes.

_____ 5. Loose fitting clothes are dangerous because they can get caught in machines.

3 IDENTIFY SAFETY HAZARDS

A PAIRS. **Match the danger with the accident that might happen.**

_c_ 1. There is a wire on the floor.

____ 2. A can of paint has just spilled on the floor.

____ 3. There are too many boxes on a high shelf.

____ 4. A large knife has been left on the worktable.

____ 5. Those workers are using a table saw without goggles.

____ 6. A man using a machine has loose clothing.

a. You could cut yourself with it.

b. It might get caught in the machine.

~~c. You might trip.~~

d. They might fall on someone.

e. You might slip.

f. They could injure their eyes.

B CLASS. **Talk about the safety signs. What do they mean? Have you ever seen them at a worksite? Where did you see them?**

C GROUPS. **Look at the workplaces in the box. Choose one. What safety hazards do you think you might find there? Discuss.**

> construction sites   factories   hospitals   hotels   restaurants

Can you... identify safety hazards at work? ☐

Respond appropriately to correction

Listening and Speaking

1 BEFORE YOU LISTEN

Have you ever made a mistake at work? What happened? Why did it happen? What did your boss say to you? How did you answer?

2 LISTEN

CD3 T8

A Listen. Margo, the office manager, is talking to Jason, a new office assistant. What is the problem?

CD3 T8

B Read the statements. Then listen again. Write *T* (true) or *F* (false).

__T__ 1. The copy machine next to Mr. Yang's office is not working.

_____ 2. Jason checked all of the copy machines in the morning.

_____ 3. Margo did not tell Jason to check the copy machines.

_____ 4. When the machines are broken, Margo can always fix them.

_____ 5. Jason apologizes to Margo.

C PAIRS. Discuss your opinion. Did Margo correct Jason in a good way? Did Jason respond the right way? Why or why not?

3 **CONVERSATION**

A Listen and read the conversation.

Margo: Jason, Mr. Yang just called me. He told me that the copy machine next to his office isn't working.

Jason: It isn't?

Margo: That's right. Did you check all the copy machines and printers this morning?

Jason: Well, I checked almost all of them, but maybe I forgot about that one. I'm sorry.

Margo: OK, Jason. I know you're new here. But remember: You need to check all of the copy machines and printers first thing when you come in. We need to make sure they're working. If there's a problem, we need to fix it. If we can't fix it, we have to call service repair.

Jason: I understand, Margo. I'll make sure it doesn't happen again.

Margo: OK, very good.

4 **PRACTICE**

A PAIRS. Practice the conversation.

B ROLE PLAY. PAIRS. Make conversations based on the situations.

Student A: You are the employer. Tell the employee something he or she did wrong. Use the situations or your own ideas.

Student B: You are the employee. Use one of the apologies. Then change roles.

Situations
Your employee forgot to give you a message.
Your employee made too many personal calls at work.
Your employee didn't wear his or her safety equipment.

Apologies
I'm sorry. I'll do better next time.
I'm sorry. It won't happen again.
I'm sorry. I'll do it over.

Follow instructions

Grammar

Reported speech: commands and requests with *tell/ask*

Direct Speech		Reported Speech
Check the printers.	→	The manager **told me to check the printers**.
Please call service repair.	→	The manager **asked me to call service repair**.
Don't come late again.	→	She **told him not to come late again**.

Grammar Watch

When you change direct speech to reported speech, make sure to change pronouns and possessives.

He said to Maria, "Please take my calls." He asked **her** to take **his** calls.

1 PRACTICE

CD3 T10

A Read and listen to a phone message. What does the caller want? Circle the correct answer.

> Hello, Boris? This is Richard. Listen, I left a phone number on the pad on my desk in the back. Could you check if it's there and get me the number? Thanks. My number here is 890-555-4567.

a. Boris asked Richard to leave a number for him.
b. Richard asked Boris to give him his phone number.
c. Richard asked Boris to call him and give him a phone number.

B Unscramble the sentences. Then write them in your notebook.

1. Mr. Kwang / the employees / to set up the display / told

2. asked / to check that all items have prices / them / he

3. warned / he / not / to come late / them

4. he / to recycle the papers / them / told

5. them / expected / he / to work late

6. they / him / asked / to explain / the time-off policy

Read the questions and statements. Rewrite the statements. Use reported speech and pronouns.

1. What did Mr. Lan tell Alex? ("Restock the batteries.")

   Mr. Lan told him to restock the batteries.

2. What did Ms. Alvarado ask Marta to do? ("Please check my work.")

3. What did Ms. Kahn tell Joe? ("Replace the products that we sold.")

4. What did Ms. Rice ask Jen to do? ("Please work the register today.)

5. What did Mr. Smith say to Bob and Leticia? ("Don't worry about the store window.")

6. What did Mr. Lan say to Susan? ("Don't make so many personal calls at work.")

Show what you know! Follow instructions

STEP 1. GROUPS OF 3. Choose a workplace you know well from the box or from your own experience.

construction site   hospital   office   restaurant   store   warehouse

STEP 2. ROLE PLAY. Make a conversation about the workplace you chose.

Student A: You are the manager. Give your employee instructions.

Student B: You are the employee. Ask questions to make sure you understand.

Student C: Take notes. Write down every instruction you hear.

A: *Put the boxes in the storage room.*

STEP 3. Student C: Report to the class. Tell the class what Student A said. Use reported speech.

C: *Elena told Amir to put the boxes in the storage room.*

Can you...follow instructions? ☐

1 **REVIEW**   For your Grammar Review, go to page 253.

2 **ACT IT OUT**   What do you say?

STEP 1. CLASS. Review the conversation on page 181 (CD3 Track 9).

STEP 2. ROLE PLAY. PAIRS. Role play the situation below.

> **Student A:** You are the manager. Your assistant forgot to order inventory for the kitchen. Now there is no coffee and no paper towels. The employees at the company are complaining. Talk to your assistant.

> **Student B:** You are the employee. On Friday, you forgot to order inventory. Listen to your boss and apologize.

3 **READ AND REACT**   Problem-solving

STEP 1. GROUPS. Read about Maya. Maya's boss never says nice things about her work. He only complains when she makes a mistake. When she forgets to do something, he gets very angry and shouts at her. Maya is a hard worker who doesn't make many mistakes. She likes her job and the money is good, but she really doesn't like her boss.

STEP 2. GROUPS. Discuss. What is the problem? Give Maya advice. What can she say to her boss the next time he criticizes her?

4 **CONNECT**   For your Self-evaluation Activity, go to page 261.
For your Team Project, go to page 271.

Which goals can you check off? Go back to page 165.

Going to the Doctor

10

Preview

Have you ever been to a hospital in the United States? What experiences have you or your family had with hospitals or doctors?

UNIT GOALS

- [ ] Recognize hospital departments
- [ ] Reschedule a doctor's appointment
- [ ] Talk about feelings about doctors
- [ ] Identify parts of the body
- [ ] Read and interpret health history forms
- [ ] Talk about symptoms
- [ ] Talk about immunizations
- [ ] Talk about medical procedures and concerns

1 WHAT DO YOU KNOW?

A Look at the pictures. The words describe departments or places in a hospital. Which words do you know?

B Match the pictures with the words. Write the numbers.

Places in a hospital

_____ admissions

_____ emergency room (ER)

_____ intensive care unit (ICU)

_____ laboratory

_____ maternity ward

_____ nurse's station

_____ pediatrics

_____ physical therapy

_____ radiology/imaging

_____ surgery

CD3 T11

C Listen and check your answers. Then listen and repeat.

Learning Strategy

Make connections

Make cards for five places in a hospital. Write the place on the front of the card. Write what patients do there on the back. Example: laboratory/get a blood test

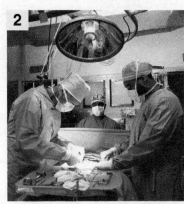

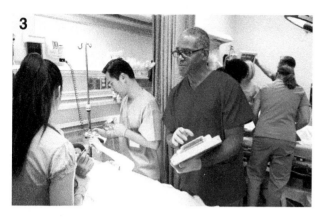

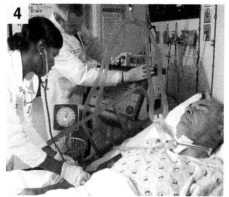

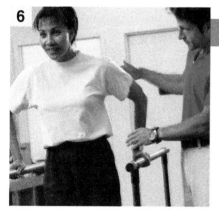

WORD PLAY. **Look at the telephone numbers. Then read the situations. Write the telephone numbers you should dial.**

ER	7790	ICU	9089
ADMISSIONS	8790	LABORATORY	9091
RADIOLOGY	7450	CLINIC	9087

1. You had surgery and need a follow-up appointment. You dial ___9087___.

2. Your cousin had a heart attack. She's in serious condition. You want to find out visiting hours. You dial _____.

3. You want to schedule an appointment for a chest X-ray. You dial _____.

4. You need to schedule some blood tests before an operation. You dial _____.

5. Your uncle went to the emergency room two hours ago. You want to find out if the doctor has seen him yet. You dial _____.

Show what you know!

GROUPS. **Discuss. Which places in hospitals have you been in or visited?**

Can you...recognize hospital departments? ☐

Reschedule a doctor's appointment

Listening and Speaking

1 BEFORE YOU LISTEN

What are your biggest problems with making or going to doctor's appointments? Discuss the ideas in the box.

inconvenient office hours
long waiting time on the phone
waiting a long time for an appointment
waiting a long time in the clinic

2 LISTEN

CD3 T12

A Yao Chen is talking to a medical receptionist. Listen and circle the correct answers.

1. Mr. Chen is calling _____.
   a. to make an appointment
   b. to cancel an appointment
   c. to speak to the doctor

2. Mr. Chen wants to see the doctor _____.
   a. on Thursday at 3:00
   b. on Friday at 3:00
   c. today at 4:00

CD3 T13

B Another patient, Ms. Ledesma, calls the medical receptionist. Read the statements. Then listen. Circle the correct answers.

1. Ms. Ledesma wants to get an appointment for _____.
   a. today at 4:00
   b. today at 5:00
   c. Thursday at 5:00

2. Ms. Ledesma's problem is _____.
   a. she's sleeping too much
   b. she can't sleep and she's tired
   c. she isn't hungry

3. The receptionist _____.
   a. gave Mr. Chen an appointment
   b. gave Mr. Chen's appointment to Ms. Ledesma
   c. did not find a good time for Ms. Ledesma to come in

3 CONVERSATION

Pronunciation Watch

We pronounce the –ed ending as an extra syllable only after the sounds /t/ and /d/.

CD3 T14

A **Listen to the words. Notice the sound of the -ed ending. Then listen and repeat.**

One syllable	Extra syllables
book*ed* = /t/	frustrat*ed* = /ɪd/
confus*ed* = /d/	remind*ed* = /ɪd/

CD3 T15

B **Say the words to yourself. Write the words in the correct columns. Then listen and check your answers.**

> bored   exhausted   shocked   embarrassed   worried

-ed = /t/	*-ed* = /d/	*-ed* = extra syllable /ɪd/

CD3 T16

C **Listen and read the conversation.**

Office Assistant: Hello, Westside Health Center.

Mr. Chen: Hi. This is Yao Chen. I have an appointment with Dr. Barnes for today at 4:00, but I need to cancel.

Office Assistant: OK, Mr. Chen. Would you like to reschedule?

Mr. Chen: Yes, I would. Can I come in next Thursday at 3:00?

Office Assistant: Sorry, we're all booked. How about Friday at 3:00?

Mr. Chen: I think that's OK.

4 PRACTICE

A PAIRS. **Practice the conversation.**

B ROLE PLAY. PAIRS. **Make a similar conversation. Cancel and reschedule an appointment with a doctor. Change the names, days, and times.**

Can you...reschedule a doctor's appointment?   ☐

Talk about feelings about doctors

Grammar

Participial Adjectives

Vito is **confused**.

The instructions are **confusing**.

Grammar Watch

• Participial adjectives end with *-ing* or *-ed*.

• Use *-ing* for someone or something that causes a feeling.

• Use *-ed* for the person who has the feeling.

• Some adjectives do not have an *-ing* form, or we do not use the *-ing* form often. For example: *relieved, stressed, tired,* and *worried*.

• See page 287 for a list of common participial adjectives.

1 PRACTICE

A **Circle the *-ed* forms. Underline the *-ing* forms.**

1. I'm worried about my health because I haven't seen a doctor for a few years.

2. The hospital has so many departments and floors that I get confused and don't know where to go.

3. It's frustrating when you have to wait months for an appointment.

B **Complete the sentences with the correct words from the box.**

> frightening   frustrating   relieved   stressed   tiring

1. I'm really _____. The hospital charged me $900 for that operation.

2. I was _____. The clinic didn't charge me for that visit.

3. It's _____ when I try to make a doctor's appointment. The doctor's office is closed evenings so I have trouble calling.

4. My son thinks that doctors are _____. He cries when he sees them.

5. It's _____ to wait a long time for the doctor. Sometimes I fall asleep in the waiting room.

A Circle the correct word.

1. I had to wait in the ER for hours before the doctor could see me. It was very **bored / boring** to stay there so long.

2. Everyone was **shocked / shocking** to hear that Luz's uncle had cancer.

3. Lately I've been **exhausted / exhausting**. I hope I'm not sick.

4. It's really **frustrated / frustrating** when I go to Greenville Clinic. The doctors never have time to explain anything.

5. I'm **frustrated / frustrating** because the doctors never seem to understand what I'm saying.

6. I don't like going to the doctor because I'm **embarrassed / embarrassing** when I take my clothes off.

B Complete the questions. Use the *-ed* or *-ing* form of the verbs.

1. Do you feel like doctors are _____ in you and care about your health? (interest)

2. Is it _____ for you to make doctor appointments? (frustrate)

3. Are you _____ to have a doctor of the opposite sex? (embarrass)

4. Are you often _____ when you talk to doctors? (confuse)

5. Do you think that hospitals are _____? (frighten)

6. Are you often _____ about medical bills? (worry)

Show what you know!   Talk about feelings about doctors

GROUPS. **Discuss. Talk about experiences with doctors and hospitals in the United States. Use some of the questions in Exercise B and your own ideas.**

A: *Have you ever been confused by a doctor?*
B: *Yes, I have. Once the doctor said, "Say, 'Ah.' " I didn't understand. He repeated it and I thought he was strange. Then he spoke slowly and said, "I want you to open your mouth and say, 'Ah' ". Finally I understood, and he was able to examine my throat.*

Can you...talk about feelings about doctors? ☐

Life Skills

1   IDENTIFY PARTS OF THE BODY

A GROUPS. **Look at the diagram of the human body. Write the number of the part of the body next to the word that describes it. Look at page 281 if you need help.**

_____ bladder

_____ brain

_____ esophagus

_____ gall bladder

_____ heart

_____ kidneys

_____ liver

_____ lungs

_____ large intestine (colon)

_____ muscles

_____ small intestine

_____ stomach

B CLASS. **Compare your answers.**

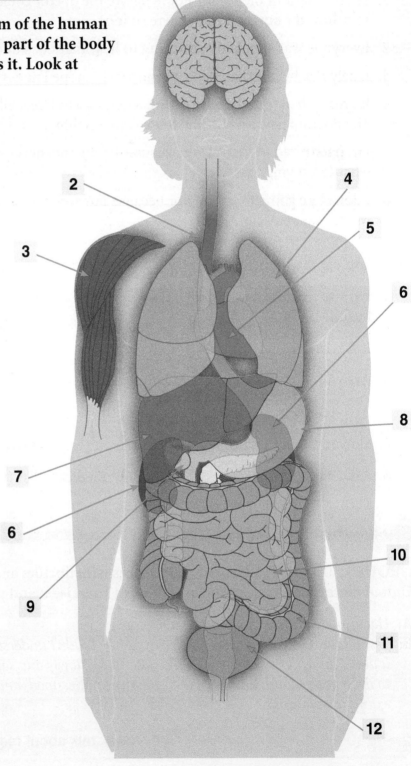

A CLASS. **Read the medical history form. Discuss new words.**

MEDICAL HISTORY FORM _____

Patient Name __Rostov, Natasha__   Today's Date ____3/24/10____

Have you been under a doctor's care in the last two years?   ☑ Yes ☐ No
If yes, for what? __High blood pressure__

Have you ever been hospitalized, had a major operation,
or a serious illness?   ☐ Yes ☑ No
If yes, for what? _____

Have you taken any medications during the past year?   ☑ Yes ☐ No
If so, what medicine? __High blood pressure medicine__

Do you have any allergic reaction to any medication?   ☐ Yes ☑ No
If yes, please list _____

Do you have any of these conditions? Check (✔) Yes or No.

Heart (disease)	☐ Yes	☑ No	Asthma	☐ Yes	☑ No
Chest pain	☑ Yes	☐ No	Allergies	☐ Yes	☑ No
High blood pressure	☑ Yes	☐ No	AIDS	☐ Yes	☑ No
Stroke	☐ Yes	☑ No	HIV	☐ Yes	☑ No
Diabetes (Type 1/Type 2)	☐ Yes	☑ No	Emphysema	☐ Yes	☑ No
Cancer	☐ Yes	☑ No	Tuberculosis	☐ Yes	☑ No

B PAIRS. **Discuss the questions about the form.**

1. What health problems does Natasha have now?

2. What medications is Natasha using?

3. Why does the form ask about allergic reactions to medications?

C **Turn to page 282. Complete the medical history form about yourself.**

*Can you...*identify parts of the body?   ☐

Talk about symptoms

Listening and Speaking

1 BEFORE YOU LISTEN

When you go to a doctor, what questions does the doctor usually ask you? How much time does he or she spend with you? Do you usually come with questions for the doctor?

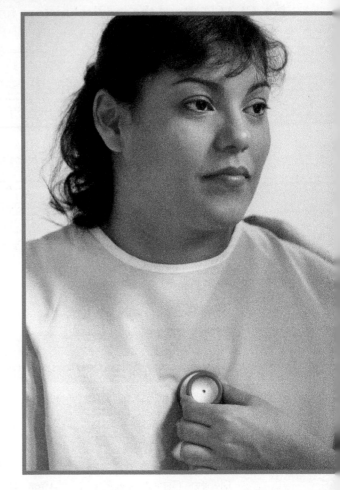

2 LISTEN

CD3 T17

A Ms. Ledesma is seeing Dr. Barnes. Listen to the first part of the conversation. What does the doctor ask her to do?

CD3 T17

B Read the statements about Ms. Ledesma. Then listen again. Write *T* (true) or *F* (false).

_____ 1. She has trouble sleeping at night.

_____ 2. She has lost some weight.

_____ 3. When she comes home, she is very tired.

_____ 4. She has stress at work.

_____ 5. She does not like to weigh herself.

CD3 T18

C Read the statements. Listen to the rest of the conversation. Circle the correct answers.

1. Dr. Barnes thinks the problem with Ms. Ledesma is _____.
   a. high blood pressure   b. heart disease   c. high cholesterol

2. Dr. Barnes tells Ms. Ledesma to _____.
   a. sleep more
   b. stop medication
   c. eat healthy and exercise

3. Dr. Barnes doesn't like to give medication because it often _____.
   a. makes patients sleep too much
   b. makes patients gain weight
   c. is not necessary

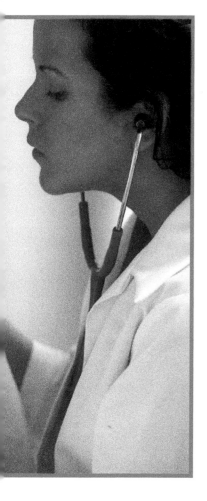

3 CONVERSATION

Pronunciation Watch

Stressed syllables take longer to say than unstressed syllables. The time it takes to say a sentence depends on how many stressed syllables there are.

CD3 T19

A Listen to the sentences. Notice that the length of time to say the sentences is the same. Then listen and repeat.

Work hard.   She's working hard.   She's been working hard.

CD3 T20

B Listen and read the conversation.

Dr. Barnes: Good afternoon, Ms. Ledesma. What seems to be the problem?

Ms. Ledesma: I feel terrible. I haven't been sleeping well. I fall asleep and I wake up after a couple of hours.

Dr. Barnes: Hmm. Anything else?

Ms. Ledesma: Well, I've been trying to lose weight like you said, but I can't. I come home exhausted, and I eat too much.

Dr. Barnes: Is anything bothering you?

Ms. Ledesma: My job. They fired two people last month, so the rest of us have been working twice as hard.

4 PRACTICE

A PAIRS. Practice the conversation.

B MAKE IT PERSONAL. GROUPS. Talk about different times when you or a family member was sick. Did you have the symptoms in the box or other symptoms? What did you do? Did you go to the doctor? Did you go to the emergency room?

chest pains or neck pain	loss of appetite
coughing	nausea
fatigue	shortness of breath
high fever	weight loss

Talk about symptoms

Grammar

Present Perfect Continuous				
	Have/Has	*Not*	*Been*	*Verb + -ing*
He / She The medicine	**has**	not	**been**	**working.**
I / We / They	**have**			

······ **Grammar Watch**

We use the present perfect continuous to show that the action began in the past and is still continuing.

1 PRACTICE

A **A nurse is teaching some students about diabetes symptoms. Underline the examples of the present perfect continuous.**

My patient is a 40-year-old male. He has been losing weight. He says that lately he's been very thirsty and tired. His wife says he hasn't been watching his diet, and he hasn't been exercising much. I think he may have type 2 diabetes. Fortunately, this can usually be controlled with diet, exercise, or medicine.

B **Complete the sentences. Use the present perfect continuous and the verbs in parentheses.**

1. My uncle _____ chest pains.
   (have)

2. My husband _____ for the past two weeks.
   (cough)

3. I _____ with sharp pains in my stomach.
   (wake up)

4. My son is 12 years old. For the last week, he _____ about leg pains.
   (complain)

5. My sister _____ a high fever.
   (run)

Ms. Lesdema is seeing her doctor again. Complete the conversation. Use the present perfect continuous.

Dr. Finkel: Good afternoon, Ms. Lesdema. How _____ since
(you / do)
I saw you last?

Ms. Lesdema: _____ chest pain. And I have trouble breathing
(I / feel)
when I walk.

Dr. Finkel: Hmm. Well, _____? You said you were going to quit.
(you / smoke)

Ms. Lesdema: No, _____. I gave it up.
(I / not / smoke)

Dr. Finkel: And _____ your high blood pressure medication?
(you / take)

Ms. Lesdema: Yes, I have. Every day. And _____ two times a week.
(I / exercise)

Dr. Finkel: Good. But try to exercise four times a week. It's important.

And _____ your diet? _____ salty
(you / watch)   (you / stay away from)
foods and alcohol?

Ms. Lesdema: Well, _____ any alcohol and _____ chips.
(I / not / drink)   (I / not / eat)

Show what you know!   Talk about symptoms

GET READY. **High blood pressure and high cholesterol can cause heart disease, a heart attack, or a stroke.**

ROLE PLAY. PAIRS. **Pretend you are a doctor and patient.**

Student A: You are a doctor. Your patient has high cholesterol. Ask how your patient has been doing. Has the patient been:

- exercising
- eating fruit and vegetables
- eating fewer eggs, less butter
- eating whole grains
- taking medication

Student B: Answer the doctor's questions. Then change roles.

Can you...talk about symptoms? ☐

Reading

1 BEFORE YOU READ

GROUPS. Discuss. What does it mean if you are immune to a disease?
Why is immunization important for children?

2 READ

CD3 T21

Listen and read the web page. Was your answer in Before You Read correct?

http://www.mayaclinic.com

Immunizations FAQ

| Home | About Us | Services | New Studies | Clinics |

Fifty years ago, many children got sick or died every year from diseases like measles. Today, children in the United States almost never get these diseases because they get vaccinated with shots. Every year, these immunizations protect millions of children from deadly illnesses.

What kinds of diseases do children get shots for?
Today, most children get nine **vaccinations** that protect them against thirteen different diseases. These include rubella, measles, mumps, diphtheria, chicken pox, and polio.

Can my child get a disease from the shots?
No. **Vaccines** don't give your child the disease. Your child might have a mild reaction to a shot. For example, he or she might get a slight fever—but only for a day or two.

I don't have insurance. Can I get these shots for free?
Yes. Special programs like the Vaccines for Children (VFC) give free vaccines to children without Medicaid or other insurance. Most family doctors **participate** in VFC. If your doctor doesn't participate, he or she can tell you where to go.

When do my children need to get the vaccines?
Children get different vaccines at different ages. For some immunizations, children need only one **dose** of the vaccine. Other immunizations **require** two or three doses. Your doctor will give you a schedule for your child's shots and go over it with you. Make sure your children have had all their shots before the first day of school. Most children need

to show proof of immunization before they can start school.

What happens if my child misses an appointment for a shot?
Your doctor can still give your child the next shot. But be sure the doctor's office has your address, and let them know if you move. Then they can remind you when it's time for the next shots. Remember, all the information you give to your doctor is **confidential**. The doctor will not tell anyone else your information.

Immunizations are important both for your child's health and for the health of your community.

3 CHECK YOUR UNDERSTANDING

A Read the article again. Circle the main idea.

a. Immunizations are dangerous for children.

b. Immunizations keep children safe from diseases.

c. Immunizations aren't available to many children.

B Write *T* (true) or *F* (false).

____ 1. When children get a vaccine, they sometimes get a low fever.

____ 2. If a family doesn't have insurance, the children can't get their shots.

____ 3. Children get all their vaccines at the same time.

____ 4. If your children don't get vaccines, they are at risk for certain diseases.

> **Reading Skill:**
> Interpreting Graphics
>
> Looking at graphics like titles and headings help you to understand what an article is about.

C PAIRS. Look at the headings in boldface in the article. What questions are asked?

4 VOCABULARY IN CONTEXT

Look at the boldfaced words in the article. Guess their meanings. Then complete the sentences with the correct words.

1. _Vaccines/Vaccinations_ are shots that make you immune to diseases.

2. For some vaccines your child needs to receive more than one _____.

3. Doctors are not allowed to tell anyone your information without your permission.
Your information is _____.

4. Some doctors don't belong to the VCF program. But most _____.

5. Schools _____ students to get vaccinated.

6. Most children do not get a serious _____ to shots.

Show what you know! Talk about immunizations

GROUPS. Discuss. What can parents do if they have a young child who is afraid of getting shots? How can they make the child feel better?

Can you...talk about immunizations? ☐

Write about an experience with a doctor

Writing

1 BEFORE YOU WRITE

A GROUPS. Discuss. Talk about an experience you or your family had with a doctor or at the hospital.

B Tetanus is a dangerous disease. You can get tetanus when you cut yourself. Read Drew's story.

> Once I was working on a construction site. I cut my hand badly and I had to go to the emergency room. They took care of my hand and gave me some medicine. Then the nurse asked me if I had ever had a tetanus shot. I hadn't, so she told me I had to get one. When she said that, I felt sick. I don't like getting shots even though I'm 6 feet tall and 220 pounds. I looked away from the nurse. She put something cold on my arm. Then she said she was done! I was surprised. I didn't feel any pain at all. I was happy and relieved it was over.

2 WRITE

Write a paragraph about a visit to a doctor or a hospital. Write about yourself or about someone you know. Why were you there? What happened?

3 CHECK YOUR WRITING

☐ Did you explain the reason for the visit to the doctor or hospital?

☐ Did you say what happened?

☐ Did you say how you felt during or after the visit?

☐ Did you indent your paragraph?

☐ Did you check for spelling and grammar?

Talk about medical procedures and concerns

Listening and Speaking

1 BEFORE YOU LISTEN

GROUPS. Discuss. Most people worry before a hospital stay. What are common worries?

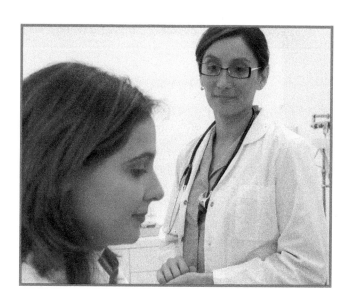

2 LISTEN

CD3 T22

A Listen to a conversation between a patient and a doctor. Why is Mrs. Garcia talking to the doctor? Circle the correct answer.

a. She wants to lose weight.

b. She's going to have an operation.

c. She's been sad and depressed.

CD3 T22

B Read the questions. Then listen again. Write *T* (true) or *F* (false).

_____ 1. The doctor is worried about Mrs. Garcia.

_____ 2. Mrs. Garcia is worried about having an operation.

_____ 3. Mrs. Garcia is worried her family will have a hard time when she is away from home.

_____ 4. Mrs. Garcia is stressed because she will miss work.

CD3 T22

C Read the questions. Then listen again. Circle the correct answers.

1. What does the doctor suggest? Mrs. Garcia should call _____.
   a. a relative or friend   b. her neighbor   c. her employer

2. Mrs. Garcia is afraid to ask some of her relatives for help because _____.
   a. they aren't healthy   b. they're busy   c. they don't want to help

3. What is Mrs. Garcia's solution? She is going to ask her _____ for help.
   a. sister   b. cousin   c. friend

Talk about medical procedures and concerns

Grammar

Preposition + Gerund			
I'm	worried	**about**	**missing** work.

Grammar Watch

- Prepositions are words like *in, of, to, at, about,* and *on.*
- Common expressions with gerunds: *be afraid of, believe in, complain about, think about.*

1 PRACTICE

A Read the paragraph. Find the prepositions + gerunds. Circle the prepositions. Underline the gerunds.

Before a hospital visit people are often nervous about different things. Most people are nervous (about) being away from their family. People are often afraid of being in pain and they are concerned about missing work. Often people are worried about paying for the medication they need after a visit. But these days, hospital stays are often short, doctors are well trained, and there are excellent pain medications.

B Unscramble the sentences. Write the words in the correct order. Write them in your notebook.

1. not / looking forward / to / taking / that blood test / I'm
2. he's / on / getting / for his family / planning / health insurance
3. my cousin / is / paying for an operation / worried / about
4. some people / complaining / are / about / getting sick at that hospital
5. thinking about / most doctors are / giving their patients / the best care that they can
6. some people / but I think they're important / don't believe in / checkups / getting

PRACTICE

Look at the website from the Maya Clinic. Patients write questions for the medical staff. Complete the sentences. Add the correct prepositions and the gerund form of the verbs in parentheses.

⊗ ◯ ⊕ ◀ ▶ ↻ http://www.mayaclinic.com   ?

Maya Clinic

About Us | Services | Join | Message Boards | Newletter

Frequently Asked Questions

Q: I'm afraid ___of getting___ heart disease. How do I know if I am at risk?
                1 (get)

A: Common risk factors for heart disease are high blood pressure, high cholesterol, smoking, and being overweight.

Q: I'm worried _____ heart disease because my father had it. Is it true it runs
                        2 (get)
   in families?

A: Yes, heart disease can run in families. That does not mean you will get it. You need to watch your diet, exercise, and see a doctor regularly.

Q: I want to make sure I'm healthy and don't get breast cancer. I'm thinking

    _____ mammogram. Can I get one for free?
     3 (have)

A: Yes, there are some clinics that give them for free. Call 1-800-4-CANCER.

Q: My husband complains _____ tired all the time. I want him to go see the
                     4 (be)

   doctor, but he doesn't believe _____ medicine. He's not afraid
                      5 (take)

   _____ sick, but I'm afraid for him. We have two little children.
     6 (become)

A: Tell him he needs to see the doctor. If he doesn't want to go, tell him it's important for your children.

Show what you know!   Talk about medical procedures and concerns

GROUPS. Talk about health matters that you are afraid of, worry about, think about, complain about, plan on, or believe in.

Can you... talk about medical procedures and concerns? ☐

1 REVIEW   For your Grammar Review, go to page 254.

2 ACT IT OUT   What do you say?

STEP 1. CLASS. Review the conversations on page 195 (CD3 track 20) and page 197.

STEP 2. ROLE PLAY. PAIRS. Make up a conversation between a doctor and patient.

> **Student A:** You are a patient. You are seeing a doctor for a follow-up appointment. You haven't been taking your blood pressure medication. You haven't quit smoking, and you still eat salty foods like chips. You really don't like exercise.

> **Student B:** You are a doctor. You told your patient to quit smoking and stop eating salty foods. You prescribed high blood pressure medication during the last visit and told your patient to exercise four times a week. You just tested your patient's blood pressure, and it's gotten worse. Ask your patient questions. Has he or she followed your advice? Tell your patient how important a healthy lifestyle is.

3 READ AND REACT   Problem-solving

STEP 1. **Read about Hilda and Federico.**

Hilda Garcia's husband, Federico, has diabetes. His doctor prescribed medication. Federico is supposed to exercise and check his blood sugar every day. The doctor also told him not to eat foods with a lot of sugar. Lately Hilda noticed Federico is in a very bad mood. When she was hanging up his coat, she found candy bar wrappers in the pocket. She realized he has been eating candy bars, even though the doctor told him not to. Hilda is very concerned.

STEP 2. GROUPS. **What is the problem? Talk about Hilda's problem. What can she do?**

4 CONNECT   For your Community-building Activity, go to page 261.
For your Team Project, go to page 272.

> Which goals can you check off? Go back to page 185.

Money Matters

Preview

Do you use a bank?
Why or why not?
How do you usually
pay big bills?

UNIT GOALS

- [ ] Use bank services wisely
- [ ] Talk about uses and risks of credit cards
- [ ] Budget expenses
- [ ] Read utility bills and save money on utilities
- [ ] Talk about housing

1　WHAT DO YOU KNOW?

A Look at the pictures and words. The words describe money and banking. Which words do you know?

B Match the pictures with the words. Write the numbers.

Money and banking

_____ ATM/debit card

_____ ATM withdrawal

_____ balance

_____ bank statement

_____ bank teller

_____ check

_____ credit card

_____ deposit slip

_____ transaction register

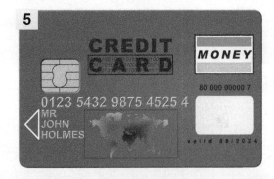

C CD3 T23　Listen and check your answers. Then listen and repeat.

Learning Strategy

Use context

Make cards for five words. Write the word on the front of the card. Write a sentence using the word on the back.

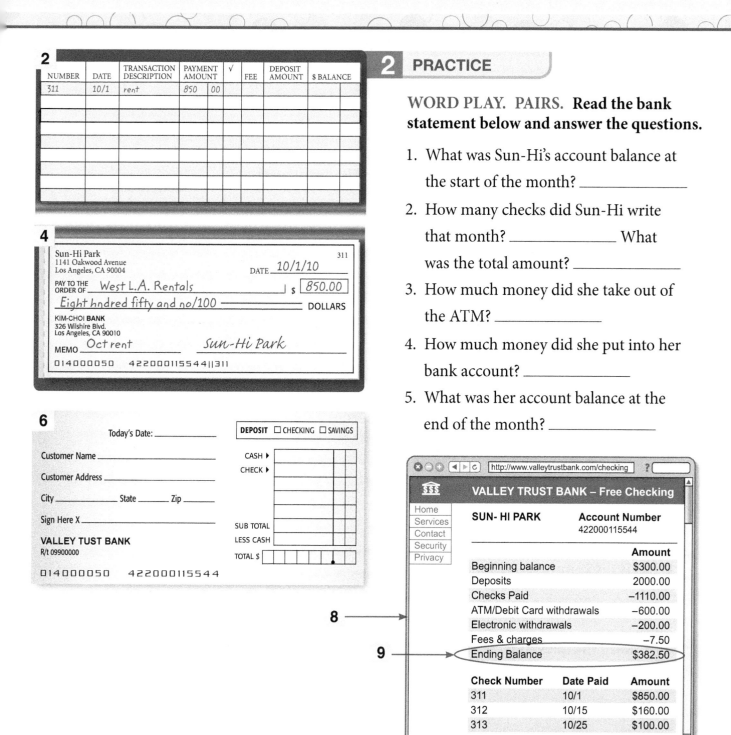

2

NUMBER	DATE	TRANSACTION DESCRIPTION	PAYMENT AMOUNT		√	FEE	DEPOSIT AMOUNT		$ BALANCE	
311	10/1	rent	850	00						

4

Sun-Hi Park
1141 Oakwood Avenue
Los Angeles, CA 90004
311

DATE _10/1/10_

PAY TO THE ORDER OF _West L.A. Rentals_ | $ _850.00_

Eight hndred fifty and no/100 ———— DOLLARS

KIM-CHOI **BANK**
326 Wilshire Blvd.
Los Angeles, CA 90010

MEMO _Oct rent_   _Sun-Hi Park_

⑈14000050   422000115544∥311

6

Today's Date: _____

DEPOSIT ☐ CHECKING ☐ SAVINGS

Customer Name _____

Customer Address _____

City _____ State _____ Zip _____

Sign Here X _____

VALLEY TUST BANK
R/t 09900000

⑈14000050   422000115544

	CASH ▶	
	CHECK ▶	
SUB TOTAL		
LESS CASH		
TOTAL $		

8 →

9 →

WORD PLAY. PAIRS. **Read the bank statement below and answer the questions.**

1. What was Sun-Hi's account balance at the start of the month? _____

2. How many checks did Sun-Hi write that month? _____ What was the total amount? _____

3. How much money did she take out of the ATM? _____

4. How much money did she put into her bank account? _____

5. What was her account balance at the end of the month? _____

http://www.valleytrustbank.com/checking   ?

$$$ **VALLEY TRUST BANK – Free Checking**

Home
Services
Contact
Security
Privacy

SUN- HI PARK   **Account Number**
                        422000115544

	Amount
Beginning balance	$300.00
Deposits	2000.00
Checks Paid	−1110.00
ATM/Debit Card withdrawals	−600.00
Electronic withdrawals	−200.00
Fees & charges	−7.50
Ending Balance	$382.50

Check Number	**Date Paid**	**Amount**
311	10/1	$850.00
312	10/15	$160.00
313	10/25	$100.00

Show what you know!

GROUPS. **If you have a bank account, do you read your statement? Why are bank statements and transaction registers useful? What can happen if you don't use them?**

Listening and Speaking

1 BEFORE YOU LISTEN

A GROUPS. Discuss. Do you use direct deposit? Why or why not? What are the advantages or disadvantages?

> When you have *direct deposit*, your employer puts your paycheck in your bank account electronically.

B Read the ad. What is a cash bonus?

Zenith Bank

- ✓ Free checking when you bank online or use direct deposit.
- ✓ Open your account today and get a $50 cash bonus.
- ✓ Open a free savings account with just $25.

What are you waiting for?
Banking has never been so easy.

2 LISTEN

CD3 T24

A Listen to the radio commercial from Zenith Bank. What is the commercial about?

a. savings accounts   b. checking accounts

CD3 T24

B Read the questions. Then listen again. Circle the correct answers.

1. What happens if you have direct deposit?
   a. You get a free checking account.   b. You pay fees for an account.

2. To get a cash bonus, when do you need to open an account?
   a. on or before April 3   b. on or after April 3

3. How much is the bonus?
   a. $100   b. $50

CD3 T24

C Listen again. Write two ways to open an account.

1. _____   2. _____

Pronunciation Watch

When we start a sentence with the word *if*, the voice pauses at the comma. The voice goes down at the end of the sentence.

CD3 T25

A Listen to the sentences.

If you have direct deposit, / you get free **check**ing.

If you have a computer, / you can bank on**line**.

CD3 T26

B Listen and repeat the sentences.

1. If you want to open a bank account, you need to show ID.

2. If you deposit a check, you need to write out a deposit slip.

3. If you have direct deposit, your employer puts your paycheck in your account.

CD3 T27

C Roberto is at Zenith Bank with a New Accounts Clerk. Listen and read the conversation.

Clerk: Hi. How may I help you?

Roberto: Hi. I'd like to open a free checking account.

Clerk: Sure. There are a couple of ways to qualify. First of all, if you have direct deposit, you get free checking.

Roberto: Hmm. Well, I don't have direct deposit.

Clerk: OK, then there is a second way to qualify. Do you have a computer? If you bank online, you can get free checking.

Roberto: Oh, sure. I use the Internet all the time.

Clerk: Great. All you have to do is bank online at least twice a month.

4 PRACTICE

A PAIRS. Practice the conversation.

B MAKE IT PERSONAL. GROUPS. Discuss. Do you bank or shop online? Why or why not? What are two advantages and two disadvantages?

Use bank services wisely

Grammar

Present real conditionals	
If Clause	**Result Clause**
If you bank online,	you get free checking.

Result Clause	**If Clause**
You get free checking	if you bank online.

Grammar Watch

- You can use the simple present in the *if* clause.
- You can use a modal, for example *(can, should, must)* in the result clause.

  *You **can** get free checking if you have direct deposit.*
- You can use an imperative in the result clause.

  *If you want free checking, **open** an account with Zenith.*
- When the *if* clause comes first, use a comma between the clauses.

1 PRACTICE

A Circle the *if* clauses. Underline the result clauses.

When you have a checking account, it's important to keep good records. (If you pay by check,) write down the check number, the amount, and the date in your transaction register. If you do, you can keep better track of the checks you wrote. Before you pay by check, make sure there is enough money in your bank account. If you write a check for too much money, there are consequences. First, the check will bounce and the bank will charge you a fee. If you write two bad checks, the bank may charge you $40 or more!

B Unscramble the sentences. Write them in your notebook. More than one answer is possible.

1. if / you can hurt your credit / you write bad checks

2. you want to buy a house or car / if / you need good credit

3. if / businesses can refuse to take checks from you / you write bad checks

4. if / you can ask the bank / you need a new transaction register

5. you lose your checks / if / you need to call the bank

2 PRACTICE

A **Combine the sentences to make one real conditional sentence.**

1. You can use it to buy things at stores. You have an ATM/debit card.

   If you have an ATM/debit card, you can use it to buy things at stores.

2. You do a transaction at the ATM. You need to type in a secret PIN.

   _____

3. Tell the bank in two days or less. You lose your ATM/debit card.

   _____

4. Someone steals your ATM/debit card. They can take money out of your bank account.

   _____

5. Call the credit card company immediately. Your credit card is missing.

   _____

B **PAIRS. Read the situations. How can you keep your personal information safe in these situations? Discuss. Write your answers in your notebook. Use present real conditionals.**

1. Your credit card expires. What should you do with it?

   If your credit card expires, you should cut it up and throw it away.

2. You lose your checkbook. What should you do?

3. You have old bank statements. What should you do with them?

4. You are alone late at night at an ATM. What should you do?

Show what you know! Use bank services wisely

GROUPS. Antoneta Deba has a bank account with Grace Bank. She just got an e-mail. It says Antoneta needs to e-mail her personal information so her bank account will be up-to-date. What should Antoneta do?

Can you...use bank services wisely? ☐

Reading

1 BEFORE YOU READ

A PAIRS. Look at the credit card statement. What was the balance from last month and this month? What are the charges from the credit card company?

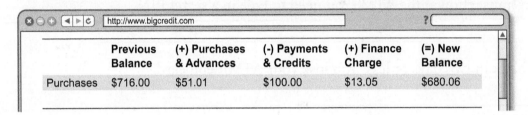

	Previous Balance	(+) Purchases & Advances	(-) Payments & Credits	(+) Finance Charge	(=) New Balance
Purchases	$716.00	$51.01	$100.00	$13.05	$680.06

B Look at the words and their definitions.

interest = the extra amount you pay to a credit card company each month to borrow an unpaid balance on your card

interest rate = the percentage (%) that a lender charges on the unpaid balance you owe

2 READ

CD3 T28

Listen and read the article.

How to Be Credit Card–Wise

Are you in credit card **debt**? If so, you're not alone. According to a new survey, the average family has a monthly **balance** of $5,100 and they can't **pay off** this debt. How do so many people get into credit card debt?

When you use your credit card you are actually borrowing money from the credit card company. Most credit card companies don't require you to pay the full amount you owe each month. Instead, you can just pay a part of it—the **minimum**. However, then you have to pay interest to the credit card company. Sometimes the interest rate is 24% or higher. This interest makes things cost more. Let's say you buy a TV for $1,000 and your interest rate is 24%. If you pay only the minimum each month, it could take you six years to pay for the TV. It will

also cost you $1,573.49. The extra $573.49 is all interest that you pay the credit card company. So how can you use credit cards **wisely**? Try these tips:

1. Don't use more than one or two credit cards.
2. If you go out shopping, leave your credit card at home and pay in cash. Use credit cards only for emergencies or big items like a refrigerator.
3. If you pay your credit card late, you will pay a **penalty** —for example, a charge of $50. Make sure to always pay at least the minimum on time.

Follow these tips to save money and protect yourself from interest and finance charges.

3 CHECK YOUR UNDERSTANDING

A **Read the article again. What is the writer's purpose? Circle the best answer.**

a. to convince us not to use credit cards

b. to help people avoid dangers of credit cards

c. to tell an interesting story about credit cards

> **Reading Skill:**
> Identifying author purpose
>
> Writers have a purpose (reason) for writing. Their purpose is to give information, make an argument, or entertain. Sometimes a writer has more than one purpose.

B **Read the statements. Write *T* (true) or *F* (false).**

_____ 1. You pay interest on a credit card when you pay your full balance.

_____ 2. When you pay interest, you are paying for the right to borrow money.

_____ 3. Credit card companies make money from interest.

_____ 4. When you owe a lot of interest on your credit card, it can be hard to pay off the balance.

4 VOCABULARY IN CONTEXT

Look at the boldfaced words in the article. Guess their meanings. Complete the sentences with the correct words.

1. She's in a lot of _____ because she has expensive student loans.

2. I paid my bill late so I had to pay a _____ .

3. You can shop _____ if you buy things on sale and use coupons.

4. My brother said it will take him five years to _____ his car loan.

5. Last month my credit card _____ was over $500 because I bought a stove.

6. I can't afford to pay my entire bill now so I'm paying the _____ .

Show what you know! Talk about uses and risks of credit cards

GROUPS. Discuss. What are other things you should or shouldn't do with credit cards? What should you do if you see charges that you didn't make on your credit card?

Can you... talk about uses and risks of credit cards? ☐

Writing

1   BEFORE YOU WRITE

A GROUPS. **What are your financial goals two years from now? Five years from now?**

B PAIRS. **Read about Alessandra's financial goal. What steps will she take to meet her goals?**

> My family left Russia and came to the Houston, Texas when I was 15 years old. My parents had a hard life and always wanted me to go to college. At first my English wasn't good, but later I went to the University of Houston. Now I have a job as an engineer. My financial goal is to pay back my student loans. To do this, I'm living in my parents' apartment and I'm paying the bank $100 each month.

C **Complete the chart. Write a financial goal you have for the future. Then write the steps you will take to meet this goal.**

Your financial goal	Steps to reach your goal

2   WRITE

Write a paragraph about your financial goal and the steps you will take to reach your goal. For example, do you want to buy a house or car? Save to go back to school? Use the writing model as an example.

3   CHECK YOUR WRITING

☐ Did you mention your financial goal?

☐ Did you tell the steps you will take to reach your goal?

☐ Did you indent your paragraph?

Budget expenses

Listening and Speaking

1 BEFORE YOU LISTEN

GROUPS. Look at Roberto and Ana Salazar's budget. How much money did they make last month before and after taxes? Circle the amount. Then add up their expenses. Write their total expenses. Did they have money left over? How much money was left?

2 LISTEN

CD3 T29

A 🔘 Listen to the radio show. Adelyn Juste talks about budgeting. What is the main idea? Circle the best answer.

a. People don't like to budget.

b. People need to change their spending habits.

c. People need to budget for their future.

Month of January		
Income		
	Gross income	2800.00
	Taxes	165.20
	Net income	2634.80
Savings	———	———
Expenses		
Housing	Rent	975
Food	Groceries	330
Transportation	Car insurance	400
	Car loan	200
	Gas and repairs	250
Utilities	Gas and electric	150
	Cell phone	50
Children's	Clothing	10
Medical	Pharmacy	25
Entertainment	Cable	60
	Miscellaneous	30
Total Expenses		

CD3 T29

B 🔘 Read the questions. Then listen again. Circle the correct answers.

1. What percentage of Americans don't budget?
   a. 6   b. 60   c. 16

2. What does Adelyn say people need to budget for?
   a. emergencies   b. financial goals   c. a and b

CD3 T29

C 🔘 Look at the budgeting steps. Then listen again. Put the steps in the correct order, according to the article. Write *1, 2, 3, 4.*

_____ Figure out your expenses.

_____ Write down your net income.

_____ Check to see if your budget is realistic.

_____ Build savings into your budget.

Budget expenses

Grammar

Future Real Conditional

If Clause	Result Clause		
If you save some money each month,	you	**will** **might**	be ready for an emergency.

Result Clause			*If* Clause
You	**will** **might**	be ready for an emergency	if you save some money each month.

1 PRACTICE

Read the article. Circle the *if* clauses. Underline the main clauses.

The Furniture Guy

In Seattle, Washington, Lloyd Evans helps people save money on furniture for their apartments. He finds and gives away used furniture to refugees from war-torn countries. (If Lloyd learns of a family who needs help,) he will spend extra time to meet their personal needs. Lloyd keeps extra furniture in a storage space until he finds someone who wants it. If people want furniture and visit Lloyd's storage space, they will find three rooms of sofas, beds, tables, chairs, cribs, TVs and other furniture.

The refugees are very thankful to Lloyd. If you visit Lloyd's house, you will see African drums and Kurdish paintings—gifts from the families Lloyd has helped.

PRACTICE

A Complete the tips to save on transportation. Circle the correct form of the verb.

1. If you (carpool) / **will carpool**, you'll spend less money on transportation.

2. If you **get / will get** a monthly bus pass, you'll save on bus fare.

3. Your car will last longer if you **change / will change** the oil regularly.

4. You might save money on repairs if you **fix / might fix** your car.

5. If you **take / will take** good care of your car, it will last longer.

6. You will pay less in gas if you **don't drive / won't drive** too fast.

B Complete the tips to save on groceries. Make future real conditionals with the verbs in parentheses. More than one answer is sometimes possible.

1. If you _____ the supermarket's weekly flyers, you _____ which items
           (read)   (know)
   are on sale.

2. If you _____ coupons, you _____ less.
           (use)   (pay)

3. You _____ only the things you need if you _____ a shopping list.
         (buy)   (use)

4. If you _____ at farmers markets, you _____ less for fruit.
          (shop)   (pay)

5. You _____ less for some items if you _____ the store brand.
         (pay)   (buy)

6. If you _____ supermarket prices, you _____ if you're getting a good deal.
        (compare)   (know)

Show what you know! Budget expenses

GROUPS. **Look at the categories in the box. What are ways you can save money on these things? Discuss.**

> appliances   children's clothes and shoes   furniture   transportation

Can you...budget expenses? ☐

Life Skills

1 UNDERSTAND UTILITIES

A **GROUPS.** Which utilites do you pay for? Gas? Electric? Heat? Hot water? Which are included in your rent?

B Look at Roberto's electric bill. Circle the amount he must pay this month.

Your Account Number	More phone numbers	Seneca Energy
987 654 320 3	24-Hour Service and info	PO Box A
Roberto Salazar	(800) 427-2000	Monterey Park, CA 94175
1801 E South Street		www.senecaenergy.com
Long Beach, CA 90805		

Billing Period	Meter Number	Next meter reading date on or about Sep 06 2010
From 07/09/10 to 8/09/10	06076856	

Previous Charges	Account Balance
Total Amount Due at Last Billing	155.01
Payment –Jul 16 2010 Thank You	155.01CR
Previous Balance	.00

Current Charges	Amount
Customer Charge 30 Days	4.93
Gas and Electricity Charges	140.07
Taxes and Fees	4.78
Total Gas Charges Including Taxes and Fees	149.78
Total Amount Due	**149.78**

Current Amount Past Due if not paid by Aug 31, 2010. A late charge of $5.00 may apply.

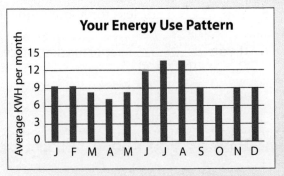

Your Energy Use Pattern

Energy Tip: We measure energy by the kilowatt-hour (KWH). When you read your utility bill, KWH shows how much energy you used.

Special DiscountYou may be eligible for California Alternate Rates for Energy (CARE) program. For more information and to request an application, please call 1-800-772-5050.

A Look at the bill again. Write *T* (true) or *F* (false). Correct the false statements.

_____ 1. Roberto's bill last month was 155.01.

_____ 2. His bill last month was for the same amount as this month.

_____ 3. The bill this month is due July 16.

_____ 4. Robert paid his bill last month and does not owe a balance.

_____ 5. Robert can apply for a special plan to pay less money for his energy.

_____ 6. If Robert pays his bill late, there is no fee.

B PAIRS. Look at the graph at the bottom of the bill. Answer the questions.

1. What does the graph show?
   a. Robert's energy use next year   b. Robert's energy use each month

2. During which months did Roberto use the least electricity?
   a. July and August   b. April and October

3. The KWH shows
   a. the money you spend on energy   b. the energy you use each hour

4. During which months did he use the most electricity? Why?

_____

_____

C GROUPS. PROBLEM SOLVE. Find ways to lower your utility bills.

STEP 1. GET READY. Check (✓) the things you do to save money on your utilities.

_____ I turn off the lights when I leave the room.

_____ I turn off the air conditioner when I leave home.

_____ I use fans instead of the air conditioner.

STEP 2. GROUPS. Discuss. What are other ways to save money on your utilities?

Can you...read utility bills and save money on utilities? ☐

Ask about appliances and utilities

1 BEFORE YOU LISTEN

A PAIRS. When you look for an apartment, you might look at classified ads. Read the ads. Write the abbreviations next to the words.

Oak Street	**Argos Boulevard**	**Tremont Street**	**Cabela Ave.**
2 BR/1 BA in 2 family house	Lg 2 BR/2 BA	2 BR/ 1 BA	2 BR/ 2 BA
New refrig., elec. stove	Sunny EIK, laundry in	$1,200/month	gas, elec. & water incl.
Cable TV incl.	basement	Close to freeways	gas stove incl.
H/HW incl.	Quiet neighborhood w/	Lg LR, EIK	Near downtown
$1,000/month	good schools	Elec. stove incl., Gas incl.	$1,100/month
Avail. now	$1100/month	street pkg.	Sec. dep. = $500
Call 555-817-2847	No sec. dep. req.	Liam_Caroll@yahoo.com	Call 555-310-3110
A	Call 555-801-2709		
	B	**C**	**D**

_____ available   _____ electric/electricity   _____ living room

_____ bathroom   _____ heat/hot water   _____ parking

_____ bedroom   _____ included   _____ security deposit required

_____ eat-in kitchen   _____ large   _____ with

B GROUPS. Discuss. Which things are most important to you in an apartment?

2 LISTEN

CD3 T30

A Listen. Roberto is calling Valeria, a real estate agent, about an apartment. Look at the ads. Which apartment is he calling about?

CD3 T30

B Listen again. Answer the questions.

1. What appliances are included?
   a. refrigerator and gas stove   b. electric stove   c. refrigerator and electric stove

2. What utilities are included?
   a. heat and hot water   b. gas   c. gas, electric, and water

3. When will Roberto meet the rental agent?
   a. at 3:00   b. at 3:30   c. at 4:00

3 CONVERSATION

CD3 T31

A 💿 **Listen to the sentences. Then listen and repeat.**

I'd like to find an apartment in a good school district.

How much do you want to spend?

We need to live close to downtown.

I'd like to come see it.

CD3 T32

B 💿 **Listen and read the conversation.**

Valeria: Hello. W & M Management Company.

Roberto: Hi. I'm looking for a two-bedroom apartment.

Valeria: OK, sure. How much do you want to spend?

Roberto: No more than $1,200. And we need to live close to downtown.

Valeria: Let me see. Hmm. I've got a great two-bedroom apartment on Cabela Avenue.

Roberto: Does it come with appliances?

Valeria: Yes, a refrigerator and a gas stove.

Roberto: How much is the rent?

Valeria: $1,100.

Roberto: Are utilities included?

Valeria: Yes, gas, electric and water.

Roberto: That's sounds good! I'd like to come see it.

> ### Pronunciation Watch
> The word *to* usually has a weak pronunciation. In conversation, *want to* often sounds like "wanna."

4 PRACTICE

A PAIRS. **Practice the conversation.**

B ROLE PLAY. PAIRS. **Make a similar conversation. Use the ads on page 220 or bring in your own.**

C MAKE IT PERSONAL. GROUPS. **Discuss. Have you had trouble finding housing? Do you have trouble with your appliances or utilities?**

Grammar

Gerunds and Infinitives as Objects of Verbs

Verb + gerund	Verb + infinitive
I **don't mind living** in an apartment.	I **need to** live close to the city.

Grammar Watch

- Some verbs are used ONLY with a gerund (*mind, feel like, finish*).
- Some verbs are used ONLY with an infinitive (*afford, agree, hope, intend, mean, need, offer, plan, promise, wait, want*).
- Some verbs are used with both gerunds and infinitives (*like, love, prefer, start*).
- See 288 for more information.

1 PRACTICE

> *lease: a contract that allows someone to live in an apartment or house etc for a specific time period in exchange for rent*

A Read the paragraph about the rental lease. Underline the infinitives. Circle the gerunds.

My husband and I are going to rent an apartment in Long Beach. We plan <u>to sign</u> a lease tomorrow. The lease is for one year. The rent is $850 a month. The lease says the landlord promises to pay for heat, water, and gas. We need to pay electric and trash. The landlord is nice and he offered to pay for new locks. We appreciated getting the help. I'm sure we'll like living there, but if we want to move, we need to give the landlord one month's notice. If we don't, we lose our security deposit.

B Complete the sentences. Circle the correct form of the verbs.

1. We don't mind **to live** / (**living**) in an apartment, as long as the neighbors are quiet.

2. We hope **to get** / **getting** an apartment in a neighborhood with a good school.

3. I want **to find** / **finding** an apartment that has all utilities included.

4. Would you mind **to wait** / **waiting** for a few minutes? The landlord is on his way.

5. We need **to save** / **saving** money for the security deposit.

6. Do you plan **to move** / **moving** in next week?

A Complete the conversations. Write the correct form of the verbs.

1. **A:** Do we need ___to pay___ both the first month's rent and the security deposit?
       (pay)

   B: Just the the first month's rent—I can wait a day _____ the security deposit.
       (get)

2. **A:** When do you intend _____ in?
       (move)

   B: As soon as we finish _____. Maybe on Friday?
       (pack)

   A: OK, that's fine. I don't mean _____ you. We'd just like _____ when
       (hurry)   (know)

   you're coming. And remember, no one is allowed _____ in after 5:00 P.M.
                                              (move)

3. **A:** Do you plan _____ cable?
       (get)

   B: How much is it?

   A: The apartment is cable ready. So if you feel like _____ it, call the cable
       (get)

   company. The cable packages start at $45 a month.

   B: I don't think we can afford _____ it right now.
       (get)

CD3 T33

B Listen and check your answers.

Show what you know! Talk about housing

GROUPS. Talk about the kind of housing you want or need. Use the words in the box and your own ideas.

can afford/can't afford	don't mind	hope	like/don't like
need/don't need	plan/don't plan	prefer	want/don't want

I don't want to live on the first floor, because my neighborhood is not that safe.
I don't mind living on a high floor, even if I have to climb a lot of stairs.

Can you...talk about housing? ☐

1 **REVIEW**   For your Grammar Review, go to page 255.

2 **ACT IT OUT**   What do you say?

STEP 1. CLASS. **Review the conversation on page 221. (CD3 Track 32)**

STEP 2. PAIRS. ROLE PLAY.

Student A: You are looking for an apartment. Ask the realtor questions. Talk about: • utilities included with the rent • appliances included with the apartment • move-in requirements (deposit, first or last month's rent) • housing preferences (location, appliances, cost, size)	**Student B:** You are a real estate agent. Answer Student A's questions.

3 **READ AND REACT**   Problem-solving

STEP 1. **Read about Monika. Then look at Monika's budget.**

Monika Cichon is a single mother with two children. She is in credit card debt. She owes the credit card company $5,000. She needs to save $200 a month to pay back the company.

STEP 2. GROUPS. **What is the problem? Give Monika advice. What can she cut out of her budget? What can she cut down on?**

Month of March		
Income		
Total Income	Gross income	1600
	After taxes	94
	Net income	1506
Expenses		
Housing	Rent	600
Food	Groceries	250
	Eating out	60
Transportation	Bus fare	70
Utilities	Gas and electric	100
	Cell phone	50
Personal	Clothing/shoes	50
	Pharmacy	60
Children	Clothing/shoes	40
	Books/toys	25
Medical	Clinic	60
	Prescriptions	50
Entertainment	Cable	80
Savings		0

4 **CONNECT**   For your Community-building Activity, go to page 262.
For your Team Project, go to page 273.

Which goals can you check off? Go back to page 205.

Washington, D.C.

Preview

Washington, D.C., is the capital of the United States. The U.S. government is located there. Have you ever been there? What do you know about it?

UNIT GOALS

☐ Talk about favorite places

☐ Read a subway map

☐ Talk about the government

☐ Talk about famous U.S. presidents

1 WHAT DO YOU KNOW?

A Look at the map. It shows places of interest in Washington, D.C. Which places do you know?

CD3 T34

B Listen to the names of the places on the map. Point to the pictures and repeat.

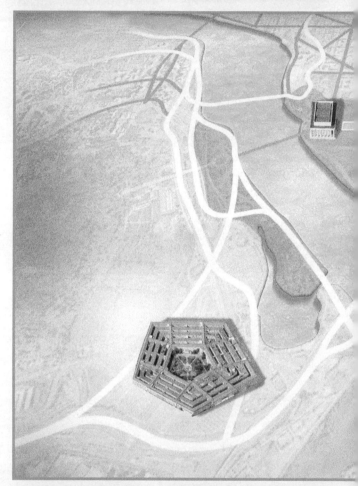

Places in or near Washington, D.C.

1. the White House
2. the Supreme Court
3. The Capitol
4. the Jefferson Memorial
5. the Washington Monument
6. the Lincoln Memorial
7. the U.S. Treasury
8. the Smithsonian American Art Museum
9. the Pentagon
10. the National Air and Space Museum

Learning Strategy

Translate

Make cards for the words *memorial, museum, court, monument, treasury,* and *national*. Write these words on the front of six cards. Write the word in your language on the back.

3

4

WORD PLAY. GROUPS. Look at the vocabulary. Write the names of the places.

1. There are famous works of American art here. _____

2. Judges explain the law here.

    _____

3. The president and his family live here. _____

4. Economists work here to make sure the U.S. economy is good.

    _____

5. The Department of Defense works here to keep the U.S. safe.

    _____

6. In this building, the Senate and the House of Representatives write laws. _____

7. This building has a large collection of airplanes and rockets.

    _____

7

8

Show what you know!

GROUPS. Discuss. Which places in Washington, D.C. would you like to visit? Why?

9

10

Talk about favorite places

Listening and Speaking

1 BEFORE YOU LISTEN

Have you ever taken a tour of a city? Where did you go?
What did you see? Would you recommend it to a friend?

tour: a short trip through a place to see it

2 LISTEN

CD3 T35

A Listen to a conversation between Tao and Hua. What is their relationship? They are _____

a. strangers   b. relatives   c. friends

CD3 T35

B Read the statements. Then listen again. Write *T* (true) or *F* (false).

__F__ 1. Hua just came back from a trip to Washington, D.C.

_____ 2. The Oval Office is a room in the White House.

_____ 3. The Blue Room is a room at the Supreme Court.

_____ 4. At the National Air and Space Museum you can see rocket ships.

_____ 5. Hua will probably visit Washington, D.C., again.

_____ 6. Hua is not interested in seeing the National Air and Space Museum.

3 CONVERSATION

A 🔘 **Listen to the pronunciation of *did you*. Then listen and repeat.**

did you ("didja")

Where did you go?
Did you go to Washington?
What did you see?
What did you like the most?

CD3 T37

B 🔘 **Listen to the sentences. Circle the words you hear.**

1. Where **do** / **did** you live?

2. What **do** / **did** you like the best?

3. **Do** / **Did** you like the museum?

4. Where **do** / **did** you go for vacation?

5. What **do** / **did** you like to do?

CD3 T38

C 🔘 **Listen and read the conversation.**

Tao: So, Hua, what did you like the most about Washington?

Hua: Hmm. I guess my favorite place was the White House. We went on a tour of the rooms inside. I liked seeing them—especially the Red Room, the Blue Room, and the Oval Office. What about you?

Tao: I liked seeing the White House, but my favorite place was the National Air and Space Museum.

Hua: What did you see there?

Tao: They've got a lot of things. Rocket ships, rocks from the moon and Mars, and lots of airplanes. It has the largest collection of planes in the world.

Hua: Wow, I'm sorry I missed it. I'll have to go next time.

the Oval Office

4 PRACTICE

A PAIRS. **Practice the conversation.**

B MAKE IT PERSONAL. GROUPS. **Talk about a city you know well. What is the best time of year to visit the city? What is the best thing to see and do?**

Grammar

Superlatives: -est, most, least, one of the most

It has	**the**	**largest**	collection of airplanes	in the world.
It is	**the most**	**popular**	museum	in Washington.
	the least	**expensive**	restaurant	around.

Grammar Watch

- *Good, bad,* and *far* have irregular forms of the superlative:
  good → the best   bad → the worst   far → the farthest

- We often use *one/some of the* with a superlative.
  It is one of the most beautiful sites in Washington, D.C.

- See page 289 for spelling rules with the superlative.

1   PRACTICE

**Read about the Cherry Blossom Festival.
Underline the examples of the superlative.**

One of Washington's <u>most popular</u> events of the year is the Cherry Blossom Festival. There are 3,000 cherry trees in Washington, D.C. Japan gave the trees to the capital in 1912 as a gift. It was one of the best gifts ever! The cherry trees are the most beautiful when they blossom in April. Visitors from all over the world come to see them. Unfortunately, this time of year is also the most crowded with the longest lines. So, if you want to enjoy the Cherry Blossom Festival, get up early. Most people agree that Washington's Cherry Blossom Festival is one of the most interesting and most unusual events they have seen.

Complete the sentences about the museums in Washington, D.C. Use the superlative form of the verbs.

1. The Smithsonian Institute is the <u>largest group of museums</u> in the world.
   (large / group of museums)

2. The National Air and Space Museum is _____ in the
   (one of / popular / museums)
   country. It has _____ of airplanes and aircraft in the world.
   (big / collection)

3. The National Gallery of Art has _____ in the
   (some of / fine / art)
   world. A lot of the art was given by Andrew Carnegie, who was

   _____ in the United States.
   (one of / rich / men)

4. At the National Museum of Natural History

   you can see the Hope Diamond. The Hope

   Diamond is _____ in the
   (one of / famous / diamonds)
   world. It is also _____
   (one of / blue / diamonds)
   ever found.

5. At the National Museum of American History

   you can also see some of the dresses worn by the first ladies.

   These are _____ in the history of fashion.
   (some of / beautiful / dresses)

Show what you know!   Talk about favorite places

GROUPS. Look through this unit at the pictures of places in Washington, D.C. Which place is the most interesting? The most beautiful? The best for children? Give your opinion and a reason why.

Can you...talk about your favorite places?   ☐

Read a subway map

Life Skills

Different cities have different names for their metro rail systems. For example:
New York = the subway
Chicago = the "L"
Washington = the metro

1 READ A SUBWAY MAP

A Washington, D.C. has a metrorail and bus system. Look at the map.

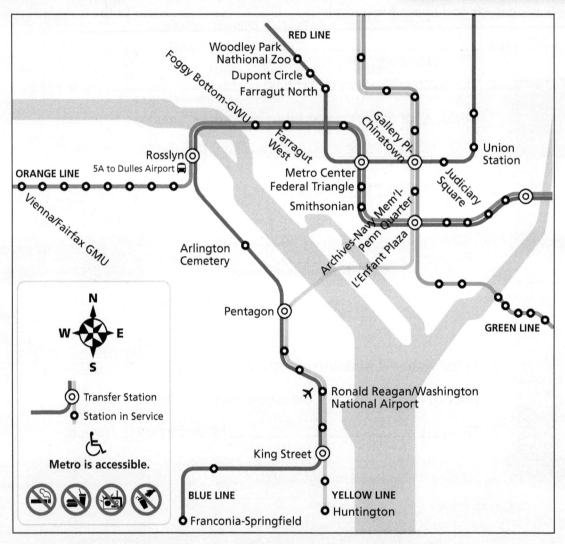

B PAIRS. Discuss the questions about the Metrorail System Map.

1. What is the difference between the symbols o and ⊚?

2. What does 🦽 is accessible mean?

3. What things can you not bring on the metro?

4. What do the symbols N, S, W, E mean?

PAIRS. **Answer the questions about the Metrorail System Map.**

1. If you are on the orange line at Rosslyn going to Vienna/Fairfax GMU, are you going north, south, east, or west? _____

2. The Metrorail has different colors to show train lines. How many train lines are there? _____

3. Which two lines go to the Smithsonian? _____

4. You are at Farragut North on the Red Line. You want to go to the Smithsonian. Which station do you have to transfer at? _____

5. Which station offers a bus shuttle to the airport? _____

3 ASK FOR AND GIVE DIRECTIONS

CD3 T39

A **Read and listen to the conversation at a Metro station. Mohani is asking directions.**

Mohani: I'm trying to get to the Washington National Airport. But I'm not sure how to get there. Do I have to change lines?

Agent: Yes. This stop is Judiciary Square. You need to go one more stop on the red line. Get off at Gallery Place. Then change to the yellow line or blue line.

Mohani: The yellow or blue line?

Agent: Yes, they both go to National Airport. The yellow line train will say Huntington. The blue line train will say Franconia-Springfield.

Mohani: When I get to the Washington National Airport stop, do I need to catch a bus?

Agent: No, the airport is right there.

B PAIRS. **Practice the conversation.**

C ROLE PLAY. **Make similar conversations.**

Student A: You want to visit the Pentagon. You're at Metro Center.

Student B: Give directions to the Pentagon station. Now change roles. Student B, you want to visit the National Zoo at Woodley Park. You're at the Smithsonian station.

Student A: Give directions.

Can you...read a subway map? ☐

Listening and Speaking

1 BEFORE YOU LISTEN

A PAIRS. Discuss. What would you like to know about the U.S. government and its capital? If you could ask a tour guide questions, what would you ask?

Tour guides show tourists a city. They ride on buses with the tourists, and talk about and visit buildings.

Tour bus at Union Station, Washington, D.C.

2 LISTEN

CD3 T40

A Listen to a tour guide in Washington, D.C. Write the three places the tourists are going to see:

_____ _____ _____

CD3 T40

B Read the statements. Then listen again. Write *T* (true) or *F* (false).

_____ 1. The president works in the White House, but his family lives somewhere else.

_____ 2. The Capitol is where Congress makes laws.

_____ 3. Senators work in the House of Representatives.

_____ 4. The Supreme Court is the highest court in the United States.

_____ 5. The Supreme Court makes laws.

_____ 6. All the laws need to follow the U.S. Constitution.

Pronunciation Watch

A compound noun is made up of two words used together as a noun. We usually stress the first word in a compound noun.

A CD3 T41
Listen to the compound nouns. Notice the stress. Then listen and repeat.

- **White** House
- **book**bag
- **rest**room
- **vis**itor center

B CD3 T42
Underline the compound noun in each sentence. Put a dot over the stressed syllable. Then listen and check your answers.

1. We visited the White House in Washington.

2. I had to check my handbag and camera.

3. My favorite room was the Blue Room.

4. We saw rocket ships at the museum.

5. I left my cell phone in the car.

C CD3 T43
Listen and read the conversation.

Guide: We are about to enter the White House. And please don't forget: no handbags, bookbags, food and beverages, cameras, strollers, or video recorders are allowed inside the White House.

Visitor 1: But I have a baby. Can't I take the baby in the stroller?

Guide: I'm sorry, strollers are prohibited.

Visitor 1: Is there a place where I can store the stroller?

Guide: I'm sorry. We don't have any storage. But you can leave it outside.

Visitor 2: Excuse me. Where are the restrooms?

Guide: The closest restrooms are in the White House Visitor Center.

4 PRACTICE

A GROUPS OF 3. Practice the conversation.

B MAKE IT PERSONAL. GROUPS. Have you ever visited a famous place? What was it? Where was it located? Who were you with?

Talk about the government

Grammar

The Simple Present Passive

	Be	Past Participle	[*by* + person or thing]	
The White House	**is**	**located**		at 1600 Pennsylvania Avenue.
The White House and its gardens	**are**	**visited**	by 6,000 tourists	every day.

Grammar Watch

- We usually do NOT use the passive voice. We use the passive voice when
  – we don't know who did the action, or
  – the person or thing who did the action is not important.

- See page 290 for more information on the passive voice.

1 PRACTICE

See page 283 for more information on the three branches of government.

Read about the U.S. government. Underline the present passives.

   In the United States, power is shared between federal and state governments. The federal government is <u>separated</u> into three branches.

- **The first branch is the Legislature.** It's called Congress. It makes new laws which are signed by the president. Congress is made up of two parts—the Senate and the House of Representatives.

- **The second branch is the Executive.** It is headed by the president. The president controls many things, like foreign affairs and the armed forces. The president also enforces the laws. Many important decisions are made by the president, but he or she does not make the laws.

- **The third branch is the Judiciary.** This branch includes the Supreme Court. The Supreme Court is the highest law court in the United States. It decides if laws follow the U.S. Constitution.

2 PRACTICE

A **Complete the paragraph about the White House. Use the simple present passive.**

The White House __is located__ at 1600 Pennsylvania
(locate)
Avenue, Washington, D.C. It _____ by 6,000
(visit)
people every day! Why is it so popular? One reason is

that it has many famous rooms. The Oval Office is a famous room that _____ by
(use)
the president. Important decisions _____ in the Cabinet Room. There are also
(also / make)
beautiful rooms that _____ after colors.
(name)
These rooms _____ the Blue Room, the
(call)
Red Room, and the Green Room. Big parties

_____ in the Red Room. Beautiful
(host)
flowers _____ in the Blue Room. Guests
(display)
_____ in the Green Room. Many important
(entertain)
leaders of other countries _____ there.
(welcome)

Fun facts about the White House

There are 132 rooms, 35 bathrooms, and 6 levels in the Residence. Visit the White House online at www.whitehouse.gov.

B **The Executive makes laws about federal holidays. Complete the sentences with the simple present passive.**

1. Veteran's Day and Memorial Day _____ every year to remember our soldiers.
(observe)
2. Martin Luther King, Jr. _____ on Martin Luther King Day.
(remember)
3. Independence Day _____ on the Fourth of July.
(celebrate)
4. On President's Day, Presidents Washington and Lincoln _____.
(honor)

Show what you know!   Talk about the government

GROUPS. Look at page 284. Discuss the U.S. holidays. When are they celebrated? How are they celebrated? Why are they celebrated?

Can you...talk about the government? ☐

Reading

CLASS. The U.S. Constitution is the highest law of the United States. It gives many rights to citizens. What are some rights and freedoms people have in the United States?

CD3 T44

Listen and read the article.

Freedom of *Religion* in the *United States*

Behrouz was born in Iran. Now he lives in Seattle, Washington. "Everything was new to me," Behrouz said about coming to the United States, "The freeways, the huge stores, the cars—I just took it all in."

Behrouz felt **overwhelmed** in his new country at first. But why did he come? Behrouz and his family **fled** from Iran. He and his family are Bahai. Their religion is not accepted in Iran. In Iran, the Bahai can be **arrested** at any time and put in prison. They can also have trouble getting jobs or going to school. Their money, house, or car can be taken away at any time. Behrouz came to the United States for freedom of religion.

Many people like Behrouz come to the United States because it protects all religions. The U.S. Constitution guarantees this freedom. People can **practice** any religion. They can worship at a church, temple, mosque, or synagogue. In some countries it can be dangerous to go to a public place of **worship**. In the United States, public places of worship are everywhere. When you drive through Los Angeles or any other big U.S. city, you will see hundreds of religious buildings— Catholic and Protestant churches, synagogues and mosques, even Buddhist,

Hindu, and Bahai temples. In fact, the United States has more religions—1,700—than any other country in the world.

Not everyone in the United States has a religion or believes in a god, and the U.S. Constitution protects this right, too. The name of God is found on money and in U.S. law courts, but the government is not allowed to make an **official** religion. In some countries, the government does not allow any religion at all or it controls religion. Here, it is the choice of each person.

Map

GEORGIA
ARMENIA
TURKEY
SYRIA
IRAQ
JORDAN
KUWAIT
BAHRAIN
QATAR
SAUDI ARABIA
UZBEKISTAN
TURKMENISTAN
AZERBAIJAN
IRAN
AFGHANISTAN
PAKISTAN
UNITED ARAB EMIRATES
OMAN

3 CHECK YOUR UNDERSTANDING

A PAIRS. Read the article again. Discuss. What is the main idea? Write a few sentences that summarize the main idea. Then compare your sentences with another pair of students.

B Read the statements. Write *T* (true) or *F* (false).

_____ 1. In the U.S, there are 170 different religious groups.

_____ 2. The U.S. government protects religion.

_____ 3. In the U.S., people don't have to belong to a religious organization.

_____ 4. Canada has more religions than the U.S. does.

Reading Skill:
Summarizing

When you summarize a text, you state or write the most important ideas or information in the text. Summarizing helps you check your understanding and helps you remember what you read.

4 VOCABULARY IN CONTEXT

Look at the boldfaced words in the article. Guess their meanings. Then complete the sentences with the correct words.

1. Many families have _____*fled*_____ from their countries because of wars.

2. In some countries, people who have a certain religion are _____ and put in jail.

3. When people come to the U.S., they often feel _____ at first because the language and culture are different from their own.

4. Churches, mosques, temples, and synagogues are all places of _____.

5. In the former Soviet Union, many people couldn't _____ their religion.

6. In some countries, like Saudi Arabia, there is one _____ religion.

Show what you know! Talk about rights and freedoms

GROUPS. Do you know anyone who came to the U.S. because they could not practice their religion in their native country? Is freedom of religion important to you?

Can you... talk about rights and freedoms? ☐

Talk about famous U.S. presidents

Listening and Speaking

1 BEFORE YOU LISTEN

Read about President Abraham Lincoln and the Civil War.

President Abraham Lincoln

Abraham Lincoln was president during the U.S. Civil War. The U.S. Civil War was a war between the northern and the southern states. It took place from 1861 to 1865. The war was fought over slavery. The South wanted slavery and the North did not. The North won the war. In 1865, slavery in the United States ended in all of the states.

2 LISTEN

CD3 T45

A 📀 Read the statements about President Lincoln. Then listen to a tour of the Lincoln Memorial. Write *T* (true) or *F* (false).

_____ Abraham Lincoln was the sixth president of the United States.

_____ Lincoln was born in Illinois.

_____ Lincoln came from a poor family.

_____ Lincoln taught himself law and was a lawyer before he was president.

_____ Lincoln was president at the time of the Revolutionary War.

_____ Lincoln freed the slaves in the rebel states in 1863.

_____ Lincoln shot someone.

B PAIRS. Compare answers.

CD3 T46

Listen and read the conversation.

Sasha: So, what do you want to do after the tour?

Galina: Well, we could go shopping or go back to the National Mall.

Sasha: We saw the museums at the Mall already.

Galina: I know. But I like walking around outside on the Mall. And we haven't seen the Washington Monument yet.

Sasha: What does your tour book say about the Monument?

Galina: Let's see . . . it was built between 1848 and 1884. There are 897 steps. You can climb up to the top or take an elevator, and you can look out at the view.

Sasha: Wow. Let's go there. I'd like to see it. As long as I can take the elevator.

the National Mall

A PAIRS. Practice the conversation.

B ROLE PLAY. PAIRS. Make conversations about places to see in Washington.

The National Zoo is free and has 2,000 animals, Giant Pandas, Bird House, butterfly room, and elephants.

Chinatown is downtown and has 20 Chinese and other Asian restaurants, nightlife, entertainment, and shopping.

Grammar

Past Passive

Subject	*Be*	Past participle	
Lincoln	**was**		president in 1861.
		elected	
Lincoln and Washington	**were**		for two terms.

1 PRACTICE

A Read about the first president, George Washington. Find the past passives. Circle the forms of *be*. Underline the past participles.

George Washington was born in 1732. He had very little school education, but he taught himself many things, like how to read maps. He was chosen as the head of the Colonial Army in 1776. Washington was a hero and an excellent commander. His army fought to be free from the British in the Revolutionary War. Washington's army won. The British were defeated and went back to Britain. America had won its freedom.

George Washington

B Complete the paragraph. Use past passives.

In 1789, Washington _____ as the first president of the United States. He
            (elect)
_____ in 1792. Washington did not want to be president a third time and went
   (re-elected)
back to his home. After his death, the city of Washington, D.C., _____ after
                                                              (name)
him in his memory. George Washington's picture _____ on the U.S. dollar, to
                                                        (print)
honor him. George Washington is known as the Father of Our Country.

Show what you know!   Talk about famous U.S. presidents

GROUPS. Choose a U.S. president. Do research on the internet. Then tell the group what you learned. When was this person president? What was this president known for?

Can you...talk about famous U.S. presidents? ☐

Write about rights and freedoms

Writing

1 BEFORE YOU WRITE

A GROUPS. The U.S. Constitution and the Bill of Rights give many rights and freedoms. Do people have these rights and freedoms in your native country also?

- the right to vote
- the freedom of speech
- the freedom of the press
- the freedom of religion
- the right to a fair and fast trial

B Read Carlos Hernandez's essay. Which freedom is important to him? Why?

> For me one of the most important freedoms in the United States is the freedom of the press. This freedom means that people can write any information, opinions, and ideas they believe and print them in newspapers, magazines, and books. The news media can say what it thinks. For example, if the news media doesn't like something the U.S. government does, they write about it in the newspaper or talk about it on TV. I came to the United States from Cuba. If you write anything the Cuban government doesn't like, they put you in jail. Many reporters in my country are in jail right now. I'm happy to live in a country where we can tell our opinions without being afraid.

2 WRITE

Write about one freedom or right that is important to you. Explain why. Talk about whether you have this right in your native country or in the United States.

3 CHECK YOUR WRITING

☐ Did you talk about one freedom or right?

☐ Did you explain why this freedom or right is important to you?

☐ Did you indent your paragraph?

☐ Did you check your spelling?

REVIEW & EXPAND Show what you know!

1 REVIEW For your Grammar Review, go to page 256.

2 ACT IT OUT What do you say?

STEP 1. CLASS. Review the conversation on page 233. (CD3 track 39)

STEP 2. ROLE PLAY. PAIRS. Look at the map on page 232. Then role play the situation.

> **Student A:** You want to visit the Smithsonian museums. You don't know the Metro system well. You are at Gallery Place–Chinatown. Ask directions.

> **Student B:** You are an agent. Give directions to the Smithsonian station. Talk about:
> - Which (color) line (train) Student A has to take
> - Whether Student A has to change lines (trains)
> - The final destination of Student A's train

3 READ AND REACT Problem-solving

STEP 1. Read about Mi-Hyun Kim and Jun Park.

Mi-Hyun and Jun are leaving Washington, D.C., to go back to New York. Their flight leaves from Dulles airport at 6:00 P.M. They are at Union Station, which has trains to New York. It's already 4:30. They are afraid they will miss their flight. They *have* to be in New York tonight to go back to work tomorrow.

STEP 2. PAIRS. Discuss. What is the problem? Talk about Mi-Hyun and Jun's problem. What do you think they should do? Which solution is best? Discuss.

- They could take a taxi, but it's expensive and there is a lot of traffic.
- They can take the Metro to Dulles airport, but they might be too late to board the plane.
- They could take a train from Union Station to New York, but they will lose the money they spent on the airline tickets.

4 CONNECT For your Community-building Activity, go to page 262.
For your Team Project, go to page 274.

Which goals can you check off? Go back to page 225.

Grammar Review

Unit 1

A Complete the sentences. Use the simple present form of the verbs in parentheses.

A: _____Do_____ you _____live_____ around here?
        (live)

B: Yes, I _____. I _____ with my sister. She _____ an apartment
                            (live)   (have)
on Oak Street. What about you?

A: I _____ around here, but I _____ nearby at Bloom's, and my son _____
        (not/live)   (work)   (take)
classes at the community center. Actually, I _____ to move, and
                                              (need)
this _____ like a nice neighborhood.
     (seem)

B: It is. When _____ you _____ to move?
                                    (want)

A: As soon as possible.

B: Let me call my sister. She _____ this neighborhood well. Maybe she can help you.
                                  (know)

B Complete the paragraph. Circle the correct words.

Last November our neighbors invited us to our first Thanksgiving dinner. It was **a lot of /
many** fun. We had **some / any** turkey, **a few / a little** sweet potatoes, **any / a lot of** rice, and a
delicious salad with **a little / a lot of** nuts and a few pieces of avocado. My husband tried
a little / a few cranberry sauce, but I didn't try **any / some**. I brought **much / some** homemade
cupcakes and a cake for dessert. I think everyone liked my desserts because by the end of the
meal there weren't **any / much** cupcakes and there wasn't **many / much** cake left.

C Complete the paragraph with *used to* and the verbs from the box.

eat   go   have   see

I came to the U.S. from Brazil six years ago. My life here is different. In Brazil, I _____

my grandparents every weekend. Now, I only see them once a year. I _____ to the beach

and play volley ball or soccer on weekends. Now, I work most Saturdays, and on Sundays I

relax at home. In Brazil, my friends and I _____ all sorts of Brazilian specialties, like

fejoada. But here I only have those foods on special occasions. In Brazil, I never _____

steady work. But here I have a good job and many opportunities. So all in all I'm happy that

I'm here. I have a good future.

Unit 2

(A) Underline the correct words.

A: Maria is thinking about going back to school.

B: When?

A: **She'll probably start / She'll start probably** this spring.

B: **Will she go / Might she go** to Bronx Community College?

A: No, **she won't / she might**. **She'll go / She goes** to Lehman College. It's closer to her home.

B: How many classes **will she take / she will take**?

A: She's not sure. She **might take / will take** one or two.

B: That's great. Maria's smart, and I'm sure **she'll do / she might do** well.

(B) Complete the sentences. Use *be going to* for the future and the verbs in parentheses.

A: My job will end next week. I _____ look for a new job. (have to)

B: Where _____ you _____? (look)

A: First I'll try online. Then I _____ the newspapers. (check)

B: Did you ask around? You've got a big family. Maybe they can help.

A: Good idea. I _____ everyone next weekend at my cousin's wedding.

I'll ask around. (see)

(C) Look at Veronica's planner for next week. Write questions and short answers. Use the present continuous for the future.

Monday	Tuesday
register for English class	take the English Placement Test

1. When / Veronica / register / for an English class?
   When is Veronica registering for an English class?
   On Monday.

2. What/ Veronica / do / on Tuesday?

   _____

3. Veronica / buy books / on Thursday?

   _____

4. What day / Veronica / start her class?

   _____

Wednesday	Thursday
buy books for class	English class begins

Unit 3

(A) **Complete the conversations with words from the box.**

behind   in   out
over   up

1. **A:** I want to sign _____ for tutoring in chemistry.

   B: Good idea. Then you won't fall _____.

2. **A:** Did you hand _____ your book report for English?

   B: Yes. Now I have time to figure _____ those tough math problems.

   A: OK. When you're finished, let's go _____ your social studies homework.

(B) **Complete the conversation. Use the simple past form of the verbs.**

A: How _____ school?
  (be)

B: Great. We _____ to the museum.
  (go)

A: Which museum _____ you _____ to?
  (go)

B: The science museum.

A: What _____ you _____ ?
  (see)

B: We _____ the Leonardo da Vinci exhibit.
  (see)

A: I _____ he _____ an artist.
  (think)   (be)

B: He _____, but he _____ also a scientist. He _____ many talents.
  (be)   (be)   (have)

(C) **Complete the questions and statements. Use the correct form of the words in parentheses.**

1. I want to go to a four-year college. (I / have to / take) _____ four years of English?

2. (he / have to / take) _____ any special tests for that college?

3. When (he / should / apply) _____ for City College?

4. Your application (have to / be) _____ in by March 30 of this year.

5. The test starts at 8:00. (you / have to / be) _____ in the room by 7:55.

6. (you / should / not / come) _____ late for the test.

Unit 4

A Complete the conversations and the verbs in parentheses. Use the present perfect or the simple past. Use *for* or *since* where necessary.

1. **A:** _____ you ever _____ nights?
   (work)

   B: Yes, I _____ . I _____ the night shift _____ three months in 2006.
   (work)

2. **A:** _____ you ever _____ to a technical school?
   (go)

   B: Yes, I _____ . I _____ to ACME last year.
   (go)

3. **A:** _____ that store _____ closed for a long time?
   (be)

   B: It _____ closed _____ last year.
   (be)

4. **A:** How long _____ you _____ your own business?
   (have)

   B: I _____ my own business _____ over three years.
   (have)

5. **A:** What _____ you _____ before that?
   (do)

   B: Before that I _____ for The Wrap.
   (work)

B Complete the conversations. Build sentences with the words from the boxes.

It's difficult	for you	to always come on time
It's easy	for me	to make a mistake
It's a good idea	for us	to dress conservatively
It's hard	for him	to understand him

1. **A:** I have a job interview tomorrow. How should I dress?

   B: _____ .

2. **A:** My boss speaks very quickly. _____ .

   B: Ask him to speak more slowly.

3. **A:** Why do you and Hans always count the money twice?

   B: _____ .

4. **A:** Your friend Ivan is late for work again. Tell him I'm not happy about it.

   B: I'm sorry, Larry. The bus runs late sometimes.

   _____ .

Unit 5

A Complete the conversations. Circle the correct words or sentences.

1. **A:** Excuse me. Could we eat on the bus?
   B: Yes, you can. / Yes, you could.

2. **A: May you please / Would you please** fasten your seat belt?
   B: Oh, sure. Sorry about that.

3. **A:** There's a small carry-on bag in that corner. Is it yours?
   B: No, **mine / my** bag is on the bus.   I think it's **her / hers**.

4. **A:** My grandfather needs a new ticket. He left **his / hers** at home.
   B: No problem. Just give me his name and address.

5. **A:** Could you **put / to put** your bags under the seat in front of you?
   B: Yes, of course. / Yes, I could.

6. **A:** We **won't be able to / couldn't** leave until they clean the plane.
   B: How long will that take?

7. **A:** We **won't be able to / couldn't** leave until the other train passed.
   B: How long did that take?

8. **A: May I / Will I** help you?
   B: Thanks. How much is a return ticket to Miami?

B Read the situations. Write questions. More than one answer is sometimes possible.

1. Someone's bag is on an empty seat on the bus. Ask the person to move his bag.

   _____

2. Ask someone if it's OK to use a cell phone on the bus.

   _____

3. You are taking a train trip. Ask a friend to drive you to the train station.

   _____

4. There's a storm. Ask an agent if your bus will be able to leave on time.

   _____

Unit 6

A Complete the conversation. Circle the correct words.

A: Is there a sale at Bloom's?

B: **I think so. I'm afraid / Yes, I think** that the air conditioners are 20 percent off this weekend. Look. Here's the flyer. I'm right.

A: **Are you sure / Do you think** there's a sale on microwave ovens, too?

B: **No, I don't think so. / I think so.** It only says air conditioners.

B Read the refrigerator ratings. Compare the refrigerators. Use the words in parentheses.

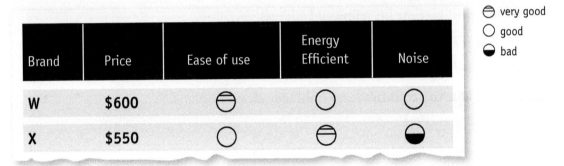

Brand	Price	Ease of use	Energy Efficient	Noise
W	$600	⊖	○	○
X	$550	○	⊖	◑

⊖ very good
○ good
◑ bad

1. (noisy)

   Brand X is noisier than Brand W.

2. (expensive)

   _____

3. (quiet)

   _____

4. (cheap)

   _____

5. (efficient)

   _____

6. (easy to use)

   _____

Unit 7

A **Complete the conversation. Write _a_, _an_, or _the_.**

A: How's Bob?

B: Fine. He's looking for _____ new car. He had _____ Grande Caravan but it used too much gas.

A: What kind does he want?

B: I'm not sure. I know he wants _____ smaller car.

A: Well I saw _____ ad for a Honda Civic at _____ community center on River Avenue. I'll tell him about _____ ad. It looked like _____ good deal.

B **Write the past continuous form of the verbs in parentheses.**

A: What caused the accident?

B: The driver _____ the road. He _____ at a map and
              (not/watch)   (look)
_____ on his cell phone.
   (talk)

A: Where were you?

B: I _____ next to the bus stop. I could see everything from there.
   (stand)

C **Combine the sentences. Use present time clauses. Begin the sentences with _When_.**

1. It rains. Use the windshield wipers and turn on the headlights.

   _____

2. He has problems with his car. He goes to the repair shop on Oak Avenue.

   _____

3. You buy a car. You need to get car insurance.

   _____

4. You speed. You use more gas.

   _____

5. She sees stop lights or stop signs. She always comes to a complete stop.

   _____

Unit 8

A Rewrite the sentences. Add the adverbs of frequency. More than one answer is sometimes possible.

1. (often) When I'm tired, I snack. _____

2. (once in a while) We go to a Chinese restaurant. _____

3. (almost never) We eat a big meal at noon._____

4. (every day) I eat a salad._____

B Complete the conversations. Use gerunds and the correct form of the verbs in parentheses.

1. **A:** When I get very hungry, I eat too much.

   B: (try / eat) _____ healthy snacks between meals.

2. **A:** My husband has high blood pressure. What should he do?

   B: Tell him to (avoid / eat) _____ salty foods.

3. **A:** I'd like my children to eat more vegetables, but they don't like them.

   B: Have you ever (think about / add) _____ vegetables to meatloaves and casseroles? Sometimes children like them that way.

4. **A:** I started to diet five weeks ago but I'm now only four pounds thinner.

   B: That's terrific. (keep / do) _____ what you're doing. It's always better to lose weight slowly. That way you keep it off.

C Rewrite each sentence. Start with a gerund.

1. It's good for your health to eat a lot of fresh fruits and vegetables.
   Eating a lot of fresh fruits and vegetables is good for your health.

2. It's hard to lose weight.

   _____

3. It's fun to cook.

   _____

4. It can be difficult to change your eating habits.

   _____

Unit 9

Ⓐ Read the conversation. Replace the nouns with *one* or *ones* whenever possible.

A: Excuse me. Are those computers on sale?

B: Which ~~computers~~? _{*ones*}

A: The computers over there. The small computers.

B: Yes, they are. They're all discounted.

A: Thanks. How much is this computer?

B: This computer is only $800 plus tax.

A: And that computer?

B: That computer is more. It's $1,400.

Ⓑ Read the conversation between Joe and his boss, Steve. Complete the sentences based the conversation.

Steve: Joe, please order some more supplies.
Joe: OK. What do we need?
Steve: Check the supply room. I know we're running low on paper.
Joe: OK. Anything else?
Steve: Yes. Answer the phone while Bill is away. He's doing some errands for me
          all afternoon. And before you leave, don't forget to hand in your time sheet.

1. (order / Steve / Joe / ask)

    _____ some supplies.

2. (Steve / tell / check / Joe)

    _____ the supply room.

3. (watch / Joe / Steve / want)

    _____ the front desk.

4. (Joe / Steve / tell / not / forget / hand in)

    _____ his time sheet.

Unit 10

A Underline the correct word.

1. I'm **interested / interesting** in what the doctor has to say.
2. The child was **frightened / frightening** by the hospital.
3. It's **embarrassed / embarrassing** to answer these questions in front of everyone in the waiting room.
4. He was **confused / confusing**. That's why he took too much medicine.
5. She was **frustrated / frustrating** that the doctor wouldn't see her that day.

B Complete the conversation with the present perfect continuous. Choose from the verbs in the box.

| eat | not/eat | exercise | feel | take | watch |

A: So, Mr. Valdez, how _____*have*_____ you __*been feeling*__? Any better?

B: A little. I _____ the pills and I _____, but I still feel tired all the time.

A: What about your diet? _____ you _____ your diet?

B: Yes, a little. We _____ out as much, and I _____ healthier meals at home.

A: Good. A healthy diet is important. Let me take your blood pressure and see how that is.

C Complete the conversations. Use the gerund form of the verb. Choose from the words in the box.

| answer | be | bring | explain | feel | ~~get~~ | miss |

1. **A:** John is worried about _____*getting*_____ an MRI.

   B: Is he afraid of _____ in a closed place?

2. **A:** I plan on _____ a list of questions to ask Dr. Lee. He's helpful.

   B: Yes. Dr. Lee is good at _____ questions and _____ things clearly.

3. **A:** My friend complains about _____ weak and dizzy. She won't see a doctor because she's afraid of _____ work.

   B: Explain to your friend that her health is more important than any job.

Unit 11

A Combine the two sentences into one real present conditional sentence. More than one answer is sometimes possible.

1. I bank online. I can save money.

   _____

2. You can save money. You open a savings account at the Bank of the U.S.

   _____

3. We use direct deposit. We can get a cash bonus.

   _____

4. You don't have to pay right away. You use a credit card.

   _____

5. You pay interest. You don't pay your entire balance on a credit card bill.

   _____

B Complete the sentences. Circle the correct words.

1. If you **pay / will pay** your bill late, you will pay a penalty.
2. If you **won't have / don't have** good credit, you will have trouble borrowing money for a house or car.
3. It **takes / will take** him five years to pay off his loan if he pays $100 a month.
4. She **isn't / won't** have trouble budgeting if she gives up her car.
5. If you **remember / will remember** your financial goals, it will be easier for you to save money.

C Complete the sentences. Circle the correct form of the verbs.

1. I hope **to find / finding** a cheap apartment near my job.
2. I keep **to look / looking** at ads in the paper and on the bulletin board at the community center.
3. Before we move, we need **to give / giving** our landlord two months notice.
4. We don't mind **to fix / fixing** things ourselves if it means paying less rent.
5. We can't afford **to pay / paying** more than $1,000 a month.
6. We need **to live / living** near a bus line.

Unit 12

A Complete the reading about Washington D.C.'s National Zoo. Use the superlative form of the adjectives.

Don't leave Washington, D.C. without visiting the National Zoo. The National Zoo is part of

the Smithsonian Institution, one of the _____ in the world.
(1. large museums and research centers)

The Zoo is also one of the _____ in Washington, D.C. Over two
(2. popular tourist attractions)

million people visit the zoo each year. The Giant Pandas are _____ and
(3. famous)

_____ loved residents of the zoo. In addition to the 2,000 different animals,
(4. good)

the National Zoo has one of the _____ in the world.
(5. good animal hospitals and conservation centers)

So be sure to make time for a trip to the National Zoo.

B Write questions in the present passive. Use the words in parentheses.

1. (What / the president's office / call) _____?

2. (Where / the Air and Space Museum / locate) _____?

3. (Which U.S. president / call / "Honest Abe") _____?

4. (What day of the week / U.S. elections / hold on) _____?

5. (What U.S. holiday / celebrate / on February 22) _____?

C Complete the sentences with the past passive. Choose from the words in the box.

> break   cancel   fill   take   wake

My brothers and I went to Washington, D.C. last week. We had some problems during our

trip. First, our flight _____. We got onto a different flight and arrived very late.

We went to our hotel. The nonsmoking rooms _____, so we got a smoking room.

The room _____ with a smokey smell. We tried to watch TV but the TV

_____. We went to sleep. In the morning we _____ by a noisy

family in the next room.

Persistence Activities

Unit 1   Sharing information through poems

A PAIRS. **Ask and answer the questions.**

What is your full name?
Where are you from?
What are some words that describe you?
What are your favorite things to do?

What is your nickname?

Nickname: A short informal name that friends or family use.

B **With your answers, write a poem about yourself.**

_____
(your full name)

from _____
(your home country)

_____ _____ _____
(three words that describe you)

_____ _____
(two things you like to do)

_____
(your nickname)

C CLASS. **Share your poem with your classmates and teacher.**

Unit 2   Finding supports or solutions

A **When you start a new English class, you may be excited but have concerns. Do you have concerns? What are they? Make a list.**

I worry about...	Possible supports or solutions
Example: I worry about getting rides to class.	Talk to other students in the class. See if you can ever carpool together.

B GROUPS. **You are not alone! Talk about your concerns. Brainstorm possible solutions.**

C **Write your ideas and your classmates' ideas for solutions to your concerns.**

Unit 3   Identifying resources for learning English

A What resources will help you learn English inside and outside class? Make a list of resources that you want to use.

> Resources are kinds of support that help you learn. For example, a public library, a friend who speaks English well, a dictionary, or a website.

1. _____

2. _____

3. _____

B PAIRS. Compare your lists. Does your partner have different resources? Do you think your partner's ideas are good? Add them to your list!

Unit 4 Checking on your goals

A PAIRS. Discuss. In Unit 2, you talked about and wrote about goals and when you want to reach them. You also thought about barriers and supports. How are you doing on reaching your goals now?

B Look at page 38. What were some important goals that you wrote down? By when do you want to reach these goals? Write in the chart.

Goal	By when?

C PAIRS. Talk about the steps you need to take to reach your goals. Have you taken any steps? Why or why not? What steps do you still need to take?

D Write your goals and the next steps you need to take in the chart.

Goals	Next steps to take	By when?

Unit 5 Identifying what is important to you

A PAIRS. Discuss. Did you travel a long way when you came to the U.S.? Do you often miss your home country? Are there times when you miss it more or less?

B What was in your suitcase when you came to the U.S.? What things did you bring with you? Write them in the box.

C What things do you wish you had brought to the U.S. that you left behind? Write them in the box.

D PAIRS. Discuss. Talk about your ideas in Exercises B and C. What are ways to feel better when you miss the things you left behind?

Unit 6 Identifying what you have learned so far

A Think about the many things that you have learned in this class so far. In your notebook, draw a mind map of what you have learned.

A *mind map* is a picture of how you connect words and ideas together.

B PAIRS. Share your mind maps. Did your partner talk about something that you forgot? Is it important to you? If so, add it to your mind map.

Unit 7   Identifying favorite activities

(A) Look at the units you have worked on so far. What types of activities have you enjoyed the most? Check (✓) the types of activities you liked best.

_____ working alone   _____ speaking activities   _____ vocabulary activities

_____ working in pairs   _____ reading activities   _____ listening activities

_____ working in groups   _____ writing activities   _____ grammar activities

(B) What did you like about your favorite activities? Write notes to yourself.

_____

_____

_____

(C) GROUPS. Discuss. Do you have the same favorite activities? Make a list. Share your list with your teacher. Your teacher can use your suggestions when planning lessons.

Unit 8   Identifying ways to reduce stress

(A) We all have stress from our responsibilities, like our families and jobs. What are ways that you can take a break or relax when you feel stress? Write your ideas.

_____

_____

_____

(B) PAIRS. Compare your ideas. Does your partner have different ideas? Are they good ideas? Add them to your list. Try them the next time you feel stress.

(C) NEW PAIRS. Share your ideas. Can you find ways to practice English when you are doing activities that relieve stress?

When I get stressed, I go for walks. While I'm walking, I look for signs in English and practice my English that way.

Unit 9   Identifying times when you succeeded at something

A Think of a time when you were successful. Write what you saw, heard, said, thought, and felt when you succeeded.

_____

_____

_____

_____

_____

B PAIRS. Compare what you wrote about in Exercise A. Discuss. Why is it important to remember the times when you succeed?

Unit 10 Identifying things you are an expert at

A GROUPS.

STEP 1. Discuss. What things can someone be an expert in? Make a list of ideas.

STEP 2. You are experts in this class. Write advice to new students. Make a list of ideas. For example, tell them what they need to do to succeed in class.

B NEW GROUPS. Join a new group. Share the ideas you wrote in Step 2. Give feedback. Say which ideas are clear and which need more information.

C GROUPS. Go back to your first group. Discuss the feedback you received. Use it to make your ideas clearer. Now write a letter of advice to new students.

Dear New Students:

Welcome to this class! We were students in this class. We want to give you some advice so that you succeed in this class!

1. Class starts at 9:00 A.M. Try to come a little early and talk to the teacher and your classmates in English.

Unit 11 Checking the progress of your goals

A Think about the hopes, dreams, and goals you talked about during this class. What were they? Do you have some additional goals now? Write all of your goals.

_____

_____

_____

_____

B Think about what you have studied in this class. Look at your textbook to help you remember. What did you learn? Does it support any of your goals? Write it in the chart.

Goal	What I learned in class that supports this goal

C PAIRS. Compare charts. Add any ideas you forgot.

Unit 12 Sharing accomplishments and memories

Congratulations! You have studied and learned a lot in this class. You also made new friends and had fun. Let's celebrate!

A On a big sheet of paper, make a poster that shows what you did and learned in class. You can write words, phrases, or draw pictures about what you learned. Save some space at the bottom of the paper.

B CLASS. Hang your posters on your classroom walls. Walk around and look at your classmates' posters. Talk to each other about your posters and write notes to each other about being together and learning English. Write about your friendships and your memories from the class.

> Ana—We had fun in English class. I will always remember you!
> Your friend, Layla

Team Projects

Unit 1   Information for newcomers MAKE A BROCHURE

TEAMS OF 4 Captain, Co-captain, Assistant, Spokesperson

GET READY **Team:** Choose a problem that people have when they move to a new country—for example:
- meeting people
- finding an apartment
- understanding English

Captain: Ask your teammates, "What can you do to solve this problem?"
Co-captain: Ask the captain the question. Keep track of the time. You have ten minutes.
Assistant: Take notes.

Materials
- 1 piece of white paper
- pens or markers
- stapler and staples

_____

_____

_____

_____

CREATE **Co-captain:** Get the materials. Then keep track of the time. You have fifteen minutes.
Team: Create a page for a brochure with helpful information for newcomers. Write a paragraph with advice on how to solve the problem you chose. Add art if you want.

REPORT **Spokesperson:** Show your page to the class. Tell the class about the problem and your ideas for solutions.

COLLECT **Captains:** Collect the page from each group. Staple the pages together to make a brochure for newcomers.

Unit 2 A Community Project MAKE A POSTER

TEAMS OF 4 Captain, Co-captain, Assistant, Spokesperson

GET READY **Team:** Imagine you are a committee that is trying to improve your community. Decide what kind of project you will organize— for example:
- having a block party
- organizing a neighborhood watch
- cleaning up the park

Captain: Ask your teammates, "What do we need to do first? Second? Third?"
Co-captain: Ask for the captain's ideas. Keep track of the time. You have ten minutes.
Assistant: Take notes.

First: _____

_____

Second: _____

_____

Third: _____

_____

CREATE **Co-captain:** Get the materials. Then keep track of the time. You have fifteen minutes.
Team: Create a poster showing the steps you will take to complete your community-improvement project. Use the information from your notes. Add art if you want.

REPORT **Spokesperson:** Show your poster to the class. Tell the class about your community-improvement project.

Materials
- large paper
- markers

TEAM PROJECTS

Unit 3   Test-Taking Tips MAKE A POSTER

Materials
• large paper
• markers

TEAMS OF 4 Captain, Co-captain, Assistant, Spokesperson

GET READY **Captain:** Ask your teammates if they think they are good or bad at taking tests, and why. Ask for ideas for what you should and shouldn't do before a test and during a test.
Co-captain: Ask for the captain's ideas. Keep track of the time. You have ten minutes
Assistant: Take notes in the chart.

Test-Taking Tips		
	You should . . .	**You shouldn't . . .**
Before a test		
During a test		

CREATE **Co-captain:** Get the materials. Then keep track of the time. You have fifteen minutes.
Team: Create a poster about how to succeed on tests. Write five or more things you should do and shouldn't do. Use the information from your chart. Add art if you want.

REPORT **Spokesperson:** Show your poster to the class. Tell the class about how to be a successful test-taker.

Unit 4 The Perfect Job DESIGN A HELP-WANTED AD

Materials
• 1 piece of white paper
• pens or markers
• stapler and staples

TEAMS OF 4 Captain, Co-captain, Assistant, Spokesperson

GET READY **Whole Class:** Ask your classmates what job they would like to have now. Find other students with the same or a similar job, and form a team of four.
Captain: Ask your teammates about the perfect job. What qualities and experience are needed? Ask for other information about the job.
Co-captain: Ask for the captain's ideas. Keep track of the time. You have ten minutes.
Assistant: Take notes in the chart.

Job	
Qualities needed	
Experience needed	
Other information (schedule, salary, etc.)	

CREATE **Co-captain:** Get the materials. Then keep track of the time. You have fifteen minutes.
Team: Write a help-wanted ad to post on the Internet. Include the information from your chart.

REPORT **Spokesperson:** Show your Internet want ad to the class. Tell the class about the job.

COLLECT **Captains:** Collect the Internet help-wanted ad from each group. Staple the ads together to make a booklet of job ads.

Unit 5 Rate the Airlines <u>MAKE A POSTER</u>

TEAMS OF 4 Captain, Co-captain, Assistant, Spokesperson

Materials
- large paper
- markers

GET READY **Captain:** Ask your teammates about an airline they have used. (If they have never flown, tell them to use their imagination.) Ask them about their experience—for example:
- Was your flight on time?
- Did your luggage arrive okay?
- How was the service?

Co-captain: Ask for the captain's information. Keep track of the time. You have ten minutes.

Assistant: Take notes in the chart.

	Name of Airline	Flight on time?	Luggage arrive?	Service good?
Student 1				
Student 2				
Student 3				
Student 4				

CREATE **Co-captain:** Get the materials. Then keep track of the time. You have fifteen minutes.

Team: Create a poster about the best airline. Use the information from your chart. Add art if you want.

REPORT **Spokesperson:** Show your poster to the class. Tell the class about the best airline.

Unit 6   Design an Electronic Item MAKE A POSTER

TEAMS OF 4 Captain, Co-captain, Assistant, Spokesperson

Materials
- large paper
- markers

GET READY **Team:** You are a design team for an electronics company. Design a new electronic item and think of a name for it.

Captain: Ask your teammates about the special features, warranty, and other information for your electronic item.

Co-captain: Ask for the captain's ideas. Keep track of the time. You have ten minutes.

Assistant: Take notes in the chart.

Type of item and its name	Special features	Warranty / Other Information

CREATE **Co-captain:** Get the materials. Then keep track of the time. You have fifteen minutes.

Team: Create an ad for the item you designed. Use the information from your chart. Add art if you want.

REPORT **Spokesperson:** Show your ad to the class. Tell the class about your electronic item and convince your classmates to buy it.

Unit 7   Transportation to school   MAKE A BAR GRAPH

TEAMS OF 4   Captain, Co-captain, Assistant, Spokesperson

GET READY   **Captain:** Ask your teammates how they get to school and how often they take each form of transportation. Ask them about the advantages and disadvantages of each.
Co-captain: Ask for the captain's information. Keep track of the time. You have ten minutes.
Assistant: Take notes in the chart.

Materials
- large paper
- markers
- rulers

Name	Bus	Train	Car	On foot (by walking)	Other

CREATE   **Co-captain:** Get the materials. Then keep track of the time. You have fifteen minutes.
Team: Create a bar graph about how your team gets to school. Use the information from your chart. Write a paragraph about the advantages and disadvantages of the most common form of transportation. Add art if you want.

REPORT   **Spokesperson:** Show your bar graph to the class. Tell the class how your team gets to school and the advantages and disadvantages of the most common form of transportation.

Unit 8   Healthy and Unhealthy Foods MAKE A POSTER

TEAMS OF 4   Captain, Co-captain, Assistant, Spokesperson

GET READY   **Captain:** Ask your teammates about their favorite foods. Ask them which ones are healthy and unhealthy, and why.
Co-captain: Ask for the captain's information. Keep track of the time. You have ten minutes.
Assistant: Take notes in the chart.

Materials
- large paper
- markers

Name	Healthy foods / Why	Unhealthy foods / Why

CREATE   **Co-captain:** Get the materials. Then keep track of the time. You have fifteen minutes.
Team: Create a poster about your favorite foods. Use the information from your chart. Add art if you want.

REPORT   **Spokesperson:** Show your poster to the class. Tell the class about your team's favorite foods and why they are healthy or unhealthy.

Unit 9 **Communications Skills** <u>MAKE A BROCHURE</u>

TEAMS OF 4 Captain, Co-captain, Assistant, Spokesperson

Materials
- 1 piece of white paper
- pens or markers
- stapler and staples

GET READY **Whole Class:** Ask your classmates what job they have or would like to have. Find other students with the same or a similar job, and form a team of four.

Captain: Ask your teammates which communication skills are important for this job. (See page 166 for a list of communication skills.)

Co-captain: Ask for the captain's ideas. Keep track of the time. You have ten minutes.

Team: Decide which three communication skills are the most important for this job and discuss why they are important.

Assistant: Take notes.

_____

_____

_____

_____

CREATE **Co-captain:** Get the materials. Then keep track of the time. You have fifteen minutes.

Team: Create a page for a brochure for new employees. Write a paragraph about the most important communication skills in the job you chose. Include information about why these skills are important. Add art if you want.

REPORT **Spokesperson:** Show your brochure page to the class. Tell the class about the important communication skills for the job you chose.

COLLECT **Captains:** Collect the page from each group. Staple the pages together to make a brochure for new employees.

Unit 10 Doctor's Visits MAKE A BROCHURE

TEAMS OF 4 Captain, Co-captain, Assistant, Spokesperson

GET READY **Captain:** Ask your teammates to compare visiting the doctor in the United States with visiting the doctor in their native countries. What is the same? What is different?
Co-captain: Ask for the captain's information. Keep track of the time. You have ten minutes.
Assistant: Take notes.

_____

_____

_____

Materials
- 1 piece of white paper
- pens or markers
- stapler and staples

CREATE **Co-captain:** Get the materials. Then keep track of the time. You have fifteen minutes.
Team: Create a page for a brochure for newcomers. Write a paragraph about visiting the doctor in the U.S. Add art if you want.

REPORT **Spokesperson:** Show your page to the class. Tell the class about how doctor's visits in the U.S. are the same as and different from visits in your native countries.

COLLECT **Captains:** Collect the page from each group. Staple the pages together to make a brochure about doctor's visits in the United States.

Unit 11 Money-Saving Tips <u>MAKE A BOOKLET</u>

TEAMS OF 4 Captain, Co-captain, Assistant, Spokesperson

GET READY **Captain:** Ask your teammates to suggest ways to save money in the United States—for example:
- eating at home
- shopping at thrift stores

Co-captain: Ask for the captain's ideas. Keep track of the time. You have fifteen minutes.

Assistant: Take notes.

_____

_____

_____

_____

CREATE **Co-captain:** Get the materials. Then keep track of the time. You have fifteen minutes.

Team: Create a page for a booklet about ways to save money in the U.S. Use the information from your chart. Add art if you want.

REPORT **Spokesperson:** Show your page to the class. Tell the class about how to save money in the U.S.

COLLECT **Captains:** Collect the page from each group. Staple the pages together to make a booklet about saving money.

Unit 12 Favorite Places MAKE A POSTER

TEAMS OF 4 Captain, Co-captain, Assistant, Spokesperson

GET READY **Captain:** Ask your teammates about their favorite place in the city where you live. Ask them where it is, what it's like, and why they like it.

Co-captain: Ask for the captain's information. Keep track of the time. You have fifteen minutes.

Assistant: Take notes in the chart.

Materials
- large paper
- markers

Name	Favorite place	Location	Description	Why they like it

CREATE **Co-captain:** Get the materials. Then keep track of the time. You have fifteen minutes.

Team: Choose one of the places you talked about. Create a poster about this place. Use the information from the chart. Add art if you want.

REPORT **Spokesperson:** Show your poster to the class. Tell the class about a favorite place in the city.

Map of the United States and Canada

RUSSIA

Chukchi Sea

GREENLAND

ICELAND

Bering Sea

Beaufort Sea

Baffin Bay

Alaska (USA)

Labrador Sea

Gulf of Alaska

Yukon Territory

Northwest Territories

Nunavut

PACIFIC OCEAN

C A N A D A

British Columbia

Alberta

Saskatchewan

Manitoba

Hudson Bay

Ontario

Quebec

Newfoundland

Prince Edward Island

New Brunswick

Nova Scotia

Maine

Washington

North Dakota

Minnesota

Michigan

New York

Vermont

New Hampshire

Massachusetts

Rhode Island

Connecticut

New Jersey

Delaware

Maryland

Bermuda (U.K.)

Montana

Oregon

Idaho

Wyoming

South Dakota

Wisconsin

Iowa

Pennsylvania

Ohio

Indiana

Illinois

West Virginia

Virginia

Nebraska

U N I T E D   S T A T E S   O F   A M E R I C A

Nevada

Utah

Colorado

Kansas

Missouri

Kentucky

North Carolina

ATLANTIC OCEAN

California

Arizona

New Mexico

Oklahoma

Arkansas

Tennessee

South Carolina

Alabama

Georgia

Mississippi

Texas

Louisiana

Florida

THE BAHAMAS

Hawaii (USA)

M E X I C O

Gulf of Mexico

CUBA

HAITI

Map of the World

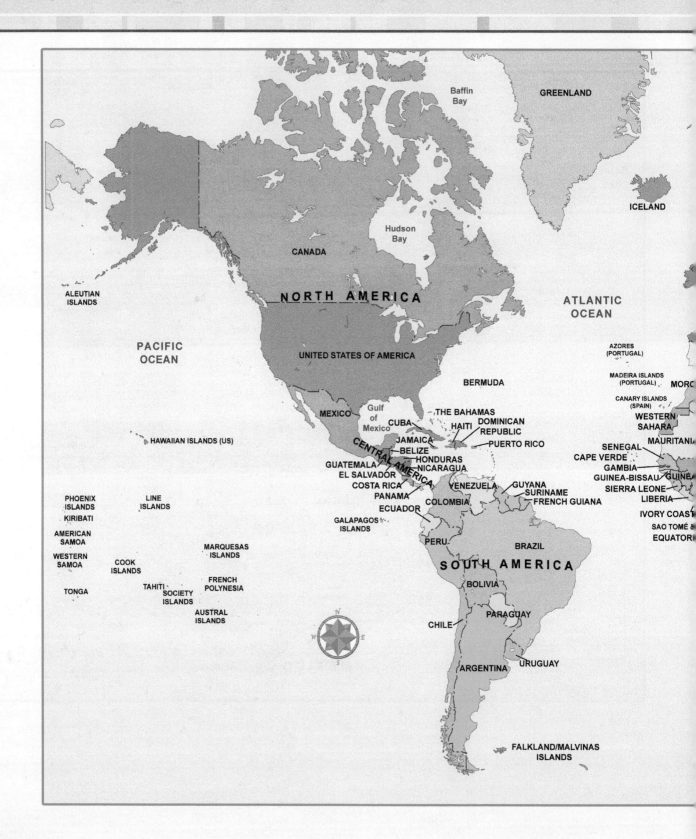

ARCTIC OCEAN

Barents Sea

RUSSIA

Bering Sea

Sea of Okhotsk

EUROPE

Black Sea
GEORGIA
ARMENIA
AZERBAIJAN
Caspian Sea
KAZAKHSTAN

MONGOLIA

ASIA

UZBEKISTAN
KYRGYZSTAN
TURKMENISTAN
TAJIKISTAN

PACIFIC OCEAN

TURKEY
Mediterranean Sea
NISIA
CYPRUS
LEBANON
ISRAEL
SYRIA
IRAQ
JORDAN
KUWAIT
BAHRAIN

IRAN
AFGHANISTAN

CHINA

NORTH KOREA
Sea of Japan
SOUTH KOREA

JAPAN

LIBYA
EGYPT
QATAR
SAUDI ARABIA
UNITED ARAB EMIRATES

PAKISTAN
NEPAL
BHUTAN

East China Sea

FRICA

GER
CHAD
ERITREA
YEMEN
OMAN
Arabian Sea

INDIA

MYANMAR BURMA
LAOS

TAIWAN

NORTHERN MARIANA ISLANDS

WAKE ISLAND (US)

DJIBOUTI
SOCOTRA (YEMEN)

BANGLADESH
THAILAND
VIETNAM

PHILIPPINES

GUAM

MARSHALL ISLANDS

RIA
CENTRAL AFRICAN REPUBLIC
SUDAN
ETHIOPIA
SOMALIA
CAMBODIA
South China Sea

YAP
PALAU

MEROON
CONGO
DEMOCRATIC REPUBLIC OF CONGO
UGANDA
KENYA

SRI LANKA

BRUNEI
MALAYSIA
SINGAPORE

FEDERATED STATES OF MICRONESIA

NAURU

RWANDA
BURUNDI
TANZANIA
MALAWI
COMOROS

INDIAN OCEAN

INDONESIA

PAPUA NEW GUINEA

SOLOMON ISLANDS

TUVALU

ANGOLA
ZAMBIA
ZIMBABWE

EAST TIMOR

Coral Sea

VANUATU

FIJI

NAMIBIA
BOTSWANA
MADAGASCAR

MAURITIUS
REUNION (FRANCE)

NEW CALEDONIA

REPUBLIC OF SOUTH AFRICA
MOZAMBIQUE
SWAZILAND
LESOTHO

AUSTRALIA

ICELAND

FAROE ISLANDS

ATLANTIC OCEAN

NORWAY
SWEDEN
Gulf of Bothnia
FINLAND

TASMANIA (Australia)

NEW ZEALAND

SHETLAND ISLANDS

SCOTLAND
North Sea

ESTONIA

UNITED KINGDOM
NORTHERN IRELAND

NETHERLANDS
LUXEMBURG
BELGIUM
DENMARK

Baltic Sea
LATVIA
LITHUANIA

RUSSIA

REPUBLIC OF IRELAND
ENGLAND
GERMANY

POLAND

BELARUS

EUROPE
FRANCE
LIECHTENSTEIN
CZECH REPUBLIC
AUSTRIA
SLOVAKIA
HUNGARY

UKRAINE

MOLDOVA

G. Gascogne
MONACO
SLOVENIA
CROATIA
BOSNIA-H.
ROMANIA
SERBIA & MONTENEGRO

ANDORRA
PORTUGAL
SPAIN
SWITZERLAND
ITALY
MACEDONIA
ALBANIA
BULGARIA
TURKEY
GREECE
MALTA

MAP OF THE WORLD   **277**

Li Chiu

342 Sycamore Street   Alhambra, CA 91803   520-555-9832   lchiu@notmail.com

OBJECTIVE

To find a full-time position as an Inventory Supervisor in Warehousing Management

WORK EXPERIENCE

Inventory Associate
IWS, Monterey Park, CA 05/08 to present
- Helped provide Quality Assurance and Inventory Control
- Built displays and organized inventory
- Checked condition of inventory
- Unloaded and counted inventory

Store Clerk
Koll's, Monterey Park, CA 03/04 to 04/08
- Worked cash register
- Provided excellent customer service
- Helped manager open and close store

SKILLS

- Knowledge of warehousing operations and workplace safety
- Knowledge of Quality Control systems
- Computer skills in Word, Excel, and Outlook
- Trilingual (English/Mandarin/Cantonese)
- Ability to work in a fast-paced, team environment
- Ability to identify and solve problems

EDUCATION

East Los Angeles College, Los Angeles, CA (B.S. expected 2013)
Iloilo Sun Yat Sen High School, China, H.S. diploma, 2004

Li Chiu
342 Sycamore Street
Alhambra, CA 91803
510-555-9832
lchiu@notmail.com

February 20, 2010

Mr. Jesse Kendall
Caruso's Inventory Specialists
3000 Overland Avenue, #200
Los Angeles, CA 90064

Dear Mr. Kendall:

I am interested in the position of full-time Inventory Supervisor, which I saw listed on JobBankUSA.com. I believe that my experience and skills in Quality Assurance and Inventory Control make me an ideal match for this position.

As my enclosed résumé shows, I have the qualifications for this position, including two years of full-time work experience at IWS in Inventory Operations. In my current Associate position at IWS, I am responsible for the quality and accurate count of a high volume of merchandise. In addition to providing quality control, I build attractive displays with my team at sites all over Los Angeles.

I would be happy to meet you to discuss this further. Please call me at 520-555-9832 and let me know a date and time that is convenient.

I look forward to hearing from you. Thank you for your consideration.

Sincerely,

Li Chiu

Li Chiu
Enc: résumé

CARUSO'S APPLICATION FOR EMPLOYMENT

PLEASE PRINT CLEARLY

NAME	ADDRESS	PHONE

If hired, can you show proof of eligibility to work in the U.S. within 3 days of hiring? ☐ YES ☐ NO

Are you 18 years of age or older? ☐ YES ☐ NO

POSITION APPLYING FOR: ☐ FT ☐ PT

AVAILABILITY: ☐ M–F DAY ☐ M–F EVE. ☐ WEEKENDS

Have you ever been fired from a job? ☐ YES ☐ NO   IF YES, what was the reason?

EDUCATION	NAME/ADDRESS	GRADUATED YES/NO	DIPLOMA OR DEGREE	YEAR	MAJOR
COLLEGE					
HIGH SCHOOL					

EMPLOYMENT HISTORY

CURRENT OR LAST EMPLOYER

EMPLOYER	ADDRESS	
SUPERVISOR	PHONE #	May we contact? ☐ YES ☐ NO
STARTING POSITION	ENDING POSITION	
DATES WORKED TO	JOB DUTIES	
SALARY/WAGE	REASON FOR LEAVING	

PREVIOUS EMPLOYER

EMPLOYER	ADDRESS	
SUPERVISOR	PHONE #	May we contact? ☐ YES ☐ NO
STARTING POSITION	ENDING POSITION	
DATES WORKED TO	JOB DUTIES	
SALARY/WAGE	REASON FOR LEAVING	

APPLICANT SIGNATURE: _____ DATE: _____

1. brain

2. esophagus

3. muscles

4. lungs

5. heart

6. kidneys

7. liver

8. stomach

9. gall bladder

10. small intestine

11. large intestine (colon)

12. bladder

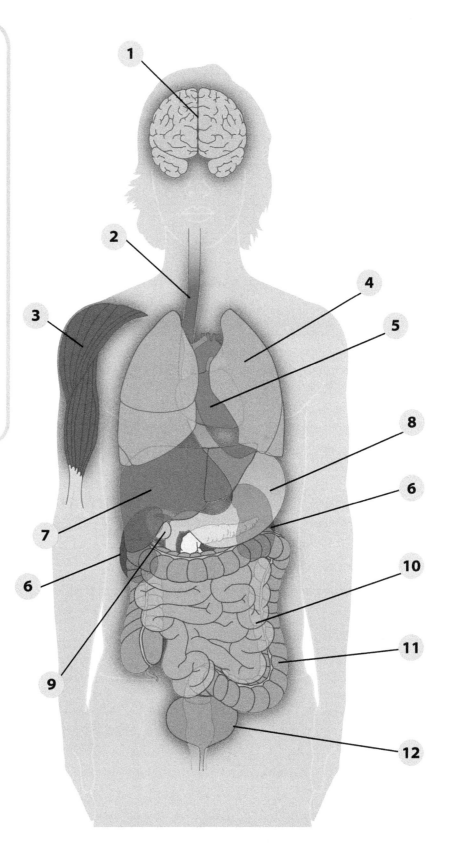

MEDICAL HISTORY FORM

Patient Name _____ Today's Date _____

Have you been under a doctor's care in the last two years? ❑ Yes ❑ No
If yes, for what? _____

Have you ever been hospitalized, had a major operation,
or a serious illness? ❑ Yes ❑ No
If yes, for what? _____

Have you taken any medications during the past year? ❑ Yes ❑ No
If so, what medicine? _____

Do you have any allergic reaction to any medication? ❑ Yes ❑ No
If yes, please list _____

Do you have any of these conditions. Check (✔) Yes or No.

Heart (disease)	❑ Yes	❑ No	Asthma	❑ Yes	❑ No
Chest pain	❑ Yes	❑ No	Allergies	❑ Yes	❑ No
High blood pressure	❑ Yes	❑ No	AIDS	❑ Yes	❑ No
Stroke	❑ Yes	❑ No	HIV	❑ Yes	❑ No
Diabetes (Type I/Type II)	❑ Yes	❑ No	Emphysema	❑ Yes	❑ No
Cancer	❑ Yes	❑ No	Tuberculosis	❑ Yes	❑ No

Have you lost or gained more than 10 pounds in the last year? ❑ Yes ❑ No
If so, give details. _____

Do you smoke? ❑ Yes ❑ No
Women: Are you pregnant? ❑ Yes _____Months ❑ No

The Three Branches of Government

The federal government has three branches. Each branch has certain powers, or things that it can do. The branches share power. They can also check, or stop, the actions of the other branches in certain ways, so there is a balace of power between branches. The columns on this page show the powers of the branches.

Legislative Branch: Congress

The legislative branch has two parts—the House of Representatives and the Senate. It has the power to:

- make laws
- declare war
- approve or disapprove of people that the president gives jobs to
- remove a Supreme Court justice (judge)
- remove the president

Executive Branch: the President

The executive branch has the power to:

- run the government
- carry out the laws
- make people obey laws
- command the armed forces
- suggest new laws
- choose Cabinet Members, Supreme Court justices (judges), other judges, and other officals
- approve or disapprove of laws made by Congress

Judicial Branch: the Supreme Court

The judicial branch has the power to:

- decide what a law means
- decide if a law agrees with the Constitution or disagrees with it
- decide if actions of the president agree with the Constitution or disagree with it
- settle arguments between the states
- protect the rights of U.S. citizens

Federal Holidays: An Overview

The U.S. Congress has marked ten holidays as "legal public holidays," when most federal government buildings are closed. Employers are not required to observe these holidays, but many employers observe six of them—New Year's Day, Presidents' Day, Memorial Day, Independence Day, Labor Day, Thanksgiving, and Christmas.

New Year's Day (January 1)

Americans celebrate the new year at home, with friends, and in gatherings. On New Year's Eve, many people have parties.

Martin Luther King, Jr. Day (third Monday in January)

This holiday honors the life of Dr. Martin Luther King, Jr., an important leader in the U.S. civil rights movement, who helped win equal civil rights for all U.S. citizens, regardless of their race. Dr. King was known for his famous speech "I have a dream". Dr. King received the Nobel Peace Prize in 1964. He was assassinated on April 4, 1968.

Presidents' Day (third Monday in February)

This holiday celebrates the first president of the United States, George Washington, and the sixteenth president, Abraham Lincoln.

Memorial Day (last Monday in May)

This holiday remembers all Americans soldiers killed in wars, including the Civil War, World Wars I and II, the Korean War, the Vietnam War and other conflicts.

Independence Day (July 4)

Independence Day is the birthday of the United States and celebrates the rights and freedoms of U.S. citizens. It honors the day that the Declaration of Independence was signed on July 4, 1776, when the American colonists declared their independence from Great Britain.

Labor Day (first Monday in September)

Labor Day honors working men and women in the U.S. For many Americans, the holiday means the end of summer and the beginning of the school year.

Columbus Day (second Monday in October)

This day remembers Christopher Columbus's first landing in the Americas, October 12, 1492.

Veterans Day (November 11)

Veterans Day remembers all of the armed forces, living or dead, who served in the United States military during times of peace or war.

Thanksgiving Day (fourth Thursday in November)

Thanksgiving is a holiday that is usually celebrated at home with a large meal when Americans give thanks for all that they have. Thanksgiving may have started in 1621 at a meal shared by English Pilgrims and members of the Wampanoag Native American tribe.

Christmas Day (December 25)

For Christians, this holiday celebrates the birth of Jesus on December 25. For other Americans, Christmas is a secular holiday.

Grammar Reference

UNIT 1, Lesson 6, page 16

Common non-count nouns

Groups of similar items: baggage, clothing, equipment, furniture, garbage, money, cash, change, traffic

Drinks and fluids: water, coffee, tea, milk, oil, soda, soup, gasoline, blood

Foods: beef, bread, butter, cheese, chicken, chocolate, ice cream, lettuce, meat, pasta, rice, salad, sugar

Materials: glass, gold, paper, wood

Gases: air, oxygen, smoke, pollution

Concepts: advice, fun, health, homework, love, information, music, news, violence, work

Languages: Arabic, Chinese, English, Spanish

Fields of study: art, computer science, engineering

Entertainment: baseball, basketball, soccer, tai chi

Activities: driving, studying, swimming, walking

Nature: weather, fog, heat, humidity, lightning, rain, snow, thunder, wind, light, darkness, sunshine, electricity, fire

Measure words*

a bit of salt

a bottle of juice

a box of cereal

a bowl of soup

a can of soda

a carton of eggs

a cup of sugar

a gallon of gasoline

a jar of jam

a quart of milk

a loaf of bread

a package of cookies

a piece of pie

a pinch of salt

a pound of rice

a slice of bread

a stick of butter

a tablespoon of oil

a teaspoon of sugar

Measure words are usually used with non-count nouns so we can count the nouns.

Grammar Reference

UNIT 2, Lesson 3, page 30

Contractions with *will*

I will	= I'll	it will	= it'll
you will	= you'll	we will	= we'll
he will	= he'll	they will	= they'll
she will	= she'll		

UNIT 3, Lesson 7, page 56

Simple past: irregular verbs

Base form	Simple past	Base form	Simple past
be	was	make	made
become	became	meet	met
buy	bought	pay	paid
catch	caught	put	put
come	came	read	read
cost	cost	ride	rode
cry	cried	run	ran
cut	cut	say	said
do	did	see	saw
drink	drank	sell	sold
drive	drove	send	sent
eat	ate	sit	sat
feel	felt	sleep	slept
find	found	speak	spoke
fly	flew	spend	spent
forget	forgot	stand	stood
get	got	steal	stole
give	gave	swim	swam
go	went	take	took
have	had	teach	taught
hear	heard	think	thought
hit	hit	try	tried
hold	held	wake	woke
hurt	hurt	wear	wore
know	knew	win	won
leave	left	write	wrote
lose	lost		

UNIT 4, Lesson 3, page 70

Contractions with the present perfect

I have	= I've
you have	= you've
he has	= he's
she has	= she's
it has	= it's
we have	= we've
they have	= they've
has not	= hasn't
have not	= haven't

Irregular verbs

Base form	Past participle	Base form	Past participle
be	been	make	made
become	become	meet	met
buy	bought	pay	paid
catch	caught	put	put
come	come	read	read
cost	cost	ride	ridden
cry	cried	run	run
cut	cut	say	said
do	done	see	seen
drink	drunk	sell	sold
drive	driven	send	sent
eat	eaten	sit	sat
feel	felt	sleep	slept
find	found	speak	spoken
fly	flown	spend	spent
forget	forgotten	stand	stood
get	gotten	steal	stolen
give	given	swim	swum
go	gone	take	taken
have	had	teach	taught
hear	heard	think	thought
hit	hit	try	tried
hold	held	wake	woken
hurt	hurt	wear	worn
know	known	win	won
leave	left	write	written
lose	lost		

UNIT 6, Lesson 6, page 116

Comparative spelling rules
Add *–er* + *than* to most adjectives with one syllable. For example:
cheap → **cheaper than**
For adjectives ending with *–y*, change the *–y* to *–ie* and add *–er*. For example:
happy → **happier than**
For adjectives ending with *–e*, add *–r*. For example:
nice → **nicer than**
For adjectives that end in a consonant + a vowel + consonant, double the consonant and add *–er*. For example:
big → **bigger than**
For adjectives with more than two syllables, add *more* before the adjective.
expensive → **more expensive than**

UNIT 8, Lesson 6, page 156

Verb + Gerund		
admit	enjoy	mind
appreciate	escape	miss
avoid	explain	practice
can't help	feel like	quit
consider	finish	recommend
delay	forgive	regret
discuss	give up (stop)	risk
dislike	keep (continue)	suggest

UNIT 10, Lesson 3, page 190

Common participial adjectives	
bored	boring
confused	confusing
embarrassed	embarrassing
excited	exciting
exhausted	exhausting
frightened	frightening
frustrated	frustrating
interested	interesting
overwhelmed	overwhelming
relaxed	relaxing
shocked	shocking
surprised	surprising
tired	tiring

UNIT 10, Lesson 10, page 202

Gerunds after prepositions

agree with	believe in	depend on
approve of	care about	disapprove of
argue with	complain about	
ask about	decide on	

UNIT 11, Lesson 10, page 222

Gerunds and infinitives as objects of verbs

Verb + Gerund

admit	discuss	finish	practice
appreciate	dislike	forgive	quit
avoid	enjoy	give up (stop)	recommend
can't help	escape	keep (continue)	regret
consider	explain	don't mind	risk
delay	feel like	miss	suggest

Verb + Infinitive

agree			
arrange	expect	pay	wait
ask	fail	plan	want
can't afford	help	prepare	wish
can't wait	learn	pretend	would like
choose	manage	promise	
decide	mean	refuse	
deserve	need	request	
	offer	seem	

Verb + Gerund or Infinitive

begin			
can't stand	forget	love	start
continue	hate	prefer	stop
	like	remember	try

UNIT 12, Lesson 3, page 230

Superlative
Add *–est* to most adjectives with one syllable. For example: **cheap** → **cheapest**   For adjectives ending with *–y*, change the *–y* to *–ie* and add *–est*. For example: **heavy** → **heaviest**   For adjectives ending with *–e*, add *–st*. For example: **nice** → **nicest**   For adjectives that end in a consonant + a vowel + consonant, double the consonant and add *–est*. For example: **big** → **biggest**   For adjectives with more than two syllables, add *the most* before the adjective.   **expensive** → **the most expensive**

UNIT 12, Lesson 6 , page 236

Passives	
Active sentence Many tourists visit The White House.	**Passive sentence** The White House is visited by many tourists.

Word List

UNIT 1

Bosnia, 6
Brazil, 6
Cambodia, 6
China, 6
Columbia, 6
cost of living, 12
Ecuador, 6

El Salvador, 6
Ethiopia, 6
Herzegovina, 6
interpreters, 12
Laos, 6
legal advice, 12
main idea, 13

mayor, 12
opportunities, 12
Peru, 6
the Philippines, 6
Poland, 6
quality of life, 12
Russia, 6

South Korea, 6
Sudan, 6
Ukraine, 6
Vietnam, 6

UNIT 2

apply, 26
contractor, 32
enroll, 26
equipment, 32
fix, 32

give up, 32
medical assistant, 29
next week, 42
obstacles, 39
real estate agent, 29

reality, 32
register, 26
short-term, 32
supports, 39
tomorrow, 42

volunteer, 26
welder, 29

UNIT 3

bring in, 51
check out, 52
design, 52
discipline, 48
do research, 46
drop out, 47, 51
falls behind, 50, 51
figure out an answer, 46
figure out, 51
fine, 52

get involved, 48
go online, 46
go over homework, 46
go over, 51
go to a parent-teacher
   conference, 46
hand in homework, 46
hand in, 50, 51
help out, 51
help someone out, 46

hit, 56
keeps up, 50
limit, 52
look up a word in a
   dictionary, 46
make fun of, 51
make up a test, 46
make up, 51
parent-teacher
   conferences, 48

performances, 52
pick on, 48, 51
renew, 52
return, 52
sign up, 51
vice principal, 48

UNIT 4

careful, 66
comfortable, 78
computer, 69
confident, 78
conservative, 78
cooperative, 66

culinary arts (cooking),
   69
dependable, 66
efficient, 66
enthusiasm, 78
hardworking, 66

health care, 69
HVAC, 69
infer, 79
make a good impression,
   78
motivated, 66

office, 69
organized, 66
pleasant, 66
punctual, 66

UNIT 5

arrivals and departures, 86
BART, 94
bins, 86
boarding pass, 86
carry-on bag, 86

connecting, 98
fees, 98
gate, 86
help, 103
kiosk, 86

luggage tags, 86
passenger, 86
prohibited, 98
responsible, 98
round-trip ticket, 86

security, 86
ticket agent, 86
transfer, 98
watch, 103
x-ray machine, 86

UNIT 6

bent, 106
brand, 112
broken, 106
cheaper, 116

convenient, 116
cracked, 106
damaged, 106
defective, 106

dented, 106
features, 112
flyers, 112
frayed, 106

leaking, 106
rebate, 118
scratched, 106
value, 112

UNIT 7

accelerator, 133
brakes, 133
bumper, 132
construction, 126
engine, 132
entrance ramp/on ramp,
 126
exit, 126
freeway/highway, 126

gas gauge, 133
glove compartment, 133
headlights, 132
hood, 132
horn, 133
ignition, 133
lane, 126
license plate, 132
obey, 138

overpass, 126
pedestrians, 138
shoulder, 126
sideview mirror, 132
slippery, 138
speedometer, 133
steering wheel, 133
suddenly, 138
tool booth, 126

tow truck, 126
traffic jam, 126
trunk, 132
turn signal, 133
vehicle, 126
windshield, 132, 133
wipers, 133

UNIT 8

administrators, 158
affordable, 158
appetizing, 158
be on a diet, 146
beverages, 158
brushing, 162
buy fresh fruits and
vegetables, 147
buy frozen dinners, 146
buying, 156
calories, 152

cavity, 160
cholesterol, 152
cook home-made meals,
 147
drink sugary beverages,
 146
eat fast food, 146
eating, 156
fat, 152
fatty foods, 147
floss, 160

flossing, 162
food choices, 157
get takeout, 146
gum disease, 160
have a snack, 146
ingredients, 152
junk food, 147
lard, 155
meal portion size, 157
nutritious, 158
pass laws, 158

physical activity, 157
runs in families, 153
satisfied, 158
school districts, 158
serving, 152
sodium, 152
TV/computer habits,
 157
x-ray, 160
your teeth, 162

UNIT 9

attend a training session, 166
balances, 172
be part of a team, 166
be responsible for something, 166
construction sites, 179
cope, 172

deal with complaints, 166
discuss a problem, 166,
exhausted, 172
factories, 179
follow instructions, 166
give instructions, 166

give someone feedback, 166
harm, 172
hospitals, 179
hotels, 179
interfere, 172
interrupted, 172
inventory, 168

quantity, 168
restaurants, 179
skimming, 172
supplies, 168
train other employees, 166
vendor, 168

UNIT 10

admissions, 186
brain, 192
chest pains, 195
confidential, 198
dose, 198
emergency room (ER), 186
esophagus, 192
gall bladder, 192
graphics, 199

heart, 192
high fever, 195
illnesses, 198
intensive care unit (ICU), 186
kidneys, 192
laboratory, 186
large intestine, 192
liver, 192
lungs, 192

maternity ward, 186
missing, 202
muscles, 192
nausea, 195
neck pain, 195
nurse's station, 186
participate, 198
pediatrics, 186
physical therapy, 186
radiology/imaging, 186

reaction, 198
require, 198
shortness of breath, 195
skin, 192
small intestine, 192
stomach, 192
surgery, 186
taking care of, 202
vaccinations, 198
vaccines, 198

UNIT 11

ATM/debit card, 206
ATM withdrawal, 206
available, 220
balance, 206

bank statement, 206
bank teller, 206
check, 206
credit card, 206

deposit slip, 206
direct deposit, 208
interest, 212
interest rate, 212

PIN (personal identification number), 211
transaction register, 206

UNIT 12

arrested, 234
court, 222
elected, 238
expensive, 226
fled, 234
located, 232
memorial, 222
monument, 222
museum, 222

national, 222
official, 234
overwhelmed, 234
place of worship, 234
popular, 226
summary, 235
the Capitol, 222
the Jefferson Memorial, 222

the Lincoln Memorial, 222
the National Air and Space Museum, 222
the Pentagon, 222
the Smithsonian American Art Museum, 222
the Supreme Court, 222

the U.S. Treasury, 222
the Washington Monument, 222
the White House, 222
tour guides, 230
tourists, 230
treasury, 222
visited, 232

Audio Script

UNIT 1

Page 8, Listen, Exercises A and B

Marco: Great game. Is this the Atlas league? I've heard about them.

Edwin: Yes. I love to come here and watch them.

Marco: Do they play every Saturday?

Edwin: Yes, unless it rains. By the way, my name is Edwin.

Marco: Hi, I'm Marco. Nice to meet you.

Edwin: Nice to meet you, too. Do you live around here?

Marco: Nearby. I live in Southside. I'm originally from Brazil.

Page 8, Listen, Exercise C

Edwin: Oh, yeah? There's a guy in the league from Brazil. He's over there, number 4.

Marco: Wait a minute, I know him! He's from my town, Corumba . . . Hey! Hector! It's me, Marco! Hi! Uh-oh. He lost the ball.

Page 14, Listen, Exercises A and B

Roger: This is 101.9 Radio New York. We turn now to events for the weekend. Ellen, could you tell us about the West Indian–American Day parade?

Ellen: Certainly, Roger. The annual West Indian–American Day parade takes place this Labor Day weekend, on Monday, Labor Day. Thousands of people will dance in beautiful costumes down Eastern Parkway in Brooklyn, New York. The costumes make this an exciting event. And don't forget the free music. You will hear calypso, rap, and reggae music played on guitars and steel drums. Last but not least, don't miss the food. This parade has terrific Caribbean food at low prices. You might want to try some rice and peas, or a little curried chicken or goat.

Roger: So, Monday, Labor Day, head to Brooklyn! Enjoy the sights, sounds, and the tastes of the West Indian–American Day Parade.

Page 20, Listen, Exercises A and B

Eva: Lucia: Edgar, are you working tomorrow?

Edgar: No, I have the weekend off.

Lucia: But you usually work on Saturdays.

Edgar: I do, but I asked for this weekend off.

Lucia: That's great. Let's go out. Why don't we go dancing!

Edgar: Dancing?

Lucia: Yeah! Remember? We used to go out all the time. We went out dancing every weekend.

Edgar: That was a long time ago!

Lucia: I know. But listen. I heard about a new restaurant, El Diamente. They play norteno, tejana, and mariachi—all the music we like.

Edgar: But I can't dance anymore. You know I've got back problems.

Lucia: Please, Edgar…

Edgar: Oh…all right…. After all, it is our anniversary.

Lucia: Oh, Edgar, you remembered! I love you! Listen. I'll ask Mom to baby-sit right now before you change your mind!

UNIT 2

Page 28, Listen, Exercises A, B, and C

Gustavo: So, Carmen, what's going on with you?

Carmen: You'll never guess! I'm going back to school.

Gustavo: Really?

Carmen: Uh-huh. I'm going to take night classes this fall.

Gustavo: Yeah? Where?

Carmen: At Los Angeles City College.

Gustavo: That's great. What will you study?

Carmen: Well, I want to be a nurse. I'd like to get an associate's degree.

Gustavo: What classes do you have to take for that?

Carmen: Well, first I have to take basic classes, like biology. Then I can apply to the clinical program.

Gustavo: How long will that take?

Carmen: I'm going to go part-time. If I work really hard, I might get the degree in three years.

Gustavo: Well, good luck. Here's an orange.

Carmen: An orange? Why an orange?

Gustavo: Don't you know? Student nurses have to practice giving shots. And they always start on an orange.

Carmen: Oh! Thanks.

Page 34, Listen, Exercises A and B

Sheng: So, Min, how's work?

Min: Oh, my new boss is terrible. I work hard, but he complains about my work a lot. Then he keeps me late, and I usually miss my bus. I'm going to look for a new job.

Sheng: I'm sorry to hear that. So are you looking for a job here at the community center?

| Min: | Yes, there are always good job postings on the bulletin board here. |
| Sheng: | Maybe you can go to a temp agency, too. Sometimes if you get a temporary job through a temp agency, it can become permanent. |

Page 34, Listen, Exercise C

Sheng:	Hey! Here's a job for you. It's a sales job.
Min:	Really? What does it say?
Sheng:	It says, "Full-time sales. Must be good with people. Good location. Flexible hours."
Min:	Where is it?
Sheng:	It's at an electronics store.
Min:	That's great! I have electronics experience. I think I'll call them. What's the number?
Sheng:	It's 555-5432.
Min:	What? That's my work number. That ad must be for my job!

Page 41, Listen, Exercises A, B, and C

And now some announcements from the Long Beach Community Center. Free classes in English and computers will start again on Wednesday, September 10. We're giving English placement tests on September 8 and 9 for new students. Space is limited, so come early. Classes are free, but you need to register in advance.

During the months of September and October, there will be a mural painting project at the corner of 5th Avenue and Dupont. This will be a special group project for people of all ages to improve our neighborhood. We'll be painting the mural every weekend from 9 until 5. Volunteers are welcome. To sign up, please call extension 6 or just drop by.

Finally, on Saturday, October 1, we're starting a food and clothing drive. Please bring in any cans or packages of food or clean clothes you don't need. And if you have time, please sign up to help distribute the food and clothes on October 20.

If you have any questions, please visit us at 89 Main Street, call us at 555-1234, or e-mail us at lbcc@gmail.com.

UNIT 3

Page 48, Listen, Exercise A

| Ted: | You're listening to WKVS, Radio Chicago. Our guest today is Kendra Williams. Kendra is a teacher in the Chicago public schools, and she's written a great book called Helping Your Child in School. Welcome. |
| Kendra: | Thank you, Ted. |

Page 48, Listen, Exercises B and C

Ted:	So, Kendra. What advice do you have for parents who want to help their kids in school?
Kendra:	Well, the first thing I tell parents is to get involved with their children's school. For example, join the parent-teacher organization, and go to school events. Some parents might feel they can't participate. Maybe they have an accent, or their grammar isn't perfect. That doesn't matter. You have the right to ask questions. And you should go to all meetings and parent teacher conferences so you'll know what's happening in the classroom.
Ted:	Any other advice to help children succeed at school?
Kendra:	Yes. I believe parents should help their children with their homework. Look it over. Talk about it.
Ted:	Hmm. I'll bet parents will learn a lot, too.
Kendra:	Yes. They probably will.
Ted:	OK. This is all good advice. But what about other problems, Kendra, that aren't about schoolwork? For example, what should a parent do if other children are picking on their child? Or if the area around the school isn't safe?
Kendra:	Those are really important questions, Ted. Well, first, they should write a note to the teacher. If the teacher can't help, the parent can see the vice principal. One of the vice principal's jobs is to make the school safe. He or she can discipline students. So, get to know your child's school and the vice principal and teachers. They can often help.
Ted:	Well, thank you so much. Your suggestions are very helpful. I'm sure our listeners have a lot of questions. After this commercial break, Kendra will answer questions. So call us at 1-800-555-WKVS …

Page 55, Listen, Exercises A, B, and C

Beatriz: Hey, Rafael. How was school?
Rafael: OK.
Beatriz: Just OK?
Rafael: Yeah.
Beatriz: What's wrong? You look really upset. Was it that homework for Mr. Meltzer? Did you get it back?
Rafael: Yeah. I got an A on it. It's not that.
Beatriz: Then what happened in school?
Rafael: Nothing.
Beatriz: I know something happened. What is it?
Rafael: It's some boys in my grade…Tommy and Mark.
Beatriz: What did they do?
Rafael: They took my lunch money.
Beatriz: When did that happen?
Rafael: On the school playground. They said they would beat me up, so I gave them my lunch money. Then in school they called me stupid. They called me a dummy. And they made fun of my name. I hate school. I'm never going back.

Page 59, Listen to a Telephone Recording, Exercises B and C

Hello, you have reached Randolph High School. Please listen to the following options.
For the principal's office, press 1.
For the vice principal's office, press 2.
For the main office, press 3.
For the counseling office, press 4
For the health clinic, press 5
For directions to the school, press 6.
For the teacher's room, press 7.

Page 60, Listen, Exercises A and B

Counselor: Hello, Mrs. Andrade. How are you?
Mrs. Andrade: Fine, thank you.
Counselor: So let's see, let me get Braulio's file. His grades were good this year, especially in math and science. He's a good student.
Mrs. Andrade: Thank you. He tries hard.
Counselor: Well, he's going to finish high school soon. But what about afterward? What would you like to see for Braulio's future?
Mrs. Andrade: We really want him to go to a four-year college.
Counselor: Oh, that's great. Well, in that case, we have to make sure he takes the right courses.

Page 60, Listen, Exercise C

Counselor: The four-year colleges want students to take certain classes. That way they are prepared for college.
Mrs. Andrade: What classes does he need?
Counselor: Well, he has to take four years of English. He also needs three years of social studies, math and science, as well as two years of a foreign language, and a semester of computer science.
Mrs. Andrade: Two years of a foreign language? Bravlio is fluent in Spanish. He can read it and write it.
Counselor: Well if he passes a test in Spanish, he doesn't have to take a foreign language. He can take math and science.

UNIT 4

Page 68, Listen, Exercises A and B

Have you ever thought about a career as a licensed technician? Things break every day. Licensed technicians are always needed to fix them. At ACME technical school, you'll learn the skills you need to become a licensed technician. We offer programs in air conditioning, refrigeration, electronics, and automotive and computer technology. Classes are held days, nights, and weekends. Study full-time or part-time in our state-of-the-art labs. We offer financial aid to those who qualify. And all programs come with free job placement services. Employers call us every day looking for you. So what are you waiting for? Call now. 1-800-ACME-FIX. That number again is 1-800-A-C-M-E-F-I-X.

Page 74, Listen, Exercises A and B

James: It's nice to meet you, Luis.
Luis: Thank you, it's nice to meet you, too, James.
James: So, I'm looking for a chef. Emilio, the assistant manager, recommended you. Can you tell me about your past restaurant experience?
Luis: Sure. I've been a line cook at El Norte restaurant for the last five years. I also owned my own café in Mexico City. And before that I worked in a couple of restaurants in Mexico for several years.
James: So why do you want to leave El Norte?
Luis: Well, I've worked there for four years. It's a very good restaurant, but I'm ready for a change. And your restaurant has a great reputation.

Page 74, Listen, Exercise C

James: Oh, so you've heard of the restaurant?

Luis: Of course. Everyone knows PJ's has great food.

James: Thank you. Now, tell me more about your experience. Have you ever planned menus or prepared meals for large groups of people?

Luis: Yes, I have. We serve a hundred people a night at El Norte.

James: And have you managed staff?

Luis: Sure, when I owned my café.

Page 81, Listen, Exercise A

Val: I'm Val Korey. We're here today with Leon Vasquez talking about the rights of employees. Leon is a career counselor at the Greenville Adult School. Today he's going to talk about our rights at job interviews. Leon, what questions are illegal for an employer to ask at a job interview?

Leon: Well, first of all, interviewers are not allowed to ask a person's age.

Val: Really? Why is that? You can usually tell a person's age just by looking at them.

Leon: That's true, but it's still illegal for an employer to ask your age. It's a way to protect older workers from discrimination.

Val: I see. Can you give us another example of an illegal question?

Leon: All right, here's a common one. Employers are not allowed to ask if someone is married or has children.

Val: Why would employers want to know that?

Leon: The employer might think that if someone has little children, they won't be dependable. They may think the mother or father will call in sick too often, or come in late.

Val: So, questions about age and family are not allowed. Are there other types of illegal questions?

Leon: Yes. There are many. For example, employers can't ask questions about religion, race, age, or national origin.

Val: Really? You mean an employer isn't allowed to ask, "Where were you born?"

Leon: That's correct.

Val: How interesting. I had no idea. Well, thanks, Leon. We have to take a break now. We'll be back after this commercial break with your questions for Leon Vasquez.

Page 81, Listen, Exercise B

Val: You're listening to ON THE AIR. I'm Val Korey. We're here today talking about the rights of employees with Leon Vasquez. Leon is a career counselor at Greenville Adult School. Today he's going to talk about our rights at job interviews. Leon, what kinds of questions are illegal for an employer to ask at a job interview?

Leon: Well, first of all, interviewers are not allowed to ask a person's age.

Val: Really? Why is that? You can usually tell a person's age just by looking at them.

Leon: That's true, but it's still illegal for an employer to ask your age. It's a way to protect older workers from discrimination.

Val: I see. Can you give us another example of an illegal question?

Leon: All right, here's a common one. Employers are not allowed to ask if someone is married or has children.

Val: Why would employers want to know that?

Leon: The employer might think that if someone has little children, they won't be dependable. They may think the mother or father will call in sick too often, or come in late.

Page 81, Listen, Exercise C

Val: So questions about age and family are not allowed. Are there other types of illegal questions?

Leon: Yes. There are many. For example, employers can't ask questions about religion, race, age, or national origin.

Val: Really? You mean an employer isn't allowed to ask, "Where were you born?"

Leon: That's correct.

Val: How interesting. I had no idea. Well, thanks, Leon. We have to take a break now. We'll be back after this commercial break with your questions for Leon Vasquez.

UNIT 5

Page 88, Listen, Exercise A

Announcement 1:

Announcer: Flight number 385 leaving for Bogota will begin the boarding procedure at Gate 13A. Passengers with small children or needing special assistance, may pre-board now.

Mother: Carlos, take your bag. We can board now.

Announcement 2:

Announcer: Attention passengers on flight number 289 to San Diego. Flight number 289 has been canceled.

Passenger A: Excuse me, I couldn't hear the announcement. Did you hear what they said?

Passenger B: Flight 289 was canceled.

Passenger A: They canceled a flight! Wait, that's our flight!

Passenger C: Oh, no, we'll miss the wedding!

Announcement 3:

Announcer: Attention passengers on flight number 870 to Caracas. The departure gate has changed. Flight number 870 will now be departing from gate 22.

Mother: What are we going to do? Samara won't be able to walk that far. She's only 3.

Father: Don't worry, I can carry her.

Announcement 4:

Passenger A: We're late!

Passenger B: Wait, Julio. I can't run that fast!

Passenger A: Keep running!

Announcer: Attention passengers: Flight number 901 is experiencing a mechanical difficulty. Boarding has been delayed. Flight number 901 will board in approximately 30 minutes.

Passenger A: You can stop running, Julio.

Page 94, Listen, Exercises A and B

Ken: Hey, Amy. It's me, Ken. I'm on BART. Sorry, I'm running late. There was a 30-minute delay. A train got stuck at 24th Street.

Amy: That's too bad. So, what time are you arriving then?

Ken: I think about 3:30. Which station should I get off at?

Amy: The Lake Merritt Station. Call me when you get there. I'll park and wait for you. Oh, I forgot to tell you. My car isn't running, but my mom will let me borrow hers. I'll be in a red Toyota Corolla.

Ken: Great. See you soon.

Page 94, Listen, Exercise C

Amy: Hello?

Ken: Hey, Amy. Where are you?

Amy: Over here, next to the taxi stand. How come I don't see you? Oh, there you are. You're wearing that polo shirt I gave you. It looks good.

Ken: It looks good? I look good.

Amy: OK, do you have all your bags?

Ken: Yeah. Wait a minute. This bag isn't mine!

Page 101, Listen, Exercise A

Announcer: Bus number 908 from Jacksonville to Miami has been canceled due to bad weather conditions. The next bus to Miami, bus number 918, will be leaving at 3:30 from gate number 24.

Page 101, Listen, Exercises B and C

Announcer: Bus number 908 from Jacksonville to Miami has been canceled due to bad weather conditions. The next bus to Miami, bus number 918, will be leaving at 3:30 from gate number 24.

Mrs. Ramirez: Hello?

Carlos: Hi, Mom. It's me.

Mrs. Ramirez: Carlos! We can't wait to see you.

Carlos: Listen, Mama. I have bad news and good news. I can't take the two o' clock bus. I missed it. I'm taking a bus at 3:30.

Mrs. Ramirez: Oh, Carlos. I made a big dinner, and everyone's coming. You won't be able to eat with us.

Carlos: I know, Mom, but we'll still be able to spend the whole Christmas day together tomorrow. I've got good news too . . . I'll be back next month for your 70th birthday.

Mrs. Ramirez: You will? Oh, that's great. But Carlos, would you do me a little favor?

Carlos: Sure, Mom.

Mrs. Ramirez: Don't tell anyone it's my 70th birthday.

Carlos: Of course not, Mom. Anyway, no one would believe you're 70.

Page 101, Listen, Exercise C

Carlos: Listen, Mom. I have bad news and good news. I can't take the two o' clock bus. I missed it. I'm taking a bus at 3:30.

Mrs. Ramirez: Oh, Carlos. I made a big Christmas Eve dinner, and everyone's coming. You won't be able to eat with us.

Carlos:	I know, Mom, but we'll still be able to spend the whole Christmas day together tomorrow. I've got good news, too . . . I'll be back next month for your 70th birthday.
Mrs. Ramirez:	You will? Oh, that's great. But Carlos, would you do me a little favor?
Carlos:	Sure, Mom.
Mrs. Ramirez:	Don't tell anyone it's my 70th birthday.
Carlos:	Of course not, Mom. Anyway, no one would believe you're 70.

UNIT 6

Page 108, Listen, Exercises A and B

Emilio:	Ana. Pull out the plug.
Ana:	What's the matter?
Emilio:	I think something burning.
Ana:	Well, what is it? What do you think is wrong?
Emilio:	Maybe it's the motor, or maybe the bag is full. Did you change the bag?
Ana:	Of course I changed the bag. It's just old.
Emilio:	When did we buy this vacuum? Do you think it's still under warranty?
Ana:	No way. This thing is at least five years old.
Emilio:	I guess we'll have to buy a new one, then.
Ana:	Good. I never liked this vacuum anyway.

Page 114, Listen, Exercise A

Luis:	Manuel, I've got a big problem.
Manuel:	What's wrong, Luis?
Luis:	I just got my cell phone bill. It was 653 dollars!
Manuel:	What? How did that happen?
Luis:	Last month I signed up for a cheaper plan with Sunphone. The plan said 900 minutes for 99 dollars. The salesperson said I could talk for 900 minutes during the day and unlimited minutes on nights and weekends.
Manuel:	So, what happened?
Luis:	Look at this bill. They charged me for both nights and weekends.
Manuel:	Did you call the company?
Luis:	I did. But they said there's nothing they can do. It's in my contract. The contract says 900 minutes a month total.
Manuel:	Call the company back. Tell them you won't pay.
Luis:	I did. They said they'll shut off my phone. What should I do?

Manuel:	Pay the bill. Then, cancel your cell phone plan and pay the cancellation fee. Then switch to Horizon. They have better plans.
Luis:	Thanks, Manuel.

Page 114, Listen, Exercise B

Luis:	Manuel, I've got a big problem.
Manuel:	What's wrong, Luis?
Luis:	I just got my cell phone bill. It was 653 dollars!
Manuel:	What? How did that happen?
Luis:	Well, last month I signed up for a cheaper plan with Sunphone. The plan said 900 minutes for 99 dollars. The salesperson said I could talk for 900 minutes during the day and unlimited minutes on nights and weekends.
Manuel:	So, what happened?
Luis:	Look at this bill. They charged me for both nights and weekends.

Page 114, Listen, Exercise C

Manuel:	Did you call the company?
Luis:	I did. But they said there's nothing they can do. It's in my contract. The contract says 900 minutes a month total.
Manuel:	Call the company back. Tell them you won't pay.
Luis:	I did. They said they'll shut off my phone. What should I do?
Manuel:	Pay the bill. Then, cancel your cell phone plan and pay the cancellation fee. Then switch to Horizon. They have better plans.
Luis:	Thanks, Manuel.

Page 120, Listen, Exercises A and B

Clerk:	May I help you?
Rachel:	Yes, I want to return this cell phone.
Clerk:	Sure . . .Is there anything wrong with it?
Rachel:	The volume doesn't work very well.
Clerk:	OK. Will that be a refund or an exchange?
Rachel:	I'd like an exchange, please.
Clerk:	All right. Do you have your sales receipt?
Rachel:	Yes, here it is. Could I exchange it for this Simsung?
Clerk:	Sure, but that's $30 more.
Rachel:	How about this Moondisk?
Clerk:	That isn't is quite as expensive…Let's see, it's $55.
Rachel:	I'll take it. But do you have any in silver?
Clerk:	I'm sorry, we're all out of silver.
Rachel:	Could you call another store to see if they have it in silver?
Clerk:	Sure. No problem.

UNIT 7

Page 127, Word Play, Exercise A

Radio traffic announcer: The time is 2:51. This is KFWB News on the 1s. Here's a look at traffic in Los Angeles. There has just been an accident on the 110 South at Manchester Avenue. Drivers are advised to take alternate routes south, Vermont or Broadway.

Page 127, Word Play, Exercise B

Radio traffic announcer: The time is 2:51. This is KFWB News on the 1s. Here's a look at traffic in Los Angeles. There has just been an accident on the 110 South at Manchester Avenue. Drivers are advised to take alternate routes south, Vermont or Broadway.

On Slauson Avenue East, there is a vehicle blocking one lane causing a traffic jam.

On the 105 East, one lane is closed for road construction from South Main Street to South Central Avenue. There is a delay of 25 minutes.

On the 405 South, an accident is in the final stages of being cleared at La Tijera Boulevard.

This is KFWB traffic news on the 1s. The next report will be at 3:01.

Page 128, Listen, Exercise A

Mechanic:	So, what can I do for you?
Li:	I'd like an oil change.
Mechanic:	No problem.
Li:	How much will that be?
Mechanic:	$29.95.
Li:	OK. How long will that take?
Mechanic:	About half an hour.

Page 128, Listen, Exercise B

Mechanic:	So, what can I do for you?
Li:	I'd like an oil change.
Mechanic:	No problem.
Li:	How much will that be?
Mechanic:	$29.95.
Li:	OK. How long will that take?
Mechanic:	About half an hour.
Li:	Good.
Mechanic:	But when was the last time you had your tires rotated?
Li:	Oh, I think about a year ago.
Mechanic:	A year? Then we should rotate the tires.

Li:	How long will it take?
Mechanic:	About 15 minutes longer.
Li:	OK.
Mechanic:	By the way, did you see there's a big dent in the back of your car?
Li:	Oh, yeah I know. I keep it that way on purpose.
Mechanic:	What? Why?
Li:	Well, a lot of people drive Subarus, so it's easier for me to know it's my car. When I'm in a parking lot, I just look for the dent, and I know it's mine.
Mechanic:	Oh.

Page 134, Listen, Exercise A

Officer:	Are you hurt, sir?
Mr. Desmond:	My neck is sore.
Officer:	Do you need an ambulance?
Mr. Desmond:	Nah, I'm OK.
Officer:	OK. License, registration, and insurance please. Mr. Desmond, can you tell me what happened?
Mr. Desmond:	Yeah, I was slowing down to make a right-hand turn onto Martine Avenue, and that car behind me was going too fast and hit me. I think she was talking on her cell phone.
Officer:	Thank you, Mr. Desmond. I've got to take a statement from the other driver . . . Stay there until I finish writing the report . . . Are you hurt, Ma'am?
Ms. Yu:	No, I'm all right, officer.
Officer:	OK. May I see your license, registration, and insurance please?...Well, Ms. Yu, can you explain what happened?
Ms. Yu:	Yes, officer. I was driving in the right hand lane. There was nothing in front of me. Suddenly this car came out of nowhere—I think it came from the left lane. It was slowing down in front of me to turn onto Martine Avenue. There wasn't time for me to stop.
Officer:	Were you talking on a cell phone?
Ms. Yu:	Err . . . No . . .
Officer:	You realize that talking on a cell phone is against the law in California, right?
Ms. Yu:	Um, no, I didn't know that. But I wasn't talking on the phone.
Officer:	Hmm. OK. I'm going to go fill out the accident report. Wait here.

Page 134, Listen, Exercise B

Officer: Are you hurt, sir?

Mr. Desmond: My neck is sore.

Officer: Do you need an ambulance?

Mr. Desmond: Nah, I'm OK.

Officer: OK. License, registration, and insurance please. Mr. Desmond, can you tell me what happened?

Mr. Desmond: Yeah, I was slowing down to make a right-hand turn onto Martine Avenue, and that car behind me was going too fast and hit me. I think she was talking on her cell phone.

Officer: Thank you, Mr. Desmond. I gotta take a statement from the other driver. . . Stay there until I finish writing the report.

Page 134, Listen, Exercise C

Officer: Are you hurt, Ma'am?

Ms. Yu: No, I'm all right, officer.

Officer: OK. May I see your license, registration, and insurance please?...Well, Ms. Yu, can you explain what happened?

Ms. Yu: Yes, officer. I was driving in the right hand lane. There was nothing in front of me. Suddenly this car came out of nowhere—I think it came from the left lane. It was slowing down in front of me to turn onto Martine Avenue. There wasn't time for me to stop.

Officer: Were you talking on a cell phone?

Ms. Yu: Err . . .No . . .

Officer: You realize that talking on a cell phone is against the law in California, right?

Ms. Yu: Um, no, I didn't know that. But I wasn't talking on the phone.

Officer: Hmm. OK. I'm going to go fill out the accident report. Wait here.

Page 141, Listen, Exercise A

Tara: This is Tara O'Neil. . . .with "Tips for Drivers."

We don't like to think about car accidents, but it's important to be ready if one happens. Do you know what to do if you have a car accident?
First, you must stop any time that you have an accident. This is for all kinds of accidents, with moving cars, parked cars, and pedestrians. If you hit something and don't stop, this is a serious felony called a hit-and-run. If you hit and run, you can go to jail or lose your driver's license.

So what do you do after an accident? First, this depends on whether you hit a parked car or a moving car.

If you hit a parked car, try to find the owner. If you can't, you must leave a note for them on their car. Write your name, telephone number, your address, and write an explanation of the accident. You also need to report the accident to the local police.

If you hit another moving car, make sure everyone is OK. If someone is hurt, call 911 for an ambulance.

Now, what other details are you responsible for after an accident?

When you have a car accident, you need to get information for your insurance company. Write down the other driver's name, address, driver's license number, license plate number, and insurance information and give them your information, too. Make sure you also call the police. They will come and do a report of the accident. You must wait for them.

Next, look carefully at your car. Has it been damaged? If you have a camera, take a photo of the damage.

When the police come, tell the officer what happened and do as he tells you. You will need to show the officer your proof of auto insurance and your driver's license. you don't have these things, you may have to pay a fine. You might also lose your driver's license. When the police officer leaves, you can go. But ask him where you can get a copy of the traffic report. You might need it later to show your insurance company. Also, write down the officer's name.

After the accident, remember, you have to call your insurance company and report the accident.

Thank you. Listen again next week for "Tips for Drivers."

Page 141, Listen, Exercise B

Tara: This is Tara O'Neil. . . .with "Tips for Drivers." We don't like to think about car accidents, but it's important to be ready if one happens. Do you know what else to do if you have a car accident? First, you must stop any time that you ever have an accident. This is for all kinds of accidents, with moving cars, parked cars, and pedestrians. If you hit something and don't stop, this is a serious felony called a hit and run. If you hit and run, you can go to jail or lose your driver's license. So what do you do after an accident? First, this depends on whether you hit a parked car or a moving car. If you hit a parked car, try to find the owner. If you can't, you must leave a note for them on their car. Write your name, telephone number, your address, and write an explanation of the accident.

Page 141, Listen, Exercise C

Tara: If you hit another moving car, make sure everyone is OK. If someone is hurt, call 911 for an ambulance.

Now, what other details are you responsible for after an accident?

When you have a car accident, you need to get information for your insurance company. Write down the other driver's name, address, driver's license number, license plate number, and insurance information and give them your information, too. Make sure you also call the police. They will come and do a report of the accident. You must wait for them.

Next, look carefully at your car. Has it been damaged? If you have a camera, take a photo of the damage.

When the police come, tell the officer what happened and do as he tells you. You will need to show the officer your proof of auto insurance and your driver's license. If you don't have these things, you may have to pay a fine. You might also lose your driver's license.

When the police officer leaves, you can go. But ask him where you can get a copy of the traffic report. You might need it later to show your insurance company. Also, write down the officer's name.

After the accident, you have to call your insurance company and report the accident.

Thank you. Listen again next week for "Tips for Drivers."

Page 148, Listen, Exercises A and B

Tanesha: Good morning. You're listening to WFUT radio. I'm Tanesha Wilson with Our Nation's Health. Today we're talking about eating habits of American workers.

According to a recent national survey, almost 1/3 of workers skip breakfast, lunch, or both almost every weekday. This can cause serious health problems. The survey also shows 89% of the workers have a snack during the work day. And more than half of the snacks consist of junk food such as potato chips, candy, or doughnuts. So why do people eat all of these snacks? The answer is, they're hungry, stressed, and they need energy. And now let's hear from some workers themselves. Here we are in the Mount Sinai Hospital cafeteria in Miami, Florida. Excuse me sir, do you work here?

Man: Yes, I do.

Tanesha: I'm Tanesha Wilson with WFUT radio. We're doing a report on eating habits. Would you mind answering a few questions?

Man: Not at all.

Tanesha: Great, thanks. Do you ever skip meals?

Man: Well, sometimes I skip breakfast if I'm late to work.

Tanesha: And do you ever snack between meals?

Man: Sure. Doesn't everyone?

Tanesha: I guess so. So, what kind of snack do you usually have at work? Fruit? Crackers?

Man: No, I usually get something from the vending machines, like chips or cookies.

Tanesha: Thank you. Well, you heard it straight from the hospital staff in Mount Sinai Hospital in Miami, Florida.

Page 153, Learn About Diabetes Exercises A and B

Radio announcer: What do you know about Diabetes? Diabetes is a disease you can develop when the sugar levels in your body are too high. Most foods we eat have sugar. Our bodies make something called insulin. This changes the sugar into the energy we need for daily activities. When you have diabetes, things go wrong. Your body does not make enough insulin or use it well.

If you don't have enough insulin, too much sugar stays in your blood. Over time, this can cause serious problems. For example, it can damage your eyes or cause heart disease. It can cause many other serious problems.

There are two types of diabetes—type 1 and type 2. More people have type 2 diabetes. Some early signs of diabetes are: being very tired, very thirsty, or losing weight. People with type 2 diabetes often have no symptoms for a long time. Everyone should go to the doctor regularly to be sure they do not have it. The doctor can look for signs of diabetes with a simple blood test.

No one knows exactly what causes diabetes. We do know that diabetes runs in some families. Overweight people are also more likely to get diabetes. There is no cure. Diabetes is a lifelong disease. However, there are ways to help control it and lead a healthy life. See your doctor regularly. Watch your diet and weight carefully and eat fewer sweet foods. Getting regular exercise is also very important. Finally, because children can also get diabetes, parents should watch their children's diet and weight, and take them to the doctor regularly. Eating healthy foods and getting exercise is just as important for children as it is for adults.

Page 154, Listen, Exercise A

Bob: Good afternoon. This is Bob Lyons, from Family Health Matters.

In the past ten years, more children have become overweight. In a recent study, the government found that about 17 percent of children and adolescents age 2 to 19 in the United States are overweight. Being overweight can cause serious health problems, like heart problems and type 2 diabetes.
Why are so many children overweight? The answers are poor eating habits and not enough physical activity. So what can parents do to stop their children from becoming overweight or help them lose weight?

Here are some tips:
First, encourage healthy eating habits.
Give your children plenty of vegetables, fruits, and whole grain foods like whole wheat bread.
Make sure your children get plenty of low-fat dairy products and lean meats like chicken and fish.
Beans are also good for protein.

Make sure that meals are not too large.
Don't give your children too many drinks or desserts with a lot of sugar or saturated fat.

What else can you do to keep your children healthy? The second important thing you can do is to increase your children's physical activity. Children and teens should get 60 minutes of physical activity most days of the week. Remember that your children will follow your example. Make sure that you are physically active and encourage your children to join you.

Here are examples of activities you can do with your children: Take a walk, ride a bike, play soccer or jump rope. Encourage your children to spend more time outside. Limit their time watching TV or on the computer.

For Family Health Matters, I'm Bob Lyons.

Page 154, Listen, Exercise B

Bob: Good afternoon. This is Bob Lyons, from Family Health Matters.

In the past ten years, more children have become overweight. In a recent study, the government found that about 17 percent of children and adolescents age 2 to 19 in the United States are overweight. Being overweight can cause serious health problems, like heart problems and type 2 diabetes.

Why are so many children overweight? The answers are poor eating habits and not enough physical activity.

Page 154, Listen, Exercise C

Bob Lyons: So what can parents do to stop their children from becoming overweight or help them lose weight?

Here are some tips: First, Encourage healthy eating habits. Give your children plenty of vegetables, fruits, and whole grain foods like whole wheat bread. Make sure your children get plenty of low-fat dairy products and lean meats like chicken and fish. Beans are also good for protein. Make sure that meals are not too large. Don't give your children too many drinks or desserts with a lot of sugar or saturated fat.

What else can you do to keep your children healthy? The second important thing you can do is to increase your children's physical activity. Children and teens should get 60 minutes of physical activity most days of the week. Remember that your children will follow your example. Make sure that you are physically active and encourage your children to join you.

Here are examples of activities you can do with your children: Take a walk, ride a bike, play soccer or jump rope. Encourage your children to spend more time outside. Limit their time watching TV or on the computer.

For Family Health Matters, I'm Bob Lyons.

Page 160, Listen, Exercises A and B

Dentist:	Well, Ho, I looked at your X-rays. Your teeth look pretty good, but when I cleaned them, your gums were bleeding a little bit. You probably need to floss more. Do you floss?
Ho:	Well, not that much.
Dentist:	Try to floss more. Flossing keeps your gums healthy.
Ho:	Isn't brushing my teeth enough?
Dentist:	Brushing after every meal is important, too. But you can't always get your teeth clean unless you floss. If you don't get all the food off your teeth, it will turn to plaque and cause cavities. And you can also get gum disease.
Ho:	What is gum disease?
Dentist:	If you have too much bacteria in your mouth, your gums get red and swollen. Look at this picture. This is a picture of gum disease.
Ho:	Ugh.
Dentist:	OK, I think we're done. Let me give you a toothbrush to take home.
Ho:	Thanks. Do you also give away dental floss?
Dentist:	Sure, here you go. And here is your free toothbrush. Is your toothbrush at home soft or hard?
Ho:	I think it's a hard toothbrush…why?
Dentist:	A soft one is better. It's easier on your teeth. See you next time. And make sure to floss.
Ho:	You had better believe I will.

UNIT 9

Page 168, Listen, Exercises A and B

Margo:	OK, you need to be sure there are enough supplies in the kitchen. First you do inventory. Start with the things on the counter. See if there are enough paper cups and paper towels. If something is missing, check in the cabinets and drawers.
Jason:	OK.
Margo:	If we don't have enough, you need to order more.
Jason:	How do I do that?
Margo:	You fill out an inventory sheet. Write down what you need under item. Then write the quantity or amount.
Jason:	Which box shows quantity?
Margo:	This one.
Jason:	OK. Then what do I do?
Margo:	Call Anthony. He's our vendor. He sells us our supplies. We give the order over the phone. Now be careful. Sometimes people order the wrong amount. Make sure you get the right quantity. Always check how many come in a box. But the most important thing is, make sure we always have enough coffee. The employees here are very unhappy without their coffee.
Jason:	Yes, Margo. I know what you mean.

Page 175, Exercises A, B, and C

Bill:	Carl, Tony is out of the office for a while and he didn't have time to finish a job. I need you to do it for him.
Carl:	No problem. What is it?
Bill:	I need you to look at a building…a condominium. I want you to take photos and finish the report for Tony. I'll check it. The bank wants the report by Friday, so we have to work quickly.
Carl:	Is there anything else?
Bill:	No, that's all. Oh…you asked to see me earlier today.
Carl:	Yes, um…I was wondering if I could leave early next Friday. My son is graduating from high school. We want to be there for the graduation.
Bill:	Sure. I don't see why not. Congratulations, by the way.
Carl:	Thanks, Bill.

Page 180, Listen, Exercises A and B

Margo: Jason, Mr. Yang just called me. He said that the copy machine next to his office isn't working.

Jason: It isn't?

Margo: That's right. Did you check all the copy machines and printers this morning?

Jason: Well, I checked almost all of them, but maybe I forgot about that one. I'm sorry.

Margo: OK, Jason. I know you're new here. But remember: You need to check all of the copy machines and printers first thing when you come in. We need to make sure they're working. If there's a problem, we need to fix it. If we can't fix it, we have to call service repair.

Jason: I understand, Margo. I'll make it sure doesn't happen again.

Margo: OK, very good.

UNIT 10

Page 188, Exercise A

Office Assistant: Hello. Westside Health Center.

Yao: Hi. This is Yao Chen. I have an appointment with Dr. Barnes for today at 4:00, but I need to cancel.

Office Assistant: OK, Mr. Chen. Would you like to reschedule?

Yao: Yes, I would. Can I come in next Thursday at 3:00?

Office Assistant: Sorry, we're all booked. How about Friday at 3:00?

Yao: I think that's OK. But let me call you back. I have to check with my boss.

Office Assistant: All right. Bye.

Page 188, Exercise B

Office Assistant: Hello. Westside Health Center.

Alvia: Hi, I'd like to make an appointment with Dr. Barnes.

Office Assistant: Who's calling please?

Alvia: Alvia Ledesma.

Office Assistant: Are you a new patient?

Alvia: No, I'm not.

Office Assistant: What's the problem, Ms. Ledesma?

Alvia: I'm tired all the time, but I can't sleep. I feel awful, and I don't know what to do.

Office Assistant: Well, we've just had a cancellation. Can you come here today at 4?

Alvia: Is it possible to come at 5?

Office Assistant: I'm sorry, I don't have anything for 5.

Alvia: OK, I'll take the 4:00 appointment.

Office Assistant: OK, great. See you this afternoon.

Page 194, Exercises A and B

Dr. Barnes: Good afternoon, Ms. Ledesma. What seems to be the problem?

Alvia: I feel terrible. I haven't been sleeping well. I fall asleep and wake up after a couple of hours.

Dr. Barnes: Hmm. Anything else?

Alvia: Well, I've been trying to lose weight like you said, but I can't. I come home exhausted, and I eat too much.

Dr. Barnes: Is anything bothering you?

Alvia: My job. They fired two people last month, so the rest of us have been working twice as hard.

Dr. Barnes: Hmm. You do have a lot on your mind. Well, let me examine you. Please step on the scale.

Alvia: The scale? Do I have to?

Page 194, Listen, Exercise C

Dr. Barnes: Ms. Ledesma, your blood pressure is high and you've gained a few pounds. I'll give you some medication for high blood pressure, but you really have to watch what you eat and do more exercise. Then you might not need the medicine. And you might even sleep better. Now, do you do any exercise?

Alvia: Not much. In the evenings, I like to watch TV. That's how I relax.

Dr. Barnes: Well, try to get some exercise. Dancing, even doing housework faster will help. Here is some information on healthy eating.

Alvia: What about sleeping pills? Or pills to lose weight?

Dr. Barnes: Let's hold off on the pills. I don't like to prescribe pills unless they're really necessary.

Page 201, Listen, Exercises A, B, and C

Mrs. Garcia: Doctor, I'm worried about next week.

Dr. Finkel: Don't worry, Mrs. Garcia. I've done many gall bladder operations. And you'll feel a lot better afterwards.

Mrs. Garcia: Oh, I'm not so worried about having the operation. I'm worried about being away from home. My husband is not used to taking care of the children. And I'm worried about missing a month of work.

Dr. Finkel: I see. Maybe you could ask a relative or a friend to help out.

Mrs. Garcia: I was thinking about asking my niece, but she's very busy. She has four children. Maybe I could call Maria, my cousin. She doesn't have a job right now, so she could probably come over to the house.

UNIT 11

Page 208, Listen, Exercises A, B, and C

Commercial: Are you tired of paying fees for your checking account? Well, if you want free checking, open an account with Zenith Bank! At Zenith Bank, we offer free checking when you have direct deposit or bank online at least two times a month. And if you open an account by April 3, you get a $50 cash bonus. So hurry! Come to your nearest Zenith Bank. Or go online to zenithbank.com.

Page 215, Listen, Exercises A, B, and C

Adelyne: I'm Adelyne Juste with Money Matters. Today we're talking about budgets. Now, most people don't like to think about budgets. In fact, 60% of Americans don't have a budget and spend more than they have. They might live this way for a while, but what happens in an emergency, such as a car accident? If you don't have a budget, you may not have money for an emergency. You'll also have trouble reaching your financial goals. So, if you want to create a budget, how do you get started? There are four steps you need to take.

First, you need to know your net income. In other words, your take-home pay. Write down how much you make each month after taxes.

Second, figure out your expenses. Write down all of the things you spend your money on each month— for example, rent, food, car payments, and utilities. Sometimes, you'll have to make a guess. For example, you may not know for sure how much you spend on gas each month.

The third step is to build savings into your budget. You have to plan to save every month for emergencies and for your long-term goals, like buying a house. Otherwise, you might not save anything, or you might not save enough. Before you decide how much you can save, look at your total expenses.

The last step is to check to see if your budget is realistic. At the end of the month, compare what you actually spent to the expenses you wrote in your budget. If you spent more than you budgeted for, you may need to spend less.

Remember, think about the big picture. What do you want for your family? What can you do to reach your goals? If you remember your reasons for saving, you'll be more motivated to keep your budget.

For Money Matters, I'm Adelyne Juste.

Page 220, Listen, Exercises A and B

Valeria: Hello. W & M Management Company.

Roberto: Hi. I'm looking for a two-bedroom apartment.

Valeria: OK, sure. How much do you want to spend?

Roberto: No more than $1200. And we need to live close to downtown.

Valeria: Let me see. Hmm. I've got a great two bedroom apartment on Cabela Avenue.

Roberto: Does it come with appliances?

Valeria: Yes, refrigerator and a gas stove.

Roberto: How much is the rent?

Valeria: $1100.

Roberto: Are utilities included?

Valeria: Yes, gas, electric and water.

Roberto: That sounds good! I'd like to come see it.

Valeria: Fine. Our rental office is open from 9:00 to 5:00. What time is good for you?

Roberto: How about 3:30?

Valeria: Hmm. I have an appointment at 4:00. Can you be here by 3:00?

Roberto: Yes, I can.

Valeria: Great. The office is at 10 Bryant Street on the first floor.

Roberto: Great. See you then.

UNIT 12

Page 228, Exercises A and B

Tao: Hey, Hua.

Hua: Hi, Tao! How are you? It's been a while since I ran into you.

Tao: I'm good. I just came back from a trip to Washington, D.C.

Hua: Really! I went there last year with my parents.

Tao: Yeah? So, Hua, what did you like seeing the most in Washington?

Hua: Hmm. I guess my favorite place was the White House. We went on a tour of the rooms inside. I liked seeing them—especially the Red Room, the Blue Room, and the Oval Office. What about you?

Tao: I liked seeing the White House. But my favorite place was the National Air and Space Museum.

Hua: What did you see there?

Tao: They've got a lot of things. Rocket ships, rocks from the moon and Mars, and lots of airplanes. It has the largest collection of planes in the world.

Hua: Wow, I'm sorry I missed it. I'll have to go next time.

Page 234, Listen, Exercises A and B

Guide: Hello, I'm Sandy Wheeler, your guide for today. Welcome, everyone, to Washington, D.C., our nation's capital. This morning we're going to visit three places. First, we're going to see the White House.

Child: That's where the president and his family live.

Guide: Um, right. We will arrive at the White House in just a few minutes. We'll go inside and visit the famous rooms. Then, after we leave the White House, our next stop will be the Capitol. That's where Congress meets to make laws.

1st Tourist: Is that where the senators work?

Guide: Yes, the senators work there, in the Senate. Congress is made up of two parts, the Senate and the House of Representatives. You might see some senators or some members of the House when we visit.

2nd Tourist: What time is lunch?

Guide: We'll have lunch after we visit Congress. Then, after lunch, we'll walk over to the Supreme Court. Now, any questions?

3rd Tourist: Can you explain . . . What exactly does the Supreme Court do?

Guide: Good question. The Supreme Court is the highest court of our land. There are many courts in the U.S., but the Supreme Court is above all the other courts. The judges there are called justices. They interpret the laws and decide if the laws follow the Constitution. Any more questions?

2nd Tourist: Yes, is the restaurant we're eating at any good?

Page 240, Listen, Exercise A

Guide: Now on your right you can see the Lincoln Memorial. It was built as a memorial for Abraham Lincoln, the 16th President of the United States. Lincoln was one of our most loved presidents.

Tourist: Could you tell us about his life?

Guide: Sure. He was born in Kentucky in 1809. He came from a very poor family and had to work hard his entire life. He taught himself law and became a lawyer. He was known for his honesty.

Tourist: When was he elected president?

Guide: Lincoln was elected president in 1860. The Civil War started soon after when the Southern states separated from the country. At that time slaves worked in the south on big farms called plantations. The Northern states wanted to end slavery. In 1863 Lincoln gave orders to free the slaves in the rebel states. In 1864 he was re-elected president. Unfortunately, in 1865 Lincoln was shot and killed. Many Americans were upset and saddened by his death. He was mourned by many people.

Index

Numeracy

account statements, 207
Budgets, 215–219, 224
Credit cards, 212–213
Utility bills, 218–219

Pronunciation

Can/can't, 89
Compound nouns, 235
Contractions with *will*, 29–30
Did you, 229
Do you, 149
Endings in *-ed*, 189
Endings in *-sion* or *-tion*, 75
Going to, 35
If clauses, 209
Inflection with questions, 161
Stressed syllables, 9, 49, 61, 75, 135, 195
Stressed words, 95, 169, 235
Th sounds, 109
Used to, 21
Want to, 221
Wh- questions, 161
Words in a phrase, 121
Yes/no questions, 161

Reading Skills

Getting the meaning, 7, 27, 87
Getting the meaning from context, 98–99
Graphics, 199
Identifying author purpose, 213
Identifying facts and opinions, 159
Identifying tenses, 42
Interpreting charts, 139
Making inferences, 79
Predicting, 32
Recognizing formatting clues, 112
Skimming, 172
Summarizing, 239
Understanding the main idea, 12–13, 33, 79, 99, 113, 139, 159, 173, 199
Using what you know, 52

Reading Topics

American cities, 12
Banking services, 209
Budgets and bills, 115, 224
Car maintenance, 129
Cell phones, 115–116
Consumer products, 110, 112, 121, 124
Credit cards, 212
Dental health, 162

Doctors and hospitals, 189, 200, 202, 204
Eating habits, 151, 163, 164
Entrepreneurs, 32–34
Exercise, 156
Future plans and goals, 27, 30, 35–39, 214
Government, 235–236
Health and work, 172
Holidays and celebrations, 15–17
Housing, 221–222
Immunizations, 198
Inventory, 169
Job interviews, 78–79
Libraries, 52
Medical symptoms, 195
Neighborhoods and neighbors, 10, 12, 22
Religious freedom, 238
Rights and freedoms, 243
School lunches, 158–158
Schools, 49, 56, 61, 64
Shopping, 112, 123
Traffic accidents, 135–136, 138–140, 144
Travel arrangements and safety, 95, 98–100, 104
U.S. presidents, 242
Washington, D.C., 229–230, 233, 241
Work experience, 69, 75–76
Working the late shift, 172
Workplace interactions, 170–171, 174, 176–177, 181, 184

Speaking Skills

Apologizing, 181
Asking and giving directions, 93, 233, 244
Asking for clarification, 4, 168–171, 171
Asking for permission, 103
Communicating with a teacher, 4, 47, 59
Giving advice, 24, 44, 64, 84, 104, 184
Giving instructions, 169, 171, 183–184
Making polite requests, 102–103
Making small talk, 8–11, 24
Rescheduling a doctor's appointment, 188–189
Responding to correction, 180–181, 184

Responding to requests, 102
Talking to a school counselor, 60

Speaking Topics

Airport travel, 89, 91
Banking services, 207–209, 211
Budgets and bills, 115, 217–219, 224
Car maintenance and costs, 129, 131, 143
Cell phones, 115, 117
Cities, 229
Community services, 41–43
Consumer products, 107, 110–113, 121, 124
Credit cards, 213
Dealing with bullies, 55, 57, 64
Dental health, 161
Describing future plans, 27, 30–31, 33
Doctors and hospitals, 188–189, 191, 200–201, 203–204
Eating habits, 149, 151, 153, 155, 164
Going back to school, 28–29, 44
Government, 237
Health and exercise, 157, 164
Holidays and celebrations, 14–15, 17, 237
Housing, 223–224
Identifying personal belongings, 97
Immunizations, 199
Job interviews, 77, 79, 81, 84
Job skills, 167
Library services, 53–54
Looking for a better job, 35, 37, 44
Medical symptoms, 195, 197
Personal information, 7, 9, 11, 13, 20–22
Problems at school, 47–49, 51, 59, 63–64
Product rebates, 119
Religious freedom, 239
Rights and freedoms, 243
School lunches, 159
Shopping, 122–123
Traffic accidents, 135, 137, 144
Traveling, 87, 95, 99–100, 104, 244
U.S. presidents, 242
Washington, D.C., 226–227, 231, 235, 241
Work experience, 67, 69, 71, 75, 77, 83, 173–174
Workplace interactions, 175, 177
Workplace safety, 179

Credits

Photo credits

All original photography by Richard Hutchings/Digital Light Source. Page 5 Charles O. Cecil/Alamy; 7 Images of Africa Photobank/Alamy; 10 Neil McAllister/Alamy; 12 Steve Skjold/Alamy; 14 Joe Kohen/WireImage/Getty Images; 15 Jake Dobkin; 16 Shutterstock.com; 20 Iakov Filimonov/123RF; 22 Peter Treanor/Alamy; 25 Chalmers Davee Library; 28(A) Fotolia.com, (B) Rob Brimson/Getty Images, (C) goodluz/Fotolia; 29(L) Construction Photography/Corbis, (M) Randy Faris/Corbis, (R) Blend Images/Alamy; 30 Brownstock Inc./Alamy; 32 Charles Gupton/Corbis; 36 Giantstep Inc/Getty Images; 39 Digital Vision/Alamy; 41 Carl & Ann Purcell/Corbis; 45 Tom & Dee Ann McCarthy/Corbis; 46-47(1) Ian Shaw/Alamy, (2) Sean Justice/Corbis, (3) Brand X/Corbis, (4) Randy Faris/Corbis, (5) Ned Coomes/Zooid Pictures, (6) Photofusion Picture Library/Alamy, (8) Blend Images - Hill Street Studios/Getty Images, (9) Tom & Dee Ann McCarthy/Corbis; 48 Luc Beziat/Getty Images; 52 White Plains Public Library; 55(Top) Brian Seed/Alamy; 56 Digital Vision/Alamy; 60 Robin Sachs/PhotoEdit; 66-67(1) Jim West/Alamy, (2) Tetra Images/Alamy, (3) Stuart Forster/Alamy, (4) Corbis Premium RF/Alamy, (5) Purestock/Alamy, (6) Robert Llewellyn/Imagestate, (7) Qaphotos.com/Alamy, (8) Jupiterimages/Creatas/Alamy; 78 Keith Brofsky/Getty Images; 82 Gg/eStock Photo; 85 Digital Vision/Alamy; 89(L) Shutterstock, (M) Shutterstock, (R) Dorling Kindersley/Getty Images; 91 Shutterstock; 94(L) Corbis Premium RF/Alamy, (R) GoGo Images Corporation/Alamy; 101(L) Hola Images RM/Getty Images, (R) Jack Hollingsworth/Getty Images; 102 Israel images/Alamy; 105 Photodisc/Alamy; 106(1) Julianne Bockius Photography/Photographers Direct, (2) RubberBall/Alamy, (3) Howard Birnstihl Photography/Photographers Direct, (4) Digital Vision/Alamy, (5) Zachariah Lindsey Heyer/iStockphoto, (6) Pat Behnke/Alamy, (7) Jerome Wilson Photography/Photographers Direct, (8) Derrick Alderman/Alamy, (9) Morris Photo Images/Photographers Direct; 110(T) Jim West/Alamy, (B) Profimedia International s.r.o./Alamy; 116(L) Shutterstock, (R) Shutterstock; 117(TL) www.currys.co.uk, (TR) iStockphoto, (BL) Ilian studio/Alamy, (BR) Dyson; 118 Photolibrary Group; 125 Thinkstock/Corbis; 128(A) Greatstock Photographic Library/Alamy, (B) Imagebroker/Alamy, (C) David R. Frazier Photolibrary, Inc./Alamy; 129(L) Ingram Publishing/Superstock Limited/Alamy, (M) Francisco Turnes/Alamy, (R) Maxim Sivyi/Photographers Direct; 131 Don Nichols/iStockphoto, Susan Van Etten/PhotoEdit, Don Hammond/Design Pics/Corbis, Zooid Pictures; 134 Ken Weingart/Alamy; 145 Gulfimages/Alamy; 146-147 (1) Dinodia Images/Alamy, (2) Radius Images/Alamy, (3) Photodisc/Alamy, (4) Angela Hampton Picture Library/Alamy, (5) Kuttig People/Alamy, (6) Greg Vaughn/Alamy, (7) Cathy Yeulet/123RF, (8) Paul J. Richards/AFP/Getty Images, (9) Shutterstock.com, (10) Blend Images/Alamy; 150 Isabel Perez/Photolibrary; 154 iStockphoto; 155 D. Hurst/Alamy, Digital Vision/Alamy, Mark Hodson Stock Photography/Alamy, Bill Aron/PhotoEdit; 156 Massimo Borchi/Corbis; 158 Brian Shumway/Redux; 160 Jupiterimages/Polka Dot /Alamy; 165 Andersen Ross/Brand X/Corbis; 166-167(1) Colorblind/Getty Images, (2) Jupiterimages/Thinkstock/Alamy, (3) John A. Giordano/Corbis SABA, (4) Blend Images/Alamy, (5) Bill Bachmann/Alamy, (6) Qaphotos.com/Alamy, (7) ImageState/Alamy, (8) Photodisc/Alamy, (9) Jupiterimages/BananaStock/Alamy, (10) Peter Arnold, Inc./Alamy; 170 Alan Gignoux/Alamy; 172 David Williams/Alamy; 177 luckyraccoon/Shutterstock; 185 Asia Images Group Pte Ltd/Alamy; 186-187(1) ER Productions/Corbis, (2) PhotoSpin, Inc/Alamy, (3) Monkey Business/Fotolia, (4) Yoav Levy/Photolibrary, (5) Randy Faris/Corbis, (6) Jupiterimages/Comstock Images/Alamy, (7) Corbis Premium RF/Alamy, (8) Thomas Northcut/Getty Images, (9) Marmaduke St. John/Alamy, (10) Photolibrary Group; 188(L) GoGo Images Corporation/Alamy, (R) Monkey Business Images/Shutterstock; 194 Blend Images/Alamy; 196 Michael Ventura/Alamy; 198 Jaimie D. Travis/iStockphoto; 201 GoGo Images Corporation/Alamy; 205 Bill Aron/PhotoEdit; 206(1) Sanjagrujic/Fotolia, (3) Fotolia.com, (5) Shutterstock, (7) David R. Frazier Photolibrary, Inc./Alamy; 210 Tony Freeman/PhotoEdit; 214 Fotolia.com; 216 Dean Rutz/The Seattle Times; 221(Left) Image Source/Getty Images; 225 Chad Ehlers/Photolibray; 226-227(1) William Manning/www.williammanning.com/Corbis, (2) Paul Conklin/PhotoEdit, (3) Steve Vidler/Photolibrary, (4) William Manning/www.williammanning.com/Corbis, (5) Rudy Sulgan/Corbis, (6) Macia Rafael/Photolibrary, (7) Shutterstock, (8) Peter Horree/Alamy, (9) Digital Vision /Alamy, (10) Smithsonian Institution/Corbis; 228 Randy Faris/Corbis; 229 Brooks Kraft/Corbis; 230 John Aikins/Corbis; 231(TL) Francis G. Mayer/Corbis, (BL) Hugh Talman/National Museum of American History/Smithsonian Institution, (R) Smithsonian Institution/Dane Penland/AP Images; 234 Rudy Sulgan/Corbis; 237 Ron Sachs/CNP/Corbis; 238 Helen King/Corbis; 240 Corbis; 241(T) idp eastern USA collection/Alamy, (BL) Gerald Hoberman/Photolibrary, (BR) Jayawardene Travel Photo Library/Photographers Direct; 242 Brooklyn Museum/Corbis.

Illustration Credits

Steve Attoe, p 190; Luis Briseño, pp.132-133, 160; Deborah Crowle, pp. 6-7, 14, 238; Brian Hughes, pp.18-19, 63; Stephen MacEachern pp 178, 226-227; Paul McCusker, p284; Luis Montiel, pp.26-27, 86-87, 126-127; Allan Moon, p43, 86, 92, 93, 179, 192, 232, 281; Steve Schulman, pp.4; Anna Veltfort, pp.3; Fred Willingham, pp.68, 88